MW01517772

SOCIOLOGY IN THE SOVIET UNION AND BEYOND

To my family
With love and hope for the future

$130.50

Sociology in the Soviet Union and Beyond

Social Enquiry and Social Change

ELIZABETH A. WEINBERG
Department of Sociology
London School of Economics

ASHGATE

Published by
Ashgate Publishing Limited
Gower House
Croft Road
Aldershot
Hants GU11 3HR
England

Ashgate Publishing Company
Suite 420
101 Cherry Street
Burlington, VT 05401-4405
USA

Ashgate website: http://www.ashgate.com

British Library Cataloguing in Publication Data
Stewart, Elizabeth A., 1942-
    Sociology in the Soviet Union and beyond : social enquiry
    and social change
    1. Sociology - Soviet Union
    I. Title
    301'.0947

Library of Congress Cataloging-in-Publication Data
Weinberg, Elizabeth Ann.
    Sociology in the Soviet Union and beyond : social enquiry and social change/ Elizabeth
Ann Weinberg.
        p. cm.
    Revised edition of: Development of sociology in the the Soviet Union: London: Routledge &
K. Paul, 1974.
    Includes bibliographical references and index.
    ISBN 0-7546-3817-0
    1. Sociology--Soviet Union--History. 2. Sociology--Study and teaching--Soviet Union. 3.
Sociology--Research--Soviet Union. 4. Sociologists--Soviet Union. 5. Social
change--Russia (Federation) I. Title.

HM477.S65W45 2004
301'.0947--dc22

2003063799

ISBN 0 7546 3817 0

Printed and bound by Athenaeum Press, Ltd.,
Gateshead, Tyne & Wear.

Contents

List of Figures

List of Tables

Acknowledgements

I wish to thank Suzanne Keller for initially stimulating my interest in the sociology of knowledge, Ithiel deSola Pool and Celia Heller for directing my early attempts to understand Soviet sociology and Gayle Durham Hollander for initiating me into the world of Soviet source materials. I owe special debts of gratitude to Merle Fainsod who guided my master's dissertation on Soviet public opinion research and Leonard Schapiro for his valuable assistance as my graduate supervisor. Eleanora Gottlieb helped me in many ways, not least in grappling with the complexities of the Russian language.

In this second edition, I want to acknowledge my graduate students' interest in the area especially Sarah Amsler who also helped with translating some of the material. I am indebted to Stephen White who warmly supported the idea of a revised edition and Jenny Law who so congenially and efficiently prepared the final manuscript with the unstinting and patient help of Alma Gibbons. I am also grateful to Soviet and Russian colleagues for encouraging me to publish a second edition so that they could read a less biased interpretation of the development of sociology in the former Soviet Union. Finally, my greatest thanks go to Angus Stewart for all of his advice and continuous encouragement in my many varied projects.

List of Abbreviations

CDSP	Current Digest of the Soviet Press
Fil Nauki	*Filosofskie Nauki (Nauchnye doklady vysshei shkoly)*
Vestnik AN SSSR	*Vestnik Akademii Nauki SSSR*
Vestnik LGU	*Vestnik Leningradskogo Universiteta:* Seriia Ekonomiki, Filosofii, Prava
Vestnik MGU	*Vestnik Moskovskogo Universiteta*: Seriia VIII - Ekonomika, Filosofiia
Vop Fil	Voprosy Filosofii

Introductory Note

The origins of the present study lie in the intersection of two areas of interest, the historical and social circumstances surrounding the development of sociology (or rather, sociologies) in different societies, and a specific 'area' of concern with the social structure and dynamics of the Soviet Union. My initial exposure to the issues and problems raised by a sociological analysis of Soviet society took place very much at the same time that the first post-'thaw' products of a reviving sociology in the Soviet Union were beginning to emerge. In addition to an interest in research findings in particular areas, there emerged a general concern with the obstacles to and the mechanisms of the acceptance of sociological enquiry in a society formally founded on the principle of planned social change through the agency of a centralized political apparatus.

Within this context, therefore, the following is a case study in the institutionalization of a discipline in a particular society. As it happened, the historical period with which the bulk of this study is broadly concerned – that of the 1960s – was characterized by a developing interest in the problematic, contingent nature of sociological enquiry in Western societies and in the social uses which that enquiry was meant to serve.* In general, the consequence has been to make clear that the 'unique' situation of Soviet sociology was more apparent than real. However, given the historical significance of the Soviet Union, an interest in the manner in which sociological enquiry has been legitimated there has continuing relevance.

Given its central focus on the problem of legitimation, the present study does not attempt a systematic assessment of the findings of Soviet sociologists. Further, it is recognized that much work, either directly sociological or relevant to sociologists, was produced in the Soviet Union by individuals and groups not calling themselves sociologists, but operating within the context of other disciplines. The assumption is made, however, that such work did not contribute directly to the institutionalization of sociology as a separate discipline. Because the focus is on the emergence of a discipline within an institutional context, the criterion for sociology is that those who produce it call themselves sociologists.

Chapter 1 puts sociology in historical perspective, tracing its development from pre-Revolutionary times to the 1956 Twentieth Congress of the Communist Party of the Soviet Union. Chapter 2 describes how the sociological aspects of Soviet Marxism, dormant during the years of the 'cult of personality', were revived

---

* See, for example, in general, A. W. Gouldner (1971), *The Coming Crisis of Western Sociology*, London, and R. W. Friedrichs, (1970), *A Sociology of Sociology*, London. For a specific study of the controversy surrounding social science at the service of government, see I. L. Horowitz (1967), *The Rise and Fall of Project Camelot*, Cambridge, Mass.

and how 'Marxist sociology' was advanced as a legitimate discipline. The second half of the chapter deals with this exercise in self-definition as it arises from the Soviet critique of 'bourgeois sociology'. Chapter 3 similarly deals with questions of the theoretical assumptions underlying research methodology, principally in so far as these relate to the process of institutionalization. The next chapter is concerned first with the institutional framework in which the sociologist worked, then with the sociologists themselves, that is, their education, regional ties, age and specialities and, finally with their journals. Chapter 5 surveys the areas of research that Soviet sociologists investigated and in particular highlights the purported relation between these research areas and wider aspects of Soviet society. This includes work on: labour; social stratification; marriage, the family, divorce and the woman's role; urban development, city planning and urban-rural relations; criminology and juvenile delinquency; and religion. Chapter 6 traces in depth the development of an area of particular significance in Soviet sociology, public opinion research. Since its initiation in 1960, the expansion and improvement of such research in a period of liberalization reflected the increasingly pragmatic trend in sociology, the growing belief among decision-makers in the functional value of such research and the greater acceptance of sociological research by the country at large. At the same time, such research affords an excellent opportunity of chronologically tracing changes in the presentation, the research methods and the approach to this type of research.

Chapter 7 also looks in depth at an area of research which was particularly significant in the Soviet context, namely time budget research or how people spend their working and non-working time. Time budget research was one of the first areas of empirical research to emerge after 1956 and was of real significance in the professional development of Soviet sociology. Chapter 8, originally published in the *British Journal of Sociology* (Vol. 43 (1) March 1992), looks at the role played by Soviet sociologists in initiating and critiquing the processes of *perestroika* and glasnost. The final chapter discusses the institutionalization of knowledge, detailing sociology's fight for legitimacy, the obstacles the discipline faced and the limits of the Soviet system up to and including glasnost and *perestroika*. In the light of the demise of the Soviet Union, the last chapter looks finally at the future of the newly evolving Russian sociology.

A few words seem necessary about some technicalities. A glossary of Russian terms appears at the end of the text. All of the words in it follow Russian spelling rules (e.g. the plural of *vuz* is *vuzy*). There are some Russian words, however, which are today quite common in English (e.g. komsomol). They are not italicized in the text, and their plurals follow English spelling rules. The Library of Congress system of transliteration has been adopted. I have also followed the Soviet practice of transposing pre-1917 orthography into new.

1
Historical Background

Up to the beginning of the twentieth century sociology was not taught in Russia as an independent discipline under that name but as an aspect of various areas of intellectual enquiry such as the 'philosophy of history', 'social foundations of economy', 'social psychology', and the like. By 1906-7, for example, Maxim Kovalevskii wrote: 'we have – in all – one chair [of sociology] in the whole Empire of 160 million inhabitants and that at a private university in the Psycho-Neurological Institute [in St Petersburg].' Kovalevskii, the first to hold the chair of sociology at the Psycho-Neurological Institute which specialized in psychiatry, neurology and experimental psychology, continued: 'I would be less surprised at the news that in Nanking or Peking a department of sociology was created than at hearing of the fact that Mr Kasso [Minister of Education] had started such a reform in Moscow or St Petersburg.'[1] By 1917, however, some universities were offering courses in sociology.

Although the formal science of sociology was hardly taught in Russian universities, the Russians were neither ignorant of nor unconcerned about social problems and ideas; quite the contrary. While it is beyond the scope of this study to discuss the work of the early Russian sociologists or to evaluate their contributions to sociology at large, it is clear that questions of the history of civilisation, the development of social ideas and ideas of progress, the nature of the state, the establishment of sociology as a distinct social science – as well as specific investigations into the family, the intelligentsia, the role of women, etc. – were ardently debated in pre-October Russia.

Strong links existed between those concerned with these questions and European thinkers. In addition to the ties which the upper classes and intelligentsia had through European languages and cultures, many Russian professors emigrated to Europe in the early part of the twentieth century. In 1901, a group of them in Paris (e.g. Kovalevskii, deRoberty, Kareev) set up a Russian section of the Higher School of Social Sciences attached to the Sorbonne; this later became the Higher Russian School of Social Sciences. The tradition of the Paris Higher School was continued when in 1905 a Higher Free School was opened in St Petersburg. It was this establishment which was the first to teach sociology as an obligatory subject.[2]

In general, Russian thought had experienced the same intellectual influences that had affected the rest of Europe, although through the process of adaption ideas were sometimes distorted. In sociology, in particular, there were extensive translations from the writings of German, French, English and American sociologists. Some Russian sociologists even argued that there were more translations of sociological works than original sociological literature.

The general impression which emerges from the various surveys of Russian social thought in this period is of the representation of a wide diversity of points of view, the satisfactory classification of which is a difficult if not impossible task. Principal among these various schools of thought were: the subjectivists, such as Lavrov, Mikhailovsky and Iuzhakov, who by accepting positivist, empiricist philosophy rejected the biological-organic and mechanist schools; the mechanists, such as Voronov and Spektorsky, who interpreted social phenomena from the viewpoint of 'social mechanics' or 'social physics'; the behaviourists, such as Bekhterev and Pavlov, who began analyzing physiological processes, proceeded to analyze nervous processes and then applied their knowledge to social phenomena; and the economic materialists, such as Plekhanov, Tugan-Baranovsky and Struve, who said that the basis of all social phenomena was economic.[3]

Articles on sociology and sociological problems were published in many weeklies and monthlies: 'rarely does an issue of one of our thick magazines fail to contain articles on some question of sociology.'[4] In 1913 Maxim Kovalevskii co-edited with E. V. deRoberty and P. A. Sorokin the first of a series of sociological yearbooks entitled *Novye Idei v Sotsiologii* (*New Ideas in Sociology*):[5] *New Ideas in Sociology* took the place of a sociology journal and helped to gain further recognition for sociology in the academic world. Under its stimulus, among other factors, the first Russian Sociological Society was established in 1916 in Petrograd (in honour of Kovalevskii).

The Post-Revolutionary Situation

The general situation in Russia after the Revolution in the 1920s and early 1930s was analogous to the slow process of re-furnishing a room. The old furniture was to be removed and replaced by the new, in a piecemeal fashion. For a while, the old and new co-existed. Gradually, however, the whole room took on a new character as the structure was re-designed.

The same process occurred in the field of sociology. The 'old philosophy' was gradually dislodged from its position in the journals and in the universities.[6] Private publications serving as the mouthpiece of 'bourgeois' views were totally eliminated by 1922. By 1924, the Department of Social Sciences at Moscow State University (which included a chair in sociology) was closed after its five-year existence. The chairs of sociology became chairs of the history of social thought; Marxist theory of society and social development became an obligatory subject.

The old idealist furnishings were to become materialist: the new structure was to be based on the *Weltanschauung* of Marxism. This transformation involved the struggle of proletarian ideology with idealism – philosophy, historiography and sociology, of which the last was accused of disseminating the legend of the absence of sociology from Marxism. In the attack on bourgeois sociology, the concepts of *narod* (nation, nationality, folk), stratification, class and progress were particular targets.[7] Marxist sociology was subsequently entrusted with applying the method of dialectical and historical materialism to social relations and with further developing historical materialism. At the same time, it was charged with popularizing and propagandizing the ideas of historical materialism and with teaching the masses about the construction of socialism.

The strongest opponents of these changes were to be found in Petrograd, the city which housed the first university to offer sociology and the first Sociology Society. Here, the discipline *qua* discipline had been most firmly entrenched prior to the Revolution. Immediately after the Revolution, Petrograd University opened a department of sociology and subsequently created a bio-sociological institute to study the relation between organic and social forces. The faculty of social sciences at the University in 1920-1 offered courses entitled the system of sociology, genetic sociology, history of sociological studies, history of socialism and criminology. In addition, there was established a society for studying the liberation and revolutionary movement of Russia. At the same time, the Kovalevskii Sociological Society was reactivated in 1920 – it had been interrupted by the death of its president, A. S. Lappo-Danilevskii, and the Revolution – and, according to a retrospective report by V. I. Klushin, its anti-Marxist direction was widely publicised by Pitirim Sorokin.[8]

Sorokin himself held a professorship at the Psycho-Neurological Institute and Petrograd University by the end of 1918. Writing from the perspective of 1925, Sorokin describes his life as a sociologist at Petrograd:

> My classes in sociology at the University became the largest and most closely attended in the whole institute, not because I was such a talented lecturer, but because sociology had now become such a vitally important subject. Not only the students, but the university clerks and the public attended my lectures. If my scientific data had favoured the Government, I should not have been sorry, because it would have made my lot much happier, but I had to present facts as they were. Being a sociologist under such conditions was a damnable business, but I had to be honest. I can hardly describe the difficulties under which I continued my work, which I knew might any day cause my arrest.[9]

Sorokin was forbidden to teach in the autumn of 1921 but he continued his research at the Research Institute of the Brain (where he 'would not be harmful to students') and at the History and Sociology Institute of the University. In September of 1922 he, along with other bourgeois thinkers, was banished from the Soviet Union. Sorokin's Petrograd colleague, K. M. Takhtarev, wrote in October 1923 that 'at the present time, chairs of general sociology at the University do not exist. Sociology has been replaced by the history of the development of social (*obshchestvennye*) forms ...'[10] By mid-1923, the department of general sociology at the university had ceased to exist, although courses listed as 'historical materialism (sociology)' continued until the mid-1930s. A department of the development of social forms was organized in place of the department of general sociology.

Qualifications to this gloomy picture of the state of sociology in Petrograd in the 1920s are offered in an analysis by the Leningrad sociologist, V. I. Klushin. He states that one of the major difficulties faced by those who sought to transform the system was the fact that the 'so-called official sociology in the university department was represented by professors who either did not hide their animosity towards Marxism or, having declared themselves to be Marxists, were no such thing and were not able to become Marxists.'[11] The non-Marxists were divided into two schools: 1) the positivists (e.g. Sorokin and Takhtarev) who, in spite of major differences, were united in their general approach to sociology as an empirical science and as an intimate of natural science, especially biology; and 2) the 'last of the Mohicans' (as Klushin calls them), a group of speculative philosophers of history of a non-Marxist kind (e.g. S. Frank and N. Karsavin). Disputes about the subject and content of sociology within and between these two non-Marxist schools – and between them and the Marxists – were the order of the day.[12]

The Marxists in Petrograd, the majority of whom were young, spent much time in the early years after the Revolution popularizing the ideas of the founders of Marxism-Leninism. Since there were only a few Marxists among university staff, they concentrated on political economy, history and the materialist understanding of history, defending these from the attacks of the bourgeois ideologists. By the middle of the 1920s, the Scientific Society of Marxists (*Nauchnoe Obshchestvo Marksistov*: NOM), which had been formed in the Worker's Faculty (*rabfak*) at the end of 1919, had become the recognized centre of Marxist philosophical and sociological thought in Petrograd. NOM's journal, *Zapiski Nauchnogo Obshchestva Marksistov* (*Transactions of the Scientific Society of Marxists*), further helped to spread the ideas of the society.

The displacement of idealism by materialism was also accomplished by the creation of scientific institutes (mostly in Moscow) where both teaching and research in the social sciences took place. In 1918, the Socialist Academy was established as the centre for Marxist research. In its socio-historical section, the general introductory courses included genetical sociology and 'general sociology (historical materialism)'; in the political-juridical section, there were courses on the sociology of crime. The Marx-Engels Institute, whose philosophy library was arranged for historical materialism *and* sociology, was formed in 1920. A year later, the Institute of Red Professors was set up for the express purpose of training professors for higher education posts (a branch was opened in Leningrad at a later stage). The preparation of Marxist-educated university teachers was also undertaken by the Sverdlov Communist University, the Russian Association of Scientific Research Institutes of the Social Sciences (RANION), and others.

The impact of the new regime was felt not only in educational and research institutions but also in publications. In 1922, the first Soviet philosophical and socio-economic monthly journal, *Pod Znamenem Marksizma* (*Under the Banner of Marxism*) was published and was soon followed by other journals which treated theoretical problems of society and general questions of social philosophy. The contributors to most of these journals and the teachers at the universities were primarily specialists in dialectical materialism and the history of philosophy. The result was that these fields were more fully represented in the published works than were the problems of (Marxist) sociology. Another reason for this was that the anti-Marxist literature was more philosophical than sociological in character and thus the criticism by the Marxists fell within the limits of the former.

During these years, several important questions on Marxist sociology were raised. These dealt mainly with the relation of method and theory in historical materialism, the relation of general and particular laws, productive forces and productive relations and the theory of the class struggle. Different interpretations of historical materialism were expressed. One treatment of historical materialism derived from mechanism whose theoretical sources were 'the subjective-idealist views of Bogdanov, the positivism of bourgeois philosophy, and the mechanistic tendencies in the natural sciences'.[13] Nikolai Bukharin appeared as the principal representative of this field in the realm of sociology; he presented an integral mechanistic conception of sociology, closely connected with the views of Bogdanov on the questions of methodology as well as on such problems of historical materialism as the origin of class, the state and ideology. Up to the beginning of the 1930s, Bukharin's book, *Teoriia Istoricheskogo Materializma – Populiarnyi Uchebnik Marksistskoi Sotsiologii* (*Theory of Historical Materialism: A Popular Textbook of Marxist Sociology*) was the centre of verbal and written discussions on historical materialism and Marxist sociology since in it he advanced the view that historical materialism *is* Marxist sociology. It was during the period of these discussions and criticisms (e.g. Bukharin's concepts were 'unhistoric', 'abstract', 'scholastic' and/or 'revisionist') that Soviet philosopher-Marxists were developing the content and structure of historical materialism as an academic discipline.[14]

A. M. Deborin and his students were critics of, and eventually successors to, the mechanists in the 1920s. Questions of historical materialism seemed to be of little importance and were even ignored in the Deborinite criticism because the Deborinites concentrated on the problems of dialectical, rather than historical, materialism. *Istoriia Filosofii VI* (*History of Philosophy VI*) notes that:

> Deborin himself and his group underrated historical materialism and declined in point of fact to work out actual problems of social development; they were not in a position to challenge the mechanistic sociological conceptions of Bukharin and others because they neither had a correct standpoint nor did they undertake thorough and concrete scientific research on the problems of social development.[15]

Deborin and his students viewed historical materialism not as sociology but only as a social *methodology*, as a totality of abstract, logical categories with which the Marxist only 'approaches' the study of the laws of different social formations, that is, historical materialism provides the 'domain assumptions' of social analysis for the Marxist.[16] Sociology, according to these views, is the task then not for philosophers but for specialists. Consequently, social theory was taken out of the boundaries of philosophy.[17]

There were thus two views about historical materialism by the end of the 1920s and the beginning of the 1930s: Bukharin's, identifying the materialist understanding of history with sociology in general (i.e. historical materialism is Marxist sociology), and Deborin's, identifying historical materialism *only* with social methodology. At the All-Union conference of historian-Marxists in February 1929 (that is, just prior to the April 1929 Sixteenth Party Congress from which the Deborinites emerged victorious), the discussion about the Marxist understanding of sociology showed quite definitely that Marxist sociology had not yet been officially defined: questions as to whether it was a theory, a methodology or both – and its consequent relation to historical materialism – clearly reflected both mechanistic and Deborinite tendencies.[18]

In the early 1930s debates continued over the question of the relation of historical materialism and Marxist sociology. These were largely a continuation of earlier arguments but refinements did occur. Some theoreticians underlined the mainly philosophical aspect of historical materialism, others saw sociology as historical materialism, while a third group considered historical materialism to be both an inseparable part of Marxist philosophy and a theory of social development.[19] In general, in comparison with the 1920s, little progress was made with regard to the development of the theory of historical materialism. Some theoretical analysis did approach less general questions about the transition to and construction of a socialist society. Advances were made in four areas in particular: works connected with theoretical questions of socialist construction were published; Leninism was established as making its own contribution to the analysis of problems of Marxist sociology; important questions were raised on culture and cultural revolution; and a number of texts and collections on historical materialism appeared, dealing with the role of ideas and the development of society, the role of the mass and related questions.[20] At the same time, with reference to the institutional context, some advance occurred through the development of the sociological groups within the Institute of Red Professors in Moscow, its branch in Leningrad and in the philosophy branch of the Communist Academy.

Before turning to sociology in the period of *partiinost'* (party mindedness, commitment to the party line), we must examine the state of empirical research since the Bolshevik victory.[21] As early as 1918, Lenin, in defining the programme of the Socialist Academy of the Social Sciences, formulated the task of developing social research. At his suggestion, a broad programme of social research was initiated. The areas under study were: 1) labour, especially the conditions and organization of labour and the influence of socio-psychological, educational and general cultural factors on labour production; 2) the economic mode of life and the income(s) of different categories of the population (e.g. the peasants); 3) class relations and questions of the theory of classes; 4) culture; 5) religion; 6) socio-economic and socio-demographic data collecting and processing; and 7) methods and techniques of social research. It has been suggested that the research was not so much sociological as socio-economic and social in character. Assessment of this position depends upon a particular theoretical stance but certainly the research did have an applied character and relied to a significant degree on having statistical data and on using simple questionnaire methods and interviews. Of all the men mentioned in connection with research on new social processes, most often cited are S. Strumilin in connection with his research on the time budgets of workers, peasants and employees (*sluzhashchie*), L. Kritsman on the (class differentiation of) peasants and the economy of the village, and S. Vol'fson on marriage and the family.

In reviewing this early period, V. Kantorovich states that sociologists 'were able to rely on data, objective in their origin, considering that statistics were widely accessible and researchers did not have to provide themselves with visas and passes to statistical materials'.[22] However, Klushin is much more critical of the researches carried out in this period: 'There was not time for concrete research, which demanded a high degree of processing and comprehension of general methodological principles and methods', because in view of their inadequate theoretical training, the few Marxists in the field of sociology devoted themselves to considering abstruse problems of the materialist understanding of history.[23]

The 1930s saw an intensification of the influence of power-political as opposed to political social influence. Just as the mechanists had been eclipsed by the Deborinites in 1929, so the Deborinites were eclipsed by the Bolshevizers in 1930-1. Philosophy and sociology were to serve the party: the disciplines were to be politicized, Bolshevized and ultimately, Stalinized.

> There is not and cannot be a philosophy [sociology] that wants to be considered Marxist-Leninist philosophy [sociology] while denying the necessity of ideational-political and theoretical leadership on the part of the Communist Party and its leading staff.[24]

From the mid-1930s to the mid-1950s, sociology as an independent academic discipline virtually disappeared in the Soviet Union. Sociology was to have no distinct place in the Marxist system since it was considered a 'bourgeois' and, consequently, non-Marxist subject. Marxism-Leninism-Stalinism took its place.

The number of courses of philosophy and sociology in *vuzy* (higher educational establishments) diminished. The teaching of Marxist philosophy was entrusted to the newly created departments of Marxism-Leninism. The departments of dialectical and historical materialism remained only in the universities and institutes where philosophy, history and literature faculties existed. Many sociological terms and concepts worked out by Marx, Engels and Lenin were no longer used: 'the very word "sociology" in this period was found to be prohibited'.[25] Only that social terminology and those social concepts to be found in the works of Stalin were recognized. The basis of sociological and philosophical commentaries became the chapter entitled 'Dialectical and Historical Materialism' in *History of the CPSU(B): Short Course*, 1938. 'When only one man was recognized as having the right to scientific creativity, all that was left to the others was to comment, popularize and – admire.'[26] To the commentaries on Stalin's pronouncements may be added those on other Marxist-Leninist classics. There was very formal discussion of such subjects as class structure, marriage and the family, religion and atheism, ethics and morals, art and aesthetics, and base and superstructure. In addition, there were general discussions of the laws of social development and the transition from socialism to communism. The net result was that theory and practice were split. There was a prevalence of 'scholasticism' (that phenomenon which describes detachment from life), the 'deducing' of life from theory, and the 'fitting' of new facts and phenomena to schemes and constructs already known.

Such sociological research as was carried out during this period occurred under the rubric of other disciplines. Ethnographers and anthropologists, for example, investigated religious behaviour and family patterns of various national, ethnic and minority groups in the outlying Soviet Republics; some did research on the kolkhozes (collective farms). Although it was mainly of a descriptive nature, this collection of data was a source of information about the impact of socialism and industrialization. It is of course also possible (though not probable) that work in sociology, as in some branches of psychology, was being done even though it was not published.[27]

Very few sociological articles appeared in journals which had once carried such articles. While Chagin suggests that gradually in the period 1939-40 some were published in *Pod Znamenem Marksizma* in which an attempt was made to go beyond the canons of Stalin's work, the journal itself was discontinued in 1944.[28] Until 1947, when the publication of *Voprosy Filosofii* (*Problems of Philosophy*) began, there was no philosophical journal in the country. However, *Bol'shevik*, the organ of the CPSU, somewhat bridged the gap. It was there, in fact, that the second stream of writing during Stalin's rule – namely, criticism of bourgeois sociology – roughly began in earnest in the middle of the 1940s. Articles on this subject were published first in *Bol'shevik* and then in *Voprosy Filosofii*.

Why was criticism of bourgeois sociology necessary? G. Aleksandrov, writing in *Bol'shevik* in 1945, suggested the answer:[29]

> Soviet philosophers are obliged to continue the work on the substantial criticism of contemporary reactionary bourgeois philosophical and sociological theories. Our scientific and teaching staffs during the last years have had little information about the state of philosophical and sociological thought abroad. However, the struggle against the ideology of bourgeois reaction as regards the most real political questions is impossible without the exposure of contemporary reactionary bourgeois philosophical and sociological theories.

Although these articles were less subtle and more polemical than those of the late 1950s and 1960s, the targets for reproach were basically the same.[30] On the whole, bourgeois sociology was continuously represented as an abstract metaphysical approach to the study of society, whereas its counterpart, historical materialism (Marxist sociology), was presented as the only scientific approach. It was Marxism, Lenin had said, which had first raised sociology to the level of science. And the theory of historical materialism was – and is – the Marxist science of society.

With the exceptions just noted, therefore, the period up to the mid-1950s represents the nadir of Soviet sociology. Only with the Twentieth Party Congress in 1956 did it experience any kind of renaissance. As Chagin says:[31]

> The Twentieth Party Congress initiated the gradual elimination of dogmatism and subjectivism in the sphere of Marxist theory and the liquidation of the consequences of the cult of personality in the sphere of Marxist sociology. This was the turning point. The 1950s – these are the years when sociology rehabilitated many lost positions, renouncing dogmatic ideas of the period of the cult of Stalin's personality and tried to become an authentic research science, relying on the practice of communist construction and the theoretical legacy of Marxism-Leninism. This was a complicated and contradictory process. The canons and dogma did not disappear at once from the content of historical

materialism. The ranks of sociologists were not re-built at once. Many still clung to the old. But the creative spirit of research continuously pierced through the dogmatic conglomerations. Soviet sociology, like all philosophy, in the 1950s defended its right to become a creative science.

What caused this to happen in the 1950s? As every Soviet account reiterates, 'After the decisions of the Twentieth Party Congress (and the subsequent Congresses leading to the Twenty-Third), the party defined the role and tasks of the social sciences, pointed out the main directions of research work, and directed the concrete study of the processes of communist construction.' Both *Pravda* and *Kommunist* published the party perspective on the solution of theoretical problems, providing the outline of the further development of philosophy and sociology.

The party and 'practice' finally produced the demand for a search for solutions to many questions raised during the Stalin era, and the first steps in the rebirth of sociology were taken.* But while the party had a last opened the door for the development of sociology, it was not until the Twenty-Third Party Congress in March-April 1966 that sociology was recognized officially as a discrete discipline with distinct functions. In the preceding decade, there had been fought out a theoretical battle which also represented (at the level of social forces) a struggle for the legitimation of sociology. It is to this theoretical debate that we now turn.

---

* In addition to these internal factors, a major stimulus to the revival of sociology in the Soviet Union came from contact with the more highly developed sociology of Eastern Europe and in particular with Polish sociology.

---

1 M. M. Kovalevskii, 'Sotsiologiia na Zapadei v Rossii', *Novye Idei v Sotsiologii,* St. Petersburg, 1913, I, pp.3-4.

2 V. I. Klushin, *Bor'ba za Istoricheskii Materializm v Leningradskom Gosudarstvennom Universitete (1918-1925 Gody)*, Leningrad, 1970, pp.11-12.

3 See J. F. Hecker, *Russian Sociology: A Contribution to the History of Sociological Thought and Theory*, London, 1934, pp.299; V. M. Khvostov, *Osnovye Sotsiologii: Uchenie o Zakonomernosti Obshchestvennykh Protesessov*, Moscow, 1920, pp.91; and P. A. Sorokin, 'Russian Sociology in the Twentieth Century', *Publications of the American Sociological Society*, XXI, December, 1926, pp.57-69.

4 N. G. Voronov, *Osnovaniia Sotsiologii*, Moscow, 1912, p.1.

5 The themes of the four published books were: 1. Sociology. Its subject and present state; 2. Sociology and Psychology; 3. What is Progress?; 4. Genetical Sociology. Contributors were both Russian and non-Russian sociologists.

6 For a discussion of the first ten years of philosophy and sociology see I. Luppol, 'Filosofiia v SSSR za Desiat let', *Obshchestvennye Nauki SSSR 1917-1927*, V. P. Volgin, G. O. Gordon and I. K. Luppol (eds.), Moscow, 1928, pp.5-24.

7 It should be noted that although bourgeois concepts were criticized, they were still discussed and different points of view were aired.

8 V. I. Klushin, 'Sotsiologiia v Petrogradskom Universitete (1920-1924)', *Vestnik LGU*, No. 5, 1964, p.70.

9 Pitirim Sorokin, *Leaves from a Russian Diary (1917-1922)*, London, 1925, p.225. He tells how, for example, he had to lecture in the dark. It is not made clear whether he lectured this way because there was no electric power or because he was scared.

10 K. M. Takhtarev, *Sravnitel'naia Istoriia Razvitiia Chelovescheskogo Obshchestva i Obshchestvennykh Form: Chast' Pervaia*, Leningrad, 1924, p.6.

11 Klushin, *Vestnik LGU*, No. 5, 1964, p.71 and his *Bor'ba za*, Chapter 2.

12 See Klushin's article and book for further discussion of the disputes.

13 B. A. Chagin, 'Razvitie Sotsiologicheskoi Mysli v SSR v 20-e Gody', *Fil Nauki*, No. 5, 1967, p.102.

14 *Ibid.*

15 M. A. Dynnik *et al.* (eds.), *Istoriia Filosofii, VI*, book 1, Moscow, 1965, p.221.

16 See A. Gouldner's discussion of this term in *The Coming Crisis of Western Sociology*, London, 1971.

17 Compare the argument of Peter Winch's *The Idea of a Social Science and its Relation to Philosophy*, London, 1960 and the ensuing debate.

18 See 'Diskussiia o Marksistskom Ponimanii Sotsiologii', *Istorik Marksist*, No. 12, 1929, pp.189-213.

19 B. A. Chagin, *Ocherk Istorii Sotsiologicheskoi Mysli v SSSR*, Leningrad, 1971, p.166.

20 *Ibid.* p.175.

21 The following discussion is based upon the generally agreed view as it emerges from: G. M. Andreeva, *Sovremennaia Burzhuaznaia Empiricheskaia Sotsiologiia; Kriticheskii Ocherk*, Moscow, 1965, p.294; P. N. Fedoseev, 'Marksistskaia sotsiologiia, ee Zadachi i Perspektivy', *Vestnik AN SSSR*, No. 7, 1966, p.3: 'Predislovie', *Sotsiologiia v SSSR*, I, G. V. Osipov (ed.), Moscow, 1966, pp.3-4; S. P. Trapeznikov, 'Razvitie Obshchestvennykh Provedeniia Konkretnykh Sotsial'nykh Issledovanii v Leningrade', *Fil Nauki*, No. 2, 1965, pp.157-60; Chagin, *Ocherk Istorii* ...

22 V. Kantorovich, 'Sotsiologiia i Literatura', *NovyMir*, No. 12, 1967, p.149.

23 Klushin, *Vestnik LGU*, No. 5, 1964, p.76.

24 M. B. Mitin, ' K Yoprosu', *Revoliutsiia i Kul'tura*, No. 19-20, 1930, p.37, cited by David Joravsky, *Soviet Marxism and Natural Science: 1917-1932*, New York, 1961, p.258.

25 G. V. Osipov, *Sovremennaia Burzhuaznaia Sotsiologiia*, Moscow, 1964, p.29.

26 B. A. Grushin, 'Sotsiologiia i Sotsiologi', *Literaturnaia Gazeta*, 25 September 1965, p.1.

27 See M. Cole and I. Maltzman (eds.) *A Handbook of Contemporary Soviet Psychology*, London, 1969, p.6.

28 Chagin, *Ocherk Istorii* ..., p.179.

29 G. Aleksandrov, 'O Nekotorykh Zadachakh Obshchestvennykh Nauk v Sovremennykh Usloviiakh', *Bol'shevik*, No. 14, 1945, p.23.

30 For a discussion of Soviet views of bourgeois sociology, see Chapter 2.

31 Chagin, *Ocherk Istorii* ..., pp.186, 189.

2
Soviet and Bourgeois Sociology

The 1956 Twentieth Party Congress of the CPSU called for liberalization in general and an end to the separation of theory and practice in particular. At that time, the discussion about sociology's renewed right to exist took the form of a debate on the classification and definition of the term sociology. Central to this discussion were questions about the tasks, the subject and the very legitimacy of concrete social (in particular, sociological) research:

> The development of society has [had] confronted us with a host of new questions concerning the economy, the social structure, the state, the family. Whereas these questions used to be raised only in very general terms, now [after the Twentieth Party Congress] we are concerned with their practical – that is, their supremely concrete – content; the daily activity of the masses in various spheres of public life raises scores of concrete 'how's' and 'why's' and demands concrete, scientific answers to these questions. [1]

In fact, empirical research on the 'how's' and 'why's' began while the philosophers were still defining and classifying sociology. While the terms of the philosophical discussion were the familiar ones of the relationship between sociology and historical materialism, the purpose of the debate was clearly to find ideological and philosophical justification for the discipline.

Within what terms was sociology established as an independent discipline? On one side of the crucial discussions were those who, following the discussions of the 1920s and 1930s, claimed that historical materialism *is* sociology. Historical materialism, it was argued, studies the general and particular laws of social development; sociology studies the general and particular laws of social development. The two are therefore identical. Because historical materialism already exists, there is no need for sociology as an independent science.[2] The central points of this position were as follows:

- Sociology is a philosophical discipline.
- According to its content, it coincides with historical materialism.
- The subject of sociology is both the general laws of development of human history and the specific laws of the functioning and development of socio-economic formations.
- Sociology, that is, historical materialism, studies social life at different levels.
- Sociology, that is, historical materialism, is also defined as an experimental, empirical science.

The term 'sociological research' is avoided and in its place is 'social research' which all social sciences perform.[3]

On the other side were those who maintained that historical materialism is not simply equivalent to sociology. Here it was argued that it is the theoretical side of sociology alone which coincides with historical materialism. (The argument implicitly conflated general theoretical and methodological questions.) The empirical or applied side of social enquiry therefore becomes an independent science, sociology. Understood in these terms, sociology is synonymous with 'concrete sociological research', based on empirical investigations.[4]

In addition to these two principal positions, there were a variety of alternatives advanced. One of these differentiated between historical materialism and sociology according to the laws which each studies. Historical materialism studies the general laws of development of society as a whole, historically defined. These general laws are manifest at all stages of societal development and in all spheres of life. Sociology, on the other hand, should study the laws pertaining both to specific formation,[5] that is, specific stages of social development, and to specific spheres of life, that is, economics, politics, etc.[6] This proposition was somewhat altered subsequently by those who argued that historical materialism studies the laws of nature, society and thought, whereas sociology specializes in the study of society alone.[7]

A further position was that which saw sociology as a science studying laws which proceed from the more general to the particular. Within this hierarchy, three major distinctions were made. The first distinction refers to the general laws existing during the entire course of human history. This coincides with historical materialism, with 'all-sociological' (*obshchesotsiologicheskaia*) theory. The second distinction pertains to those laws which are present in different economic formations (capitalism, socialism, communism).[8] The third distinction refers to those laws discoverable through concrete sociological research, which pertain to only one social formation.[9]

Distinct from but related to these alternative positions about the relationship between historical materialism and sociology were a series of views about the relationship between sociology and the social sciences. One of these claimed that sociology is social science in its most general form. Sociology is fuller and wider than other social sciences because it uses the results obtained from all social research and it also studies society directly. Thus sociology examines the entire system of social relations.[10]

A different view asserted that sociology – an independent science – is just one of the many concrete social sciences which study social structure. Sociology, as a social science (and not as part of philosophy), is similar to the other sciences which share with sociology the theory and method of historical materialism. Related to this view is the argument that sociological research is merely one form of social research: social research is wider than sociological research because it covers social relations in such diverse fields as economics, law and the state.[11] As against this, there is the view that each of the three branches of Marxism-Leninism – philosophy, political economy and scientific communism – conduct social research.[12] Sociological research can therefore be subsumed under any or all branches.

It should be understood that no real resolution was arrived at over these various positions which were taken up in the years following 1956. In whole or in part, many of the debates continued to the 1990s. The point which is emphasised here is that the latent significance as opposed to the manifest content of these debates was in their establishing that there was a legitimate area of discussion about the exact status of sociology and its nature as a social science. This, of course, meant accepting the initial premise of sociology's existence at all. Through a combination of the various propositions described above, sociology – for all practical purposes – won the battle for legitimation and recognition as an independent academic discipline within the Soviet Union. In so doing, it demonstrated that a science in addition to historical materialism should be created.

While there was no consensus on the above classifications, most Soviet sociologists would have agreed that in the most general sense theirs was a science which studied the laws of the functioning and development of society, a science proceeding from Marx's basic laws, embracing the socio-historic process and concerning social phenomena and their interaction. This science investigated the laws and motive forces of the origin, development and replacement of socio-economic formations. At the same time, it was concerned with the totality and interaction of social phenomena within society: sociology studies the social structure of society as a complete, organised system of social relations, institutions and social groups, interrelated with each other. Because the individual is viewed as the product of society, being both nurtured and moulded by it, society is defined as the broadest system of mutually interacting persons.

The Soviet View of Bourgeois Sociology

In general, the Soviet conception of sociology was inversely related to its view on bourgeois sociology. Since the 1920s, any means of constructing (Marxist) sociology had simultaneously been a way of combating bourgeois ideology which, according to this view, tried to construct sociology by basically ignoring historical materialism. Marxist sociology was considered to be in a state of ideological war with bourgeois sociology. The battlefield itself was the arena for, as well as the means of, an intense ideological struggle. Marxist and bourgeois sociology were enemies because they have opposing social, political and theoretical bases; their understanding of history, either materialist or idealist, was incompatible; and the former carried out 'scientific' sociological research whereas the latter was plagued by empiricism.[13]

The most obvious and basic Soviet criticism of bourgeois sociology was its class character. The interests of the bourgeoisie are the *de facto* bases of bourgeois sociological principles. The bourgeoisie, as the ruling class, needs sociology to help solve numerous problems; sociology comes to the aid of the bourgeoisie, just as it, in turn, aids sociology by readily financing research. Thus bourgeois sociology, as the executor of the direct social orders of the ruling class, 'aided' research such as Project Camelot. This naturally raised in the Soviets' mind the problem of the relationship between sociologist and client.[14]

Furthermore, bourgeois sociology acted as the disseminator of bourgeois ideology, as the 'handmaid of imperialism'.[15]   It recommended ways of strengthening the capitalist system and of rationalizing and stimulating the organization and productivity of labour.

> Modern bourgeois sociology is nothing more than a mechanical aggregate of different social myths and utopias which express the age-old dream of a class peace, social integration, solidarity, harmony, etc., while preserving private ownership of the goods and means of production and, consequently, the exploitation of man by man.[16]

Bourgeois sociology also undertook to cure the individual ills and eliminate the conflicts within capitalist society, but it completely ignored the general social process of which these ills were merely particular manifestations. The individual is taught to be a loyal member of bourgeois society and to blame not the society but him/herself for any and all difficulties.[17]

The second objection to bourgeois sociology, namely, its lack of and use of theory, is somewhat paradoxical. On the one hand, bourgeois sociology was condemned for not having a general, all-embracing theory of social development and for denying the significance of such a theory. But on the other hand, it was accused of professing idealism and metaphysics, rather than materialism and dialectics. In a similar vein, bourgeois sociology was criticized for giving credence to such diverse theories and philosophies as positivism, neo-positivism, pragmatism, personalism, existentialism, neo-Malthusianism, neo-Thomism, neo-Kantianism, and so on.[18]

Although bourgeois sociology was not guided by a single, all-embracing theory (such as historical materialism), it was recognized nonetheless that it contained more limited sociological theories. Of these, three usually appeared as targets of criticism. The first was the 'stages of growth' theory, originally proposed by W. W. Rostow as an alternative to the Marxist study of socio-economic formations. It is not difficult to understand why this came under attack, especially if it is recalled that Rostow sub-titled his theory 'A non-communist manifesto'. The second referred to the concept of 'a single industrial society' which is closely related to convergence theory. While it was accepted that the two (former) superpowers were indeed industrial countries, one was capitalist and the other socialist, and the theory negated the root differences between the two. Convergence was neither feasible nor desirable. The third theory is associated with Malinowski and Parsons, namely, the theory of structural-functionalism. While structural-functional analysis may have exposed several links in society, its limits were obvious to Soviet critics:

> In the first place, this [its limits] is explained by the disregard for the socio-economic basis of the social structure which is principally distorted by the concept of structure and function of social formations. In the second place, [this is explained] by the disregard for the genetic approach to the analysis of social phenomena [and] by the anti-historicism peculiar to functionalism. Marxist

sociology proceeds from the organic unity of the structural-functional and genetic approaches [or methods] in sociological research.[19]

The problem with the structural-functional approach to social phenomena, according to the Soviet critics, was a methodological one: the methodology of Marxism is ignored by the structural functionalists. Since Marxist sociology considered both functioning and development, the method of functionalism cannot be applied because it only discusses the former. In contrast, 'Marxism ... examines any social system as maintaining a certain stability, [while] simultaneously becoming, appearing, developing and transforming into another system.'[20]

However, latterly more Soviet sociologists stressed that the structural-functional approach was an organic part of the Marxist method of sociological – or economic – analysis. Marx in *Capital* – and Engels in his works on the family – was cited as a classical form of 'systems (structural) and functional analysis of capitalist economy as a complex dynamic system'.[21] Furthermore, 'to speak of structural-functional analysis as wholly the creation of Western sociology [and to argue that] Marxist sociology must be "re-armed" using it, means above all to ignore the real experience of the development of Marxist theory which there is at the present time'.[22]

A third major Soviet criticism of bourgeois sociology involved the connection between bourgeois sociology and social psychology or, put more accurately, the assimilation of the former by the latter. Accordingly, the objective logic of social development is overlooked and the real nature of capitalist society remains obscured behind a façade of psychic interaction between people – behind the web of individual human relations, acts and intentions.[23] Thus sociology is converted into a theory of behaviour in which no distinction is made between objective phenomena and their reflection in the minds of men. By equating the concept of 'social situation' with the concept of 'social-psychological', 'purely ideal' phenomena are analysed without regard for their dependence on and conditioning by material factors.[24] Thus the human psyche becomes the fundamental basis of society and the role of economics is ignored.

At the same time that bourgeois sociology was censured for gravitating towards social psychology, it was accused of marrying empiricism. Lacking a general theory and refusing to show general social patterns, bourgeois sociology then became equated with empirical research. The particular (i.e. the fact) is raised upon a pedestal and the general (i.e. the law of the historical process) is ignored.[25]

As a result, social life is compartmentalised. This partially happens because 'society' itself is thought of as a mechanistic aggregate of individuals', as an aggregate of isolated social beings.[26] Man, the individual, is discussed in the abstract, outside of classes, outside of social groups. What follows is the growth of separate sociological disciplines – for example, the sociology of religion or the sociology of the family – each concerned with carrying out petty studies. These researches, non-historical by nature and devoid of generalized theory, tackle specific, and not long range, problems, the 'solution' to which aims at adapting people to the existing system. Even the use of objective methods is nullified by a subjective interpretation of data. And even in the best cases of this 'factology', only the relations existing at the surface of social life are discovered.

The definition and criticism of bourgeois sociology in the 1966 *Kratkii Slovar' po Filosofii* (*Short Dictionary of Philosophy*) aptly sums up the Soviet view.

> In capitalist countries sociology is a branch of knowledge [which has] developed a network of institutions in which a large number of concrete researches is conducted. The majority of these researches bears a practical character and is subsidised by private firms and monopolies. Contemporary bourgeois sociology is separate from philosophy. It ceased being a general theory of social development, having been split into a multiplicity of separate 'sociologies' – labour, political life, education, family, leisure, sport, etc. Empiricism prevails ... Sociology, in point of fact, is converted into social psychology ... Thus, in spite of sociology's declaration of 'independence' from philosophy, bourgeois sociologists inevitably proceed from definite philosophical theories, as a rule idealistic and metaphysical. The inability of bourgeois sociology to give a general picture of the development of social life is explained by the fact that the bourgeoisie, as the class which has lost its *raison d'etre*, is not interested in the knowledge of the general laws of history which predict its demise. The class function of bourgeois sociology consists in working out practical means for smoothing over social conflicts, in justifying and defending capitalism. [This is] accompanied by attacks on communism ... Fearing to recognize the progressive development of society, bourgeois sociology prefers the concept of 'social change(s)' to the concept of 'progress' ... Criticism of contemporary bourgeois sociology and its methodological bases is one of the important tasks of Marxist sociology. [27]

In spite of this blanket criticism, it should be noted that, in more sophisticated Soviet writings, Western sociologists were divided into those with whom the Soviets should co-operate and those with whom co-operation was impossible. In more strictly political terms, there are two poles of thinking, one represented by C. Wright Mills and his criticism of the Cuban invasion and the American ruling elite, and the other represented by W. W. Rostow, as one of the authors of the single industrial society theory. The young radical sociologists who criticized conservative trends in the development of bourgeois sociology were favourably seen to present a new approach to sociology, especially in their 'non-conformist' research. [28]

The views presented above, gleaned from the considerable number of articles, monographs and books devoted to bourgeois sociology, represent the most general and widely held Soviet views concerning the functions and limitations of bourgeois sociology. By no means all of these arguments were found in each Soviet treatise, nor were they all upheld by everyone writing in the field. In fact, the majority of articles dealt with specific, rather than with general, areas of sociological interest. In many cases, a most detailed account of bourgeois theory and research was offered, explained and criticized. While the degree of sophistication regarding the presentation of the critiques varied considerably, the prevalent sentiment was that bourgeois sociology by its very nature was not and could not ever be Marxist sociology. Therefore those characteristics for which bourgeois sociology was criticized were considered not to be inherent in Marxist sociology.

In reviewing Soviet criticism of bourgeois sociology, it would be foolish not to note that in the first place, bourgeois sociologists criticize their own work and in the second, their criticism often falls within the range of shortcomings and criticisms noted and put forward by the Soviets. For example, Project Camelot was censured equally by Soviet and Westerner alike.[29] Or more broadly, the single industrial society theory stimulated many strong debates both for and against. However, it is not my intention to examine how valid these criticisms are, but rather to look at the positive role that the critiques of bourgeois sociology performed in terms of the development of Soviet sociology.

The invectives against bourgeois sociology helped to establish and stimulate the growth of sociology if for no other reason than that after discrediting bourgeois sociology in various ways, those who endorsed Soviet sociology could portray their own as the more superior science. Within a similar frame of 'ideological' warfare, some Soviets might have argued that they needed their own sociology to counteract both the theory and research of bourgeois sociologists.

On a more positive front, the explication of bourgeois texts made bourgeois theory and research available in Russian to a large number of people, many of whom would not have had access to the originals. In the best instances, the theory or research was presented in detail before it was criticized. Often the theories and researches were traced through a period of time, sometimes dating back to the nineteenth century. Extensive bibliographies may have accompanied the discussions. In this way the Soviet sociologist learnt about and may have consequently utilised what was happening outside the Soviet Union. In this sense his/her intellectual isolation (particularly prevalent during and immediately after the Stalinist era) was diminishing, his/her sociological horizons were broadened, and he/she may have been able to avoid some of the problems, in theory and methodology, which his/her colleagues abroad have faced and overcome. The process of adopting and adapting some aspects of bourgeois sociology becomes more apparent in the next chapter.

But before turning to that issue, it must be made clear that the discussions in the Soviet Union were about the classification and the definition of *Marxist* sociology. According to Soviet sociologists, Marxist and Soviet sociology were synonymous because the Soviets were unanimously engaged in Marxist sociology whereas the vast majority of sociologists in capitalist societies were engaged in what the Soviets typified as bourgeois sociology. Thus the generic term 'sociology' encompassed two mutually exclusive brands of sociology.

---

1 B. A. Grushin, 'Sotsiologiia i Sotsiologi', *Literaturnaia Gazeta*, 25 September 1965, p.1.

2 For a statement of this position, see the criticism of Iu. A. Levada for either attempting to separate historical materialism (or rather, all sociological theory) from Marxist sociology or create an alternative theory. First see Levada's 'Lektsii po Sotsiologii' in *Informatsionnyi Biulleten Nauchnogo Soveta AN SSSR po Problemam Konkretnykh Sotsial'nykh Issledovanii*

(Moscow, 1969) Nos. 20-21. For criticism, see 'O Lektsiakh po Sotsiologii Iu. A. Levady', *Vestnik MGU: Seriia Filosofiia*, No. 3, 1970, pp.95-6 and B. E. Kozlovskii and Iu. A. Sychev, 'Obsuzhdenie Kursa Lektsii Iu. A. Levady po Sotsiologii', *Fil Nauki*, No. 3, 1970, pp.178-85.

3 A. G. Zdravomyslov, *Metodologiia i Protsedura Sotsiologicheskikh Issledovanii*, Moscow, 1969, p.16.

4 See the following for an overall discussion of the problem: V. P. Rozhin, 'O Predmete Marksistskoi Sotsiologii', *Voprosy Marksistskoi Sotsiologii*, V. P. Rozhin (ed.), Leningrad, 1962, pp.3-6; A. Verbin and A. Furman, *Mesto Istoricheskogo Materializma v Sisteme Nauk*, Moscow, 1965, pp.141-3; B. A. Grushin, *Mneniia o Mire i MirMnenii*, Moscow, 1967, pp.3-8.

5 'Formation' is the translation for the Russian *formatsiia*, meaning stage or structure, especially as it refers to a social system. Hence, stage of social development.

6 A. I. Verbin, V. Zh. Kelle, and M. Ia. Koval'zon, 'Istoricheskii Materialism i Sotsiologiia', *Vop Fil*, No. 5, 1968, p.154.

7 G. V. Osipov, *Sovremennaia Burzhuaznaia Sotsiologiia*, Moscow, 1964, pp.373-4.

8 Some maintain that this second distinction referred only to communist formation and the third to individual social groups within this formation. Therefore, other formations (e.g. capitalism) were not studied.

9 A. M. Kovalev, 'Eshche Raz o Sotsiologii Marksizma i Nauchnom Kommunizme', *Fil Nauki*, No. 1, 1967, pp.112-13.

10 D. I. Chesnokov, 'K Voprosu o Sootnoshenii Obshchestvennykh Nauk', *Metodologicheskie Voprosy Obshchestvennykh Nauk*, D. I. Chesnokov et al. (eds.), Moscow, 1966, p.38.

11 F. Konstantinov and V. Kelle, *Historical Materialism – The Marxist Sociology*, Moscow, 1965, p.17.

12 A. G. Zdravomsyslov and M. T. Petrov, 'Trudy V. I. Lenina – Klassicheskii Obrazets Marksistskogo Konkretnogo Sotsial'nogo Issledovaniia', *Fil Nauki*, No. 2, 1963, p.3.

13 See, for example, A. M. Rumiantsev and G. V. Osipov, 'Marksistskaia Sotsiologiia i Konkretnye Sotsial'nye Issledovaniia', *Vop Fil*, No. 6, 1968, p.7.

14 V. Shliapentokh, *Sotsiologiia Dlia Vsekh*, Moscow, 1970, p.45 and N. F. Naumova, 'Nravstvennye Antonomii Sovremennoi Burzhuaznoi Sotsiologii', *Vop Fil*, No. 2, 1970, p.112.

15 The corollary to this is bourgeois sociology's function as detractor of socialism, communism and Marxist sociology.

16 G. V. Osipov et al., 'Marksistskaia Sotsiologiia i Mesto v Nei Konkretnikh Sotsiologicheskikh Issledovanii', *Fil Nauki*, No. 5, 1962, pp.21-32.

17 N. V. Novikov, *Kritika Sovremennoi Burzhuaznoi 'Nauki o Sotsial'nom Povedenii'*, Moscow, 1966, p.71.

18 One Soviet critic criticized fellow Marxist writers for confusing bourgeois philosophical beliefs with bourgeois sociological beliefs. See G. M. Andreeva, 'Priemy i Metody Empiricheskikh Issledovanii v Sovremennoi Burzhuaznoi Sotsiologii', *Voprosy Organizatsii i Metodiki Konkretno-Sotsiologicheskikh Issledovanii*, G. K. Ashin et al. (eds.), Moscow, 1963, p.90. Also M. P. Baskin's 'Krizis Burzhuaznoi Ideologii', *Sovremennaia Burzhuaznaia Sotsiologiia*, by G. V. Osipov, Moscow, 1964, p.20.

19 Strukturno-funkstional'naia Shkola', *Sotsiologiia v SSSR*, II G. V. Osipov (ed.), Moscow, 1966, p.505.

20 D. M. Ugrinovich, 'O Predmete Marksistskoi Sotsiologii', in *Ocherki Metodologii Poznaniia Sotsial'nyk Iavlenii*, D. M. Ugrinovich, O V. Larmin, and A. K. Uledov (eds.), Moscow, 1970, p.31.

21 *Ibid.* p.29.

22 If this was a change in the position, this would parallel changes in the acceptance of 'bourgeois' methods described in Chapter 3.

23 I. M. Popova, 'Mesto i Rol' Sotsial'noi Psikhologii v Amerikanskii Sotsiologii', *Vestnik MGU*, No. 5, 1960, pp.44-57.

24 G. V. Osipov, 'Nekotorye Cherty i Osobennosti Burzhuaznoi Sotsiologii XX Veka', *Vop Fil*, No. 8, 1962, pp.120-31.

25 M. N. Rutkevich and L. N. Kogan, 'O Metodakh Konkretno-Sotsiologicheskogo Issledovaniia', *Vop Fil*, No. 3, 1961, pp.123-33.

26 G. M. Andreeva, 'Metodologicheskie Osnovy Burzhuaznoi Empiricheskoi Sotsiologii', *Metodologicheskie Voprosy Obshchestvennykh Nauk*, D. I. Chesnokov *et al.* (eds.) , Moscow, 1966, p.99.

27 'Sotsiologiia', *Kratkii Slovar' po Filosofii*, I. V. Blauberg (ed.), Moscow, 1966, pp.278-80.

28 See, for example, V. S. Semenov and M. N. Gretskii, 'Marksistsko-leninskaia Nauka V Nastuplenii, *Fil Nauki*, No. 2, 1971, p.163.

29 G. Sjoberg (ed.) , *Ethics, Politics and Social Research*, London, 1969.

The Theory of Research

The more closely one examines Soviet accounts on research methods and techniques, the more one becomes aware that Soviet sociologists were as anxious as others to find those methods and techniques which would best serve to analyze social phenomena. Such differences as occurred in their writings may be traced to the Soviets' original attempts to obtain initial recognition of the most elementary ways and means of gathering, processing and analyzing information. The usual process consisted in explaining and qualifying a specific method and then appealing for its acceptance by other Soviet sociologists. Once the method had been at least partially accepted as valid for Marxist research, the sociologists pleaded for and indicated ways for its improvement. Viewed as a whole, the process represented a strategy for institutionalizing sociological research practices.

As part of this process, more and more was written about the benefits of studying the techniques employed by non-Marxist sociologists and engaging in critical borrowing of such methods. Justification for the use of such methods by Soviet sociologists had to be sought and the fact that they were used by bourgeois sociologists rationalized. Thus there was a change from perceiving methods as 'bourgeois' to seeing them as 'acceptable' in terms of their general validity and applicability. Like bourgeois sociologists, Soviet sociologists were slowly more able to weigh the pros and cons of already established methods and to develop others.

Earlier blanket criticism of various methods subsided. In its place were discussions about the significance of using such indices as the arithmetic mean, the degree of variation from the mean and the degree of error. Gradually a variety of methods – game theory, the theory of optimal programming, the theory of probability, correlation analysis – became part of the sociologist's normal equipment. By this stage, the most significant criticism was concerned with the mechanical application – potential or actual – of methods worked out in other disciplines, without due consideration of their validity for sociology.

No matter which methods were used, the Soviet researcher was seen as ideally performing certain functions. He/she was to examine the general theoretical problems of society and analyze social phenomena which appear as a result of new forms of productive, social and personal relations. His/her studies should have facilitated the 'all-round' development of the individual's personality (e.g. the 'new man'), thus linking societal with individual development in the process of building communism. By studying social phenomena, the sociologists should have been able to influence the development of society in the capacity of a social planner: they were to extract meaning and a programme of action from the 'facts' they uncovered. He/she was to share the data with state, party and public organizations which, in turn, would aid him/her in research. By analyzing the results, he/she was to provide planning agencies, enterprises and institutions – especially in the techno-economic realm – with invaluable information and 'feedback'. Pre-conceived stereotypes were to be destroyed by such research and negative phenomena (such as crime) were to be eliminated. Bearing in mind that the Soviets equated sociology with social research, the following remarks by V. A. Iadov, a leading sociologist, are a representative statement of the Soviet view of the functions of such social research:

> First, the *informational* function – sociology uncovers social problems, provides scientific description of them, and classifies and analyzes them. Then, the *critical* function – it collates new facts with those previously known, evaluates possible variations in explaining them, offers explanatory hypotheses with respect to the given sphere of phenomena ... Next, the *theoretical* function – the scholar builds a non-contradictory, integral concept, a model of the sphere under study. Next the function of *prognosis* – forecasting possible paths of development of changes in social processes and evaluating the reliability of the forecasts. And then the *'engineering'* or applied function – the sociologist proposes optimum paths for active intervention in social processes in a socially desirable direction. (Italics mine).[1]

Concrete social enquiry was (still) said to be based on historical materialism which, in effect, served as the methodology for sociology. Historical materialism should have acted in the research process as method and principle for determining subject matter, formulating hypotheses, compiling a plan of investigation and explaining results. How did it help to interpret social reality?

> The Marxist [read: historical materialist] interpretation of a social situation, free of metaphysical and idealist one-sidedness, regards it [a social situation] as a link in the general historical process, as an interconnection of material and ideological relationships, in which the economy plays a decisive but not inexorable role, and in which the common will and the conscious activity of the socialist collective are capable of accelerating to a considerable degree the course of historical development, operating in accordance with its objective guidance.[2]

Less concisely, Soviet sociologists were formally guided by the following principles of research. First of all, historical perspectives, that is, the interrelationship between the past, the present and the future must be emphasized. Social enquiry is to be grounded on history; sociological research cannot be 'photography',[3] because it encompasses the historical situation. Second, sociological research is to be based on a materialist, rather than an idealist, understanding of social phenomena; laws and interrelations are objective and determined by material circumstances. Finally, sociological research is to be intrinsically objective and scientific because historical materialism is said to be the first scientific system for understanding and then directing the development of society.

In these studies, therefore, sociologists should have shown how the general theoretical patterns were manifested and prove the reality of the theory. But he/she must also have uncovered new *zakonomernosti*.[4]

Marxism-Leninism never laid claims to predicting historical events in all their specific details. After all, every historical event contains an enormous number of crisscrossing interactions and factors that add up to the inimitable uniqueness of a particular historical phenomenon. This is why Marxism-Leninism assumes it is necessary to study the changing reality *anew*, starting from preceding generalizations and facts, in order to perceive the sources of the new, in order to use, for study, the general principles of Marxism as a methodological medium ...[5]

B. A. Grushin similarly emphasized the contributions to be made to general theory by research into an immanent reality: 'the concrete study of social reality, which always proves to be *new social reality*, perforce must enrich general theory, must as it is clear that existing theory must guide concrete research, determine its structure, methodology, etc.'[6]

Theory and methodology were therefore considered to be fundamentally united: to improve one meant to correspondingly improve the other. Some Soviet sociologists, however, did recognize the existence of two problems not unlike those faced by their Western colleagues. The first involved the connection between meta-theory and research. Here the crucial question was: How could the original theoretical positions be embodied in the concrete research methods used for retrieving and analyzing materials? The second problem was concerned with how one elevated research data to theoretical generalizations so that the research not only gave direct recommendations for practice, but also served as the basis for the further development of theory.[7]

In attempting to deal with these problems, Iadov has inserted a transition stage between the theoretical and the empirical.[8] He suggested a three-tiered, interlocking system for ascertaining objective sociological facts and drawing up a programme of research. The highest level is the philosophical and scientific world view (the paradigm) – general notions about the processes of social and natural life (e.g., dialectical and historical materialism). The second level translates the concepts of the first into sociological language. This is the level of sociological theory and hypotheses, the level at which hypotheses related to concrete social situations are advanced; in other words, the level of 'middle range' theory. The third level involves the methods and techniques required for actual empirical research. See Figure 3.1.[9]

These three levels – roughly, *Weltanschauung*, sociological theory and research methods – are Iadov's basic methodological prerequisites for establishing a programme of research. Closely connected to this scheme is his view of the three levels of methodology.[10] Dialectical materialism occupies the first level, the level of universal scientific methodology; the dialectical approach is neither a supplement nor an addition to the methods and techniques of research, but rather acts as a directive for working out these research procedures. The second and third levels are, respectively, the general and the specific methodology of sociological research and are parallel to what Iadov terms all-sociological (*obshchesotsiologicheskaia*) theory and specific sociological theory. All-sociological methodology gives instructions related to the ways of working out special sociological theories which, in turn, contain particular methodological directions.

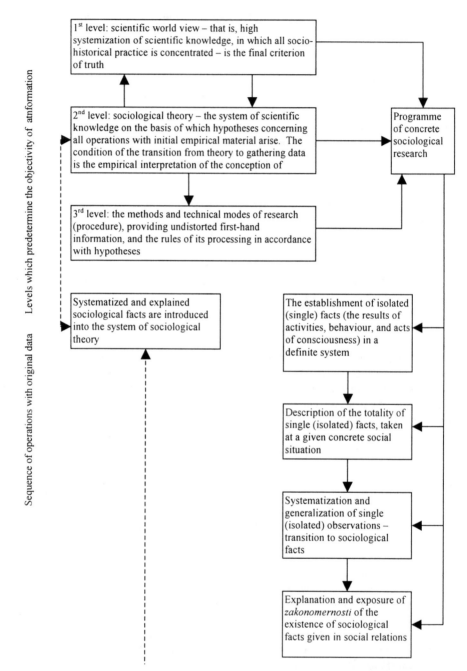

Figure 3.1 General scheme of the sequence of operations of ascertaining objective sociological facts

As is obvious, Iadov's two schema are very similar; the connection between theory and methodology is quite clear. He has further described and classified the methods and techniques to be used at the third stage. His scheme is a comprehensive picture of those areas of research methods which have been discussed and used by other sociologists in the Soviet Union.[11] As such these methods received similar, if at times less sophisticated, treatment by Soviet sociologists as they would have from other social scientists. See Figure 3.2.[12]

Iadov was certainly not the only sociologist concerned with these problems. A. M. Rumiantsev and G. V. Osipov, for example, see four levels in the system of sociological knowledge, namely:

- general sociological theory – historical materialism, the most general laws of society;
- theory of the social structure of society, which studies laws of interaction and functioning of different social systems within a given social structure;
- theory of different social systems studying specific *zakonomernosti* (regularities, patterns) of functioning of different aspects and phenomena of social life (e.g. sociology of the family, of labour, etc.);
- empirical level – research of social facts and their scientific systematization.[13]

This hierarchy represents an alternative formulation of the strategy of combining general theory with middle range theory and empirical research.

A general scheme to guide the sociologist in his research was constructed in 1967 by V. N. Shubkin who, like Iadov, was an eminent sociologist whose pronouncements carried considerable weight. The scheme was one of the first to indicate various stages of research, combining operational concepts and quantitative procedures.[14] See Figure 3.3.

In his *Metodologiia i Protsedura Sotsiologicheskikh Issledovannii* (*Methodology and Procedures of Sociological Research*), A. G. Zdravomyslov suggested five stages of research procedures: 1) working out the programme of research; 2) defining the objects and the unit of observation; 3) working out the means of gathering material; 4) gathering material; and 5) analyzing material and its generalizations. Zdravomyslov saw no principal differences between Shubkin's scheme (which underlines and isolates quantitative aspects of procedures) and his own (which graphically depicts its logical junctions).[15]

In sum, the Soviet sociologist's original concern was to legitimate a body of tools to be used for sociological research within the framework of historical materialism. This process went on over time and to some extent accounts for the methodological weakness and lack of sophistication in much early Soviet research. It also explains a growing recognition by some Soviet theorists of problems concerning the relation between theory and methods, a relation which, in more official terms, was unquestioned and unquestionable because theory and method were united.

Methods

<u>Sphere of gathering first-hand information</u>   <u>Sphere of processing first-hand information</u>

related to:

1. ascertaining single (isolated) facts	2. system of gathering first-hand information	
observation	monographic enquiry	description and classification
study of documents	complete enquiry	experimental analysis (actual and conceived experiments
questionnaires	selective enquiry	
	experimental observation (actual experiment)	statistical analysis (survey of statistical laws)
		systemic analysis
		typologization
		genetic or historical analysis
		social modelling

Techniques

<u>Sphere of gathering first-hand information</u>   <u>Sphere of processing first-hand information</u>

related to:

1. ascertaining single (isolated) facts	2. system of gathering first-hand information	
methods of qualitative control of first-hand information: adequacy validity stability	statistical equipment for selecting single (isolated) observations	logical means (for example, systemic analysis)
	methods of qualitative and quantitative levelling out of characteristics	statistical methods (descriptive statistics, statistics of deduction and ascertainment of functional connections)
measurement of quantitative characteristics of first-hand facts ('scaling')		other mathematical means, not statistical (for example, linear programming, use of the theory of graphs, mathematical modelling
		techniques of processing sociological qualitatively-quantitatively compounded characteristics (indices)

Figure 3.2 Methods and techniques

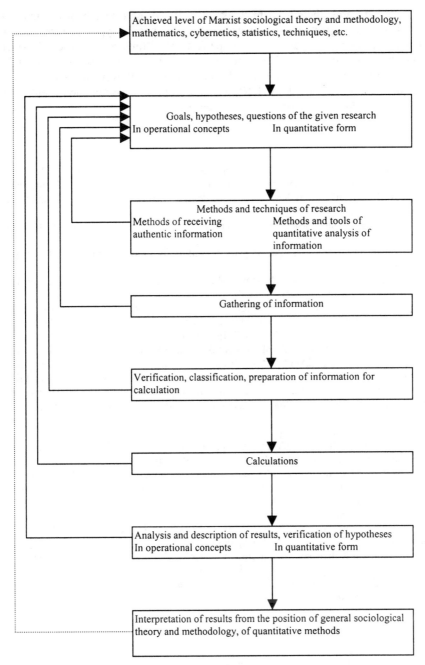

Figure 3.3 Scheme of sociological research with the use of quantitative methods

In general, their need to work out a theory of research meant that the Soviets were not great innovators with regard to specific types of research. A major exception to this has been their 'perfecting' of time budget research which studies how people allocate their time. (This research is discussed in Chapter 7.) The methods developed after much debate in the USSR were utilised in cross-national studies sponsored by UNESCO's European Co-ordination Centre for Research and Documentation in Social Sciences.

1 V. A. Iadov, 'Prestizh v Opasnosti', *Literaturnaia Gazeta*, 28 February 1968, p.11.

2 V. V. Mshvenieradze and G. V. Osipov, 'Osovny Napravleniia i Problematika Konkretnykh Sotsial'nykh Issledovanii', *Sotsiologiia v SSSR*, Vol. I, G. V. Osipov (ed.) Moscow, 1966, p.57.

3 P. N. Fedoseev, 'Marksistskaia Sotsiologiia, ee Zadachi i Perspektivy', *Vestnik AN SSSR*, No. 7, 1966, p.7.

4 *Zakonomernost'* – order; regularity; pattern; conformity to systematic/established law of nature or society.

5 A. M. Rumiantsev, 'Vstupaiushchemu v Mir Nauki', *Komsomol'skaia Pravda*, 8 June 1967, p.3. (Rumiantsev's italics).

6 B. A. Grushin, 'Sotsiologiia i Sotsiologi', *Literaturnaia Gazeta*, 25 September 1965, p.2.

7 See G. M. Andreeva's discussion in 'Metodologicheskaia Rol' Teorii na Raznykh Etapakh Sotsial'nogo Issledovaniia', *Vop Fil*, No. 7, 1964, p.16.

8 V. A. Iadov, 'Ob Ustanovlenii Faktov v Konkretnom Sotsiologicheskom Issledovanii, *Fil Nauki*, No. 5, 1966, pp.28-38. Also discussed in Iadov's *Metodologiia i Protsedury Sotsiologicheskikh Issledovanni*, Tartu, 1968, pp.20-32. See also G. M. Andreeva and E. P. Nikitin's proposals for a series of hierarchically organized levels for explaining laws ('Metod Ob'iasneniia v Sotsiologii', *Sotsiologiia v SSSR*, Vol. II, Moscow, 1966, pp.124-44).

9 Iadov, *Fil Nauki*, No. 5, 1966, p.37.

10 V. A. Iadov, 'Rol' Metodologii v Opredelenii Metodov i Tekhniki Konkretnogo Sotsiologicheskogo Issledovaniia', *Vop Fil*, No. 10, 1966, pp.27-37.

11 Iadov fails to mention one other early 'method', namely, the role of scientific and theoretical conferences. These conferences were usually listed as one of the primary methods of research.

12 Iadov, *Vop Fil*, No. 10, 1966, p.33.

13 A. M. Rumiantsev and G. V. Osipov, 'Marksistskaia Sotsiologiia i Konkretnye Sotsial'nye Issledovaniia', *Vop Fil*, No. 6, 1968, p.7.

14 V. N. Shubkin'Kolichestvennye Metody v Sotsiologii', *Vop Fil*, No. 3, 1967, p.38. Also see Shubkin's *Sotsiologicheskie Opyty*, Moscow, 1970, pp.66-7.

15 A. G. Zdravomyslov, *Metodologiia i Protsedura Sotsiologicheskikh Issledovanii*, Moscow, 1969, pp.44, 47.

4

The Sociologists

The exact number of 'sociologists' in the Soviet Union was unknown. The term itself is somewhat vague so that such a figure, if it were precisely calculable, might have included the amateur as well as the more highly skilled and educated sociologist.* For the purposes of the following discussion, however, an individual is a sociologist if he/she defined him/herself as such. What is certain is that the number of people in this broad category continually expanded.

The following profile of Soviet sociologists is divided into three main sections. The first section discusses the training of the sociologists and their complaints about its inadequacy, a deficiency which may be traced to the discipline's origin in philosophy. This question of training is then continued in an examination of the activities of institutes carrying out professional training as well as research. The second section surveys the *Sovetskaia Sotsiologicheskaia Assotsiatsiia* (Soviet Sociological Association), the only body which represented the sociologists, and closely examines the participants it sent to the Sixth World Congress of Sociology. The final section looks at the role played by journals in informing their readers of current sociological research, in linking the Soviets with other socialist countries, and in reporting Soviet, socialist and international conferences and exchanges.

Training and Research Institutes

> The sociologist's vocation is an unusual one. He must have a broad outlook and all round professional training. For this reason we consider it advisable to open sociology divisions in the universities of Moscow, Leningrad, Novosibirsk, and Kiev, and to offer specialization in this line of study for graduate students and upper-classmen in the humanities faculties.[1]

In March 1966, the noted Novosibirsk sociologist, V. N. Shubkin, published the above proposition in *Pravda*. A month later Academician A. Aleksandrov, writing in *Literaturnaia Gazeta*, reiterated the call for improving the training of sociologists: training, he said, is 'conducted on an extremely limited scale, maybe at two or three universities, on the basis of the initiative of several enthusiasts in this field ... The impression is created that in the eyes of the USSR Ministry of Higher

---

* P. N. Fedoseev stated that 'about 2000 workers in *vuzy*, scientific research institutes, party, komsomol, and trade union organizations are actively engaged in social research.' See his 'Marksistskaia Sotsiologiia, ee Zadachi i Perspektivy', *Vestnik AN SSSR*, No. 7, 1966, p.5.

and Specialised Secondary Education this science does not exist at all'.[2]   By the end of that same year, V. A. Iadov of Leningrad had joined the angry chorus:

> The USSR Ministry of Higher and Specialised Secondary Education obviously thinks sociology should continue to develop 'on a volunteer basis'. Otherwise it is difficult to explain why for the third year now the Ministry is not reacting to persistent appeals to offer the appropriate specialities in at least three of the country's universities – Moscow, Leningrad, and Novosibirsk – where there are trained specialists.[3]

The first 'sociologists' in the post-1956 era were trained as philosophers and became social scientists because they concentrated on social laws and theory. The majority of these people focused their attention primarily on ideological aspects, merely reiterating Marxist social theory on given topics; the minority became sociologists by performing actual empirical research. Data from the first All-Union Sociology Symposium held in February 1966 in Leningrad indicated that the composition of sociologists was changing. Sociologists at this conference received their education in the following fields:[4]

	per cent
Philosophy	25
History	27
Economics	10
Psychology	3
Other humanities	30.5
Technical specialists	4.5

It is quite apparent that none of the conference participants was educated as a sociologist *per se*, even though the majority were described as having been occupied with sociology for three to four years.

While there appeared to be little specific training in the discipline,* whatever training there was came under scrutiny. For example, Iadov complained in 1966 that 'the level of training of many "professional" sociologists is, alas, very low at the moment ... We have neither teaching aids on the methodology and techniques of empirical research nor specialization in sociological research in the humanities departments.'[5] Commentators at the Sukhumi Conference (April 1967) on 'Quantitative Methods in Social Research' pointed out that 'even if such a speciality were introduced in the next academic year (and the hopes of this are feeble), the first professionally trained sociologists would not appear for several years. There are extremely few people enrolled in graduate work in sociology.' Who, then, should train the sociologists? 'How could people [instructors in the

---

* For contrary evidence based on his first-hand knowledge of the situation in Moscow, see Wesley A. Fisher's letter to the editor in the November-December 1971 issue of *Problems of Communism*, p.81.

social sciences at the institutes for raising qualifications] themselves unacquainted with sociology train sociologists? Or people who are familiar with it only theoretically?[6] The general position presented by these views seems clear. The circle is complete: few places existed where those who wanted to become sociologists could be trained, while at the same time few institutions employed people capable of teaching the discipline.

There is, however, evidence contrary to this assertion. This evidence suggests that there was an apparently growing number of dissertations dealing with sociological topics. Since the beginning of 1966, data on philosophy dissertation topics and the institutions awarding philosophy dissertations were published by the Supreme Attestation Commission's (VAK) appraisal commission (*ekspertnaia komissiia*). 'Sociology' receives different treatment in these accounts.[7]

In the six reports up to the beginning of the 1970s, sociology was only once – in 1965-6 – listed as an independent discipline: in 1964-5, it was listed as 'history of philosophy (including the history of bourgeois philosophy and sociology)'; in the years 1966-9 it was coupled with scientific communism; and in the last year, 1969-70, 'sociological research' (and not sociology *per se*) was attached to historical materialism. Consequently, it was impossible to get an exact figure for theses in sociology. (Table 4.1, however, gives some indication of the fluctuating number of dissertations.)

Table 4.1   Dissertations, by year and subject

	Total	Doctorate	Candidate
1965			
Historical materialism and scientific communism	98	16	82
History of philosophy (and bourgeois sociology)	65	16	49
Subtotal	163	32	131
Total (all theses)	340	54	286
1965-6			
Scientific communism	55	3	52
Historical materialism	30	5	25
Sociology	16	2	14
Subtotal	101	10	91
Total (all theses)	340	37	303
1966-7			
Scientific communism and sociology	75	9	66
Historical materialism	38	9	29
Subtotal	113	18	95
Total (all theses)	323	43	280

The question of meeting this problem was first posed in the 1967-8 discussion when the introduction of Doctorate and Candidate degrees in Socio-political Sciences was suggested. Since then each report has re-emphasized this idea.*

To a greater or lesser extent, all of the reports discussed the themes of the dissertations in sociology. The earliest one only noted an uneven distribution of thesis topics and advocated stimulating research in the 'theoretical problems of sociology and methodological questions of concrete social sciences'. The next report again pointed to the insignificant number of theses written on the basis of concrete social research and, except for vaguely mentioning theses connected with the problems of working and free time, did not specify research topics. The 1966-7 account did elaborate the themes of the sociology dissertations including those on the changing content and character of labour and on social structure, especially on the *rapprochement* of the working class and intellectuals and on the evolution of different social groups. Two theses on time budget research – one by M. S. Aivazian and the other by V. A. Artemov (the latter's work was well known in this area) – received much praise. In the next academic year, two distinguished Soviet sociologists earned their doctorates, B. A. Grushin for 'Public opinion (methodology and methods of its research)' and V. A. Iadov for 'Methodological problems of concrete sociological research'. Out of the eleven who earned Candidate degrees, four studied problems of free time,** while the others concentrated on the problems of *byt* (daily life, customs), labour, socialist production team and spiritual interests of youth. The 1968-9 report did not specifically discuss the themes (or, more correctly, only discussed what was not examined). The final report, however, did. Doctorates were conferred on G. N. Volkov for 'Social problems of development of science and technology', D. M. Gvishiani for 'American theory of organizational management' and A. G. Zdravomsyslov for 'Theoretical and methodological problems of research of social interests'. The candidates examined methodological problems of research of society and the individual, problems of the scientific-technical revolution and its influence on social life under capitalism and socialism, and contemporary bourgeois sociology.

As might be expected, the standard of dissertations varied a great deal, outstanding being the distinguished work of Iadov, Grushin and Zdravomyslov. The authors of the reports themselves criticized the general standards of the theses for a variety of reasons, namely, lack of originality, doubling of themes, lack of theoretical and/or practical significance, themes which were too comprehensive, and insufficient application of data obtained in concrete sociological research in the fields of scientific communism, historical materialism, scientific atheism, ethics and aesthetics. On the whole, however, the authors felt that the quality of the theses was improving.

---

* The Doctor of Science degree (*doktorskaia stepen'*) is the highest academic degree, roughly equivalent to the DLitt or DSc.

The Candidate of Science degree (*kandidatskaia stepen'*) is a first post-graduate degree, roughly equivalent to an MA or MSc.

** Artemov and Aivazian were listed here as well as in the previous year.

Thus, philosophy students were writing theses in sociology and were, no doubt, getting some training in the discipline. This occurred in a few graduate or *ad hoc* seminars on theories and methods of sociology and through 'practical experience' either at universities or at research institutes. Where exactly were these people studying?

Once again, the Supreme Attestation Commission (VAK) provides an answer. While the 1964-5 information listed only the cities, the next two reports listed the specific universities, institutes and academies of sciences where philosophy (and hence, sociology) students studied; unfortunately, no indication was given as to the number of students per speciality per university or institute. Information was available regarding the names of the universities and academies of sciences by academic year and also regarding the omissions and additions per year (see Table 4.2). More specific information concerned the degree and training institutions in Moscow, the city where the majority of philosophy training took place (see Table 4.3). (In 1964-5, Moscow was only listed as one of the cities and, consequently, there was no breakdown by institutions.) The last three VAK reports did not discuss individual institutions.

Tables 4.2 and 4.3 certainly do not list all of the institutions where training took place, nor do they name all of the institutions which prepared sociologists for sociological research: scientific research institutes and *vuzy* (higher educational establishments) had sociological laboratories which did not offer degree and training programmes. The list of places for training and research continued to expand, but, on the whole, it can be divided into three types: those institutes attached to the universities and *vuzy*, those associated with the USSR and republic academies of sciences, and those linked to other organizations, such as the party, komsomol, trade unions, enterprises and journals. Thus, in any given city (depending on its size), one might have expected to find sociologists attached to one or more of these three types of institutes.

Before exploring some of the major centres of sociological research, let us enlarge the picture for Moscow. At Moscow State University, the Institute of Philosophy's Laboratory of Sociological Research worked on problems connected with equalizing the conditions of life between city and village, the influence of technological progress on workers (including socio-psychological research on the labour force), bourgeois sociology and problems of methodology. Other departments and laboratories within the University – such as the Department of Historical Materialism and the Laboratory for Labour Resources – also conducted sociological research.

The Academy of Sciences in Moscow comprehended a great number of Institutes, of which the following had units for sociological work: the Institute of State and Law (crime, delinquency and social management), Institute of Archaeology and Ethnography (culture and customs of peasants and the peoples of the USSR), Institute of Economics (social problems of technology and labour), and the Central Economic-Mathematics Institute (methodology of concrete social research and optimal economic planning). The Institute of Philosophy had a sector for studying new forms of labour and daily life which was transformed first into a Division of Concrete Social Research and then in 1968 into a full Institute of

Table 4.2   Locale of Universities and Academies of Sciences

1964-5[a]	1965-6: Additions (compared with 1964-5)[a]	1966-7: Omissions (compared with 1965-6)[a]
Moscow (exception, see Table 3)	Perm	Perm
Leningrad	Irkutsk	Tashkent
Urals	Voronezh	Kirghiz SSR, Institute of Philosophy and Law
Novosibirsk		
Bielorussian	Khar'kov	
Tomsk	L'vov	
Kazan	Latvian	
Gorkii		
Rostov		*Additions*
Krasnoiarsk Pedagogical Institute		(compared with 1965-6)
Kiev		Odessa
Tbilisi		Dagestan
Kazakh		Vil'nius
Tashkent		
Azerbaidzhan		
Erevan		
Tadzhik		
Saratov		
Kirghiz SSR, Institute of Philosophy and Law		
Academies of Sciences[b]		
1965-6: Additions		*1966-7*[c]
(compared with 1964-5)		compared with 1965-6)
Ukrainian SSR		d
Kazakh SSR		
Uzbek SSR		d
Bielorussian SSR		Missing
Kirghiz SSR		*Addition*
		Azerbaidzhan

[a] Unless otherwise noted, all are state universities.
[b] The 1964-5 list did not list Academies of Sciences.
[c] Unless otherwise noted, the 1965-6 Academies of Sciences appeared on the 1966-7 list.
[d] These Academies of Sciences have two listings, the first as the Sector of Social Sciences and the second as the Institute of Philosophy.

Table 4.3   Degree and training institutions in Moscow

1965-6	*1966-7*
Moscow State University, Philosophy Faculty	
Institute of Philosophy, USSR Academy of Sciences	
Academy of Social Sciences attached to CC CPSU	
Moscow State Pedagogical Institute	
Moscow Institute of Economy	
Higher Party School attached to CC CPSU	Missing
State Institute of Theatrical Art	
Moscow *Oblast'* Pedagogical Institute	
Social Sciences Sector, USSR Academy of Sciences	Missing
Military-Political Academy	
	Additions
	Moscow Institute of Culture
	Moscow Institute of International Relations

Concrete Social Research. The creation of this Institute within the Academy of Sciences, separated from the Institute of Philosophy, symbolized the legitimation of the discipline itself. The Institute housed five sectors: a sector of methodology, methods and techniques; a sector of the problems of development of social relations of city and country; a sector of problems of development of labour collectives; a sector of sociology and socio-psychological problems of the individual; and finally, a sector of problems of public opinion and the effectiveness of ideological work. The Academy of Sciences' Social Sciences' section also set up, in February 1966, a learned council on the problems of concrete social research to 'co-ordinate concrete social research, including sociological research, which is being conducted in the country'[8] and 'to realize links with sociological centres of the Ministry of Higher and Secondary School Education and Ministry of Culture with different public organizations, enterprises, etc'.[9]

Moscow also housed: the Institute of the World Labour Movement's Social Research Division – 'the second national centre for the field [which] seeks to stress and develop comparative studies, of both communist and non-communist countries';[10] *Komsomol'skaia Pravda*'s Public Opinion Institute (see Chapter 6);

the Central Statistical Administration of the RSFSR; and the Youth Problems Institute formed at the Komsomol Central Committee in 1964 to co-ordinate the work of fifty sociological groups and thirty-five youth centres in various towns and villages.[11]   Not separately listed here are the numerous party, enterprise, trade union and other organizations which either conducted or commissioned research (see below pp.39-41).

Another leading centre of sociological research was Leningrad where, in 1958, a sociology seminar was set up within the framework of the Soviet Sociological Association.   In October of 1960, the first sociology laboratory, attached to the Philosophy Faculty of Leningrad State University, was established. In 1963, other social science laboratories – including the sociology laboratory – entered the Union of Integrated Social Research and in 1965, the Union became the basis of the Institute of Complex Social Research, the largest research institute in Leningrad.   'In the system of the University, the Institute acts as an inter-departmental scientific centre, as a singular base of all the humanities faculties.'[12] In a 1965 report on research in Leningrad, the Institute was said to have a staff of ninety, some of whom worked at the Sociological Research Laboratory.[13]   On the whole, the Institute had three main research directions:

- social planning for industrial enterprises;
- working out optimal systems for administration and scientific organization of labour; and
- studying social problems of higher schools and the education of students.

Other institutes in Leningrad also had sociology laboratories.   The Leningrad Mechanics Institute had a group of workers studying intra-class differences; the Electro-Technical Institute worked on mass communication and mechanisms of response to socially significant information; the sociologists at the Philosophy Department of the Leningrad branch of the USSR Academy of Sciences studied the family, *byt*, and services, problems of city planning, change in the social structure, methodology of sociological research and problems of labour. Another centre for research was the Public Institute for Social Research which was established in 1963 without a paid staff.   It concentrated on problems linked with the development of technology and on the results of atheistic education.   In addition, the higher party school, the higher school of the trade union movement, and the komsomol city committee conducted research or had research done for them on a contractual basis, as did other interested organizations, such as the State Radio and Television Committee.

In Sverdlovsk, sociology was institutionalized in two places, at the University and at the Urals branch of the USSR Academy of Sciences.[14]   At the former, a philosophy sector was opened in 1965 which was transformed in 1966 into a philosophy faculty, one of whose functions was to prepare workers for sociology laboratories and instructors of social science for *tekhnikumy* and secondary schools. Research under the auspices of the University focused on three main areas: processes of raising the cultural-technical level of the working class (for example, work by Iovchuk), problems of change in the social structure (for example, Rutkevich), and the development of the spiritual life of working people (for example, Kogan). The Urals branch of the USSR Academy of Sciences had two special sociological sectors, one devoted to the problems of management and the other to research on the cultural and intellectual life of society.

While sociology was firmly ensconced in philosophy in Sverdlovsk, sociology in Novosibirsk seemed to be rooted in economics and mathematics.[15] In fact it was a Novosibirsk *kollektiv* (team) at the Siberian branch of the USSR Academy of Sciences which originally began to study time budgets in the late 1950s, thus commencing empirical research after the 'thaw'. This branch embraced the Institute of Economics and Organization of Industrial Enterprise, which studied labour resources, population movement, working and non-working time, the level of organization of labour and production, and so on, and the Laboratory of Economic and Mathematical methods of Research, which studied the problems of youth, the choice of professions, job placement, labour turnover, and the methodology, methods and techniques of concrete sociological research. The Academy's Institute of History, Philology and Philosophy also studied sociological problems of youth, social mobility and cultural development of the peoples of Siberia and the Far East, and time budgets.[16]

A further guide to the pattern of institutionalization of Soviet sociology was offered in a review of philosophy and sociology in the Ukraine.[17] There, the centres of sociology were the Institutes of the Academy of Sciences of the *SverdSotsial'nye* SSR (especially the Institute of Philosophy), the university laboratories of concrete sociological research (in Kiev, Khar'kov, L'vov, and Dnepropetrovsk), sociological groups attached to *vuzy*, polytechnic and pedagogic institutes, party committees at *raion*, city, and *oblast'* level, komsomol organizations, and the editorial boards of newspapers. The basic themes of sociological research in the Ukraine were: time budgets, change in social structure, attitudes of students to their elected specialities, the technical level of workers and their attitude toward labour, the role of public opinion in the management of industry and forms of religious belief. This has been the pattern in other established centres of sociology.

As this review of the centres for sociological work has shown, party, komsomol, trade union and other organizations were involved in training personnel and in conducting research. Courses in sociological methods for party officials, for example, were (if not already introduced) strongly suggested: 'there is no provision whatsoever for ... the methodology of concrete sociological research in the curriculum [for the training of party officials]. But it is absolutely essential that a party official be conversant with these subjects.'[18] The Academy of Social Sciences, attached to the CPSU's Central Committee, conducted yearly seminars for party officials and scientists. Some party committees established departments of Marxist sociology at evening universities and at the Higher Party Schools.[19] Other organizations set up similar facilities.

In terms of research, these organizations could have relied, in the first place, on work conducted by the research institutes, the *vuzy* or other institutions. It has been argued that such research should have enabled party workers to analyze phenomena more scientifically, gather concrete information and utilize new methods for studying social problems. The sociologists, in turn, should have benefited from collaboration with the party and other organizations because the latter could help in the development of a theory of socialist society, aid in gathering information and subsequently effect practical recommendations.[20]

In the second place, these organizations themselves carried out research of a social character by setting up research centres which united teachers, scientific personnel, and workers from party and public organizations.* A good proportion of this research concentrated on the effectiveness of ideological-political work among different social groups (for example, workers and technical intellectuals) on the effect of methods and organization of a number of trends in propaganda and agitational work, on ways of forming public opinion and on a study of the party *aktiv* themselves.[21] Other party 'research fell into the broad category of gathering information of a socio-economic and socio-political nature (for example, the work situation, contexts of crime and drunkenness).**

The exact position is not clear, but it appears that social research involving the party and other organizations was frequently carried out on a co-operative basis. A picture of the type of inter-dependence involved is provided in a discussion of some research carried out in Estonia on the influence of art. Figure 4.1, showing the organizational structure at the questionnaire stage of research, indicated the division of labour involved.[22]

From Figure 4.1 it is impossible to say precisely where co-operation ended and supervision began. It is clear, however, that many types of social research in the USSR were carried out by a combination of party workers and social scientists, an unknown number of whom were themselves party members.

---

* An example of this is the public institute of sociological research set up under the *gorkom* in Dnepropetrovsk.
** A. G. Zdravomyslov points out that this information was not concentrated and analyzed as a whole, nor did it have a systematic character. He suggested creating indices of this information gathered by the party committees.   See *Metodologiia i Protsedura Sotsiologicheskikh Issledovanii*, Moscow, 1969, p.57.

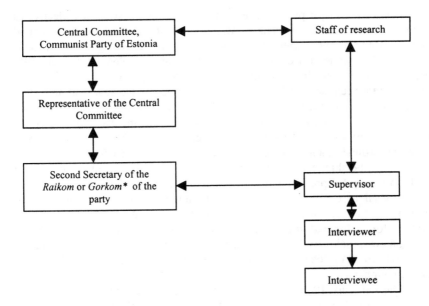

Figure 4.1 Organizational structure

Raikom – district committee of the party. *Gorkom* – urban committee, usually of the party

The Soviet Sociological Association – Sixth World Congress of Sociology

The Soviet Sociological Association was founded in 1958. According to its statutes, it was to follow two courses:

1) to participate in the activities of the International Sociological Association and disseminate Soviet sociologists' work abroad, and
2) to assist in the development of scientific research work inside the USSR.

However, at the third general meeting of the Association, held in February 1966,[23] 125 participants weighed up the work of the Association and concluded that, on the whole, the Association had fulfilled the function of guaranteeing representation of Soviet sociologists abroad, but had focused little attention on internal problems.*

---

* The first general meeting was in 1958 and the second in 1961. Since no further reference was made to a general meeting until 1966, it has been assumed that the latter is the date of the third meeting.

One of the major problems revolved around the question of collective as opposed to individual membership. At the time of the Association's second general meeting in 1961, there were twenty-four collective members, chiefly Institutes of the Academies of Sciences. In February of 1966, there were fifty collective members, and by November of 1967, seventy-nine organizations and institutions had been accepted as collective members. However, at the 1966 Leningrad meeting the question arose as to the advisability of admitting individual members into the Association. It was argued that the inclusion of individual members, most of whom were working on sociological problems, would help to unite and co-ordinate their frequently isolated efforts. Along with the motion for individual membership came a suggestion that individual members be bound regularly to inform the presidium of the Association about their research; there was also a proposal to create an institute of 'probationary candidates', the fact of admission attesting to the qualifications of the individual researcher. The suggestion for individual membership was accepted: in November 1967, the Association was said to have 580 scholars as individual members and by September 1970, 1,469 people were individual members and 273 institutions were collective members.

The February 1966 meeting also considered some motions for enlarging and improving the functions of the Association. Some members proposed that the Association conduct yearly seminars and symposia. Others suggested the creation of branch associations and research committees at the *oblast'* and/or republic level to discuss and carry out research, while others proposed the creation of a regular *apparat*, attached to the presidium of the Association, to co-ordinate sociological research. Branch associations were thereafter set up in Moscow, Leningrad, Novosibirsk, Sverdlovsk, Kiev, Kharkov, Perm, Tallinn and other large centres; twenty-four permanent research committees were established to co-ordinate the activity of sociologists.[24] In general, the training of sociologists and the publication of study aids and a journal devoted to sociology were included in the proposals which were aimed at further uniting sociologists and improving the quality of their work.

Before the Soviet Sociological Association was established, the Soviet Union was represented for the first time at the Third World Congress of Sociology of 1956 in Amsterdam. Subsequently, the Association sent delegates in increasing numbers to the Fourth Congress in Stresa in 1959, the Fifth Congress in Washington in 1962, the Sixth Congress in Evian (France) in 1966, and the Seventh Congress in Varna (Bulgaria) in 1970. Subsequently Soviet sociologists participated in international meetings.

Because many of the foremost sociologists attended, a close look at the Evian Congress's eighty-two Soviet delegates presents an excellent opportunity of supplementing this profile of Soviet sociologists.* The sample is biased in favour of the 'better' sociologists but, nevertheless, a picture of the composition of Soviet sociologists in general can be drawn.

The number eighty-two is derived from the Liste des Participants, Supplement II du Bulletin d'Information No. 3, in conjunction with a list prepared by V. S. Semenov in an article entitled 'VI Vsemirnii Sotsiologicheskii Kongress'.[25] Those whose papers were read in their absence are not included in the discussion. Of the eighty-two participants, information was found on seventy and therefore the following discussion is based on seventy. The Evian delegates are also compared with those who attended the previous Washington Congress; all but four of the eighteen Soviet participants returned to the Evian Congress.[26]

The overwhelming majority of participants in 1962 and 1966 were from the Moscow area. But whereas in 1962 only two republics were represented (seventeen participants from the RSFSR and one from Latvia), the 1966 delegation represented seven republics. The regional breakdown was as follows:

RSFSR
Moscow	44
Leningrad	6
Novosibirsk	3
Sverdlovsk	3
Volgograd	1

Ukrainian SSR
Kiev	4

Georgian SSR
Tbilisi	2

Byelorussian SSR
Minsk	1

Uzbek SSR
Tashkent	1

Latvian SSR
Riga	1

Kazakh SSR
Alma-Ata	1
	3

Unknown

	Total	70

* This part of the study was completed before the Varna conference where 300 to 400 Soviets were present, a fact which would have greatly extended an already complex examination of these sociologists.

One can generalize from these data that sociology was indeed spreading throughout the country into the national republics.

The delegates' educational background was as follows:

Doctor of Science	35
comprising	
Doctor of Philosophy	28
Doctor of Historical Science	2
Doctor of Law	1
Doctor of Economic Science	3
Doctor of Juridical Science	1
Professor	2
(listed only as Professor, no academic degree listing available: this title does not include Doctors of Science who are also professors)	
Candidate of Science	16
comprising	
Candidate of Philosophy	12
Candidate of Economic Science	3
Candidate of History	1
Unknown	17
Total	70

Two of the delegates were full members of the USSR Academy of Sciences; three were corresponding members. All in all, then, in terms of academic honours and achievement, the delegates ranked very highly: over half of the participants had doctorates or were professors, almost one quarter had candidate degrees, while the rest remain unknown. If we leave aside the figures for the unknown, then the ratio of doctorates to candidates is almost two to one. This was not the case at the 1962 Congress where the number was more evenly divided; four of the eight candidates at that Congress had, by the time of the Evian Congress, earned their doctorates. One could generalize from this that more and more practising sociologists were obtaining higher degrees.

The institutional positions of the participants have been separated into three tables, the first listing affiliation to universities and institutes, the second to the Academies of Sciences, and the last to other organizations, such as party, komsomol and journals. Individuals have been noted twice if their affiliation with more than one institution was known: a plus (+) appears for each of the two affiliations. The date of affiliation was taken to be correct as of 1966, that is, as close to the Evian Congress as possible, but I have also indicated when an individual changed his position. An asterisk (*) means that the participant was the head of his/her institute or organization. See Tables 4.4, 4.5 and 4.6.

**Table 4.4   Institutional position of the participants
I. Universities and institutes**

Moscow
  Moscow State University   <u>7</u>
    Philosophy Institute   2
      Department of Historical Materialism   1*
      Department of Scientific Communism   1   +
      Sociology Laboratory   1*   +
    Humanities Faculty
      Department of Historical and Dialectical Materialism   2*

Leningrad   <u>5</u>
  Leningrad State University
    Philosophy Faculty
      Department of Sociology and Philosophy   1
      History of Philosophy   1*
      Institute of Complex Social Research   3*   +

Sverdlovsk
  Urals State University
    Philosophy Faculty   2*   2+

Kiev
  Kiev Medical Institute
    Chair of Philosophy   1*

Tbilisi
  Tbilisi State University   1

**Table 4.5   Institutional position of the participants
II. Academies of Sciences**

Moscow, Academy of Sciences, USSR		
Institute of Philosophy	9*	3+
Theory of Culture Section	2*	
Sector of Historical Materialism	1*	
Sector of Contemporary Bourgeois Philosophy and Sociology of Countries of the West	1*	
History of World Philosophy Department	1*	+
Social Research Unit	1*	+
Sector of Psychology	1	+
Institute of History	1	
Institute of Economics	1	
Institute of State and Law	2	
Vice-President for Social Sciences, USSR Academy of Sciences (until Spring 1967)	1	+
Leningrad Branch, Academy of Sciences, USSR		
Department of Philosophy	1	+
Siberian Branch, Academy of Sciences, USSR		
Institute of Economics and Organization of Industrial Enterprise	1	
Sociology Sector	1*	
Laboratory of Economic and Mathematical Methods Social Research Section	1*	
Urals Branch, Academy of Sciences, USSR		
Sociology sectors (2)	2*	+
Academy of Sciences, Bielorussian SSR	(each*)	
Institute of Philosophy and Law		
Academy of Sciences, Kazakhstan SSR	1*	
Institute of Philosophy and Law		
Academy of Sciences, Ukrainian SSR	1*	
Institute of Philosophy		
Academy of Sciences, Georgian SSR	2	
Institute of Economics		
Academy of Sciences, Latvian SSR	1	
Academy of Sciences, Uzbekistan SSR	1	
	1	

Table 4.6   **Institutional position of the participants**
         III. Organizations: party, komsomol, trade union and journals

Moscow		
Academy of Social Sciences (attached to the Central		
Committee, CPSU)		
Department of Philosophy (became head of		
Department of Dialectical and Historical		
Materialism, early 1967)	1*	
Department of History of Soviet Society	1*	
Sociological Research Group	1*	
Higher Party School (Central Committee, CPSU)	1	+
Department of Marxism-Leninism	1*	+
Institute of Marxism-Leninism (Central Committee,		
CPSU		
Sector of Scientific Communism	1*	
Institute of the World Labour Movement (money from		
All-Union Central Council of Trade Union, yet		
formal tie to Economics Department, USSR		
Academy of Sciences)		
Social Research Division	1*	
A sector of the above	1	
Institute of International Relations (Ministry of		
Foreign Affairs)	1*	
Komsomol'skaia pravda's Public Opinion Institute	1	
Editorial Boards		
Voprosy Filosofii	2	2+
Filosofskie Nauki	5*	5+
Kommunist	1	
Voprosy psikhologii	1	+
Sovetskaia etnografiia	1	
Novosti	1*	
Soviet Sociological Association		
President	1*	+
Vice-President	1	+
Learned Secretary	1	
Institutional position unknown	10	

In addition to indicating where each participant worked, these tables put in some perspective the distribution of participants per type of institution. Thus, the number of people from the three types of institution is:

Universities and institutes	16 of whom	5 are listed twice
Academies of Sciences	34 of whom	11 are listed twice
Other organizations	24 of whom	12 are listed twice
Unknown	10	

Of the fourteen men listed twice, three were listed simultaneously under universities and Academies, eight under Academies and other organizations, and two under other organizations and universities; one was listed in two places on the table for other organizations. On the whole, the distribution emphasises the affiliation of a large number of sociologists with research institutions.

It is also evident from the tables that almost one-half of the people affiliated with universities and institutes were heads of their respective departments; almost one-third of those with the Academies headed their departments, and three-eighths of those attached to the other organizations were heads of their institutions. Therefore, taken in conjunction with academic achievement, it would appear that the 1966 participants were considerably weighty people in their professions.

What, then, were their main areas of specialization in regard to sociology?* As in the previous tables, some individuals are listed under two classifications on Table 4.7: no pattern, however, emerged from this cross-classification. (A plus (+) appears for each of the two classifications.) What did emerge is further evidence of the declining role of the 'grand theorist' philosophers and the growing research orientation of the sociologists.

In Table 4.7, the people classified under 'Marxist philosophy' included those working in dialectical and historical materialism, scientific communism, political economy, history of philosophy and culture and history of the CPSU. Ten of these people headed their departments. At least eight of them were definitely Communist Party members and at least eleven of them were over forty-five. A very similar combination of age, party membership and directorship applied to the people listed under 'nationality questions', 'international relations' and 'socialist revolution'. Thus it appears that the people in the 'philosophy-theory' category were the old-time stalwarts.

---

* Each person was classified according to publications, the conferences attended in the Soviet Union, and the meetings participated in at the Congress.

Table 4.7   Areas of specialization

Philosophy, theory		
Marxist philosophy	15	3+
Modern moderates	2	
Nationality questions (including concepts of national sovereignty, patriotism and race)	6	+
International relations (including military history, co-existence, conflicts)	3	
Socialist revolution	2	2+
Sociology, theory and research		
Social theorists	3	+
Theory and methods of bourgeois empirical research	3	+
Comparative socialist research	3	+
Methods and modelling	6	4+
Fields of concrete social research		
Labour	11	5+
Social structure	7	4+
Marriage and family	1	
Urban sociology	1	+
Criminology	1	
Law	1	
Religion, ethics, morals and values	4	+
Art and mass communication	2	
Public opinion research	1	
Time budget research	1	
Peripheral fields		
Psychology and social psychology	2	
Ethnography	1	
Demography	2	
Listed only by groups participated in at Congress		
Mass communication and leisure	1	
Leninist national policy	1	
Sociology and other sciences	1	
Unknown	1	

Quite a different picture emerges for those actually engaged in sociological research. On the whole, these were in the thirty-five to forty-five age bracket: although some in this group were older or younger, the most dynamic work seemed to be coming from the middle group. Moreover, in comparison with the older group, these sociologists were scattered throughout the country: there was less concentration in the Moscow area. In terms of their education, these sociologists were equally divided between candidates and doctorates. Only about one-third of them were in charge of their respective departments, but their ages would certainly have been the crucial factor here.

From this profile, it would appear that Soviet sociologists roughly fell into two, not quite mutually exclusive, groups. On the whole, those who were described as actually engaged in research were becoming the rule, rather than the exception.

Journals

Because Soviet sociologists did not have their own periodical, this resulted in the appearance of articles on sociology in other journals, especially in those concerned with philosophy, but also in economic, historical, political, ethnographic, juridical and anthropological journals, as well as in the daily press.

Two journals indicated that they were to be published on a regular basis. The first, *Sotsial'nye Issledovaniia* (*Social Research*), appeared six times: the first issue came out in 1965, then one in 1968, and four in 1970. It was sponsored by the Academy of Sciences' Institute of Concrete Social Research and the Soviet Sociological Association. It published articles on general problems of sociology as well as devoting issues to specific problems, such as the family and marriage or time budget research. The other journal, *Chelovek i Obshchestvo* (*Man and Society*), was first published in 1966. Its subsequent issues appeared once each in 1967 and 1968, three times in 1969, twice in 1970, and twice in 1971. It was sponsored by Leningrad State University's Institute of Complex Social Research and as such reflected the Institute's interests in problems of a sociological, psychological, economic and juridical nature. For example, articles appeared concerned with social planning and management, the individual and all aspects of labour and youth and socialization.

As a rule, however, two regularly published philosophy journals, *Voprosy Filosofii* and *Filosofskie Nauki*, carried the majority of articles on sociology.* *Voprosy Filosofii* had about twice as many articles in the field of sociology as did *Filosofskie Nauki* and its articles covered a wider range of topics. Besides informing their readers on past, present and future research in the discipline, what other functions did these journals perform?

---

* The universities and Academies of Sciences also published general journals on the social sciences which often contained articles on sociology.

From the early 1960s, the journals began quite regularly to carry reviews, summaries and/or surveys of philosophy and sociology journals from the other socialist countries. *Voprosy Filosofii* tended to review a number of journals from these countries at one time, whereas *Filosofskie Nauki* tended to investigate articles from different magazines on a specific problem (such as dialectical materialism) or to concentrate on journals from one country: this division, however, was not hard and fast. Meetings of representatives from the editorial boards of the philosophy and sociology journals in the socialist countries were reported since the first meeting in 1962. Books on philosophy and sociology from the socialist countries were reviewed. For example, in 1965 *Voprosy Filosofii* reviewed Czech publications from 1960 to 1963 and, in 1966, Polish literature on sociology for 1960-4.[27]

The journals also reported exchanges between and conferences of Soviet and other sociologists. In November of 1962, for example, an exchange between Leningrad State University and some Polish universities focused on the general questions of method and technique of sociological research and on the study of labour activity.[28] Conferences sponsored by one socialist country and attended by Soviet delegates also received coverage. Typical of these was one called in November 1966 by the Sociology Institute of the Czech Academy of Sciences, the Social Institute of the Slovak Academy of Sciences, the sociology society and the Institute of Marxism-Leninism from *vuzy*.[29] The journals reported inter-socialist conferences which, for example, discussed the problems of the social structure of socialist society or theoretical problems of labour turnover. Finally, they discussed international gatherings of which the most notable were the international sociological conferences.

The journals also aided Soviet sociologists by reporting the conferences held in the Soviet Union. The conferences themselves provided both individual and institutional contact for sociologists and they also acted as a collective platform for the discipline as a whole. While the journals undoubtedly did not cover all of the conferences, they gave a fairly good picture of the range and depth of the conference papers.

These conferences did not include meetings or seminars which were regularly scheduled (biennially, annually). Such meetings, also reported in the journals, might, for example, have discussed the work of the *vuzy*, the results and problems of co-ordinating and planning research, and the work of special seminars set up by various bodies and devoted to some problems of social science.

The journals themselves also held meetings with their readers. The readers appeared to voice their approval and/or disapproval of difference subjects, including the contents of the journal. For example, in 1965 at Cherepovets, the head of the Department of Marxism-Leninism at the Cherepovets Pedagogical Institute requested more articles on concrete sociological research (and 'not only on questions of methodology and methods'), asserting that only five such articles appeared in 1964.[30] An opposite view was expressed at a conference in Tbilisi where one man complained about the increase of non-philosophical themes in the journal, including concrete sociological research.[31] He was answered, however, by the corresponding secretary of the editorial board of *Voprosy Filosofii*, I. V.

Blauberg, who stated that since there are no specialised periodical publications on questions of concrete sociology, *Voprosy Filosofii* must study these problems. In general, all of these conferences with readers mentioned the subject of sociology and usually requested more coverage in this field.

By far the greatest task of the journals, however, was to inform their readers about current research in the discipline. In describing research, they also provided valuable information as to who was doing what – and where. In the absence of a professional periodical, these journals were the substitute, informing sociologists about their profession, the growth of the discipline and their colleagues' work. In so doing they played a significant role in the process of institutionalizing sociology in the Soviet Union.

---

1 V. N. Shubkin, 'Sotsiologiia: Problemy i Perspektivy', *Pravda*, 13 March 1966, p.3.

2 A. Aleksandrov, 'Slovo o Sotsiologii', *Literaturnaia Gazeta*, 21 April 1966, p.2.

3 V. A. Iadov, 'Sotsiologiia: Problemy i Fakty-otvetstvennost', *Literaturnaia Gazeta*, 12 November 1966, p.2.

4 E. V. Beliaev *et al.*, 'Vsesoiuznyi Simpozium Sotsiologov', *Vop Fil*, No. 10, 1966, p.156.

5 Iadov, *Literaturnaia Gazeta*, 12 November 1966, p.2.

6 V. Mikhailov and V. Perevedentsev, 'Bol'shie Ozhidaniia', *Literaturnaia Gazeta*, 14 June 1967, p.18.

7 M. F. Ovsiannikov and Iu. A. Petrov, 'O Sostoianii Dissertatsionnoi Raboty po Filosofii v 1964-5 Uchebnom Godu', *Vop Fil*, No. 2, 1966, pp.138-40; M. F. Ovsiannikov and Iu. A. Petrov, 'O Dissertatsionnoi Rabote po Filosofii v 1965-6 Uchebnom Godu', *Vop Fil*, No. 1, 1967, pp.150-3; M. F. Ovsiannikov and Iu. A. Petrov, 'O Dissertatsionnoi Rabote po Filosofii v 1966-7 Uchebnom Godu', *Vop Fil*, No. 11, 1967, pp.131-6; V. G. Afanas'ev and Iu. A. Petrov, 'O Dissertatsionnykh Rabotakh po Filosofii v 1967-8 Uchenbom Godu', *Vop Fil*, No. 1, 1969, pp.145-52; A. G. Afanas'ev and Iu. A. Petrov, 'O Dissertatsionnykh Rabotakh po Filosofii i Sotsiologii v 1968-9 Uchenbom Godu', *Vop Fil*, No. 12, 1969, pp.140-6; and A. S. Bogomolov and Iu. A. Petrov, 'O Dissertatsionnykh Rabotakh po Filosofii v 1969-70 Uchebnom Godu', *Vop Fil*, No. 1, 1971, pp.140-5. The following discussion was compiled from these reports.

8 A. Rumiantsev, T. Timofeev and Iu. Sheinin, 'Dlia Progress Nauki i Truda', *Izvestiia*, 12 May 1966, p.3.

9 G. V. Osipov 'Teoriia i Praktika Sovetskoi Sotsiologii', *Sotsial'nye Issledovaniia*, No. 5, 1970, p.22.

10 George Fischer, 'Sociology', *Science and Ideology in Soviet Society*, George Fischer (ed.), New York, 1967, p.11.

11 *Tass* report, 11 May 1965.

12 L. L. Gremiako, V. Ia. El'meev and D. A. Kerimov, 'Institut Sotsial'nykh Issledovanii', *Vop Fil*, No. 8, 1966, p.146.

13 Much of the following discussion is based on V. A. Iadov's 'O Chem Govorit Opyt Organizatsii i Provedeniia Konkretnykh Sotsial'nykh Issledovanii v Leningrade', *Fil Nauki*, No. 2, 1965, pp.157-60. See also the article by B. G. Anan'ev and A. S. Pashkov, 'Kompleksnoe Issledovanie Sotsial'nykh Problem', *Chelovek i Obshchestvo*, No. 8, 1971, pp.3-15.

14 See V. V. Kim and K. N. Liubutin, 'Razvitie Filosofskikh Issledovanii v Sverdlovske', *Fil Nauki*, No. 6, 1967, pp.125-9.
15 See E. S. Lazutkin, 'Ekonomiko-sotsiologicheskie Issledovaniia', *Vop Fil*, No. 3, 1966, pp.120-8. Also O. V. Belykh *et al.*, 'Ob Opyte Konkretnykh Sotsial'nykh Issledovanii, *Fil Nauki*, No. 3, 1966, pp.139-48. The latter was relevant for all of the centres of sociological research.
16 R. S. Rusakov and V. D. Karchemnik, 'O Rabote Instituta Istorii, Filogii i Filosofii SO AN SSR v 1969 Godu', *Izvestiia Sibirskogo Otdeleniia Akademii Nauk SSSR*, No. 6, 1970, pp.153-6.
17 R. A. Anufrieva and V. A. Vasilenko, 'Sotsiologiia na Ukraine i ee Perspektivy', *Vop Fil*, No. 9, 1967, pp.159-61.
18 V. Vol'skii, 'Partiinaia Zhizn': Krugozor Rukovoditelia', *Pravda*, 17 January 1967, p.2.
19 Iu. S. Meleshchenko, Iu. P. Smirnov and A. G. Kharchev, 'Sotsiologicheskie Issledovaniia i Partiinaia Rabota', *Chelovek i Obshchestvo*, No. 3, 1968, p.84, and R. I. Kosolapov and P. I. Simush, 'Partiinaia Rabota i Konkretnye Sotsiologicheskie Issledovaniia', *Ideologicheskaia Rabota Partiinykh Organizatsii*, A. M. Korolev and S. I. Mosiagin (eds.), Moscow, 1969, pp.234-56.
20 V. N. Malin, 'Za Nauchnyi Podkhod k Partiino-ideologicheskoi Rabote', *Problemy Nauchnogo Kommunizma*, No. 2, Moscow, 1968, p.7.
21 Meleshchenko *et al.*, *Chelovek i Obshchestvo*, No. 3, 1968, p.81, and V. Provotorov, 'Sotsiologicheskie Issledovaniia v Partiinoi Rabote', *Partiinaia Zhizn'*, No. 19, 1967, p.36.
22 M. I. Zhabskii and P. K. Lenik, 'Sotsiologicheskoe Issledovanie Massovogo Retsipienta Iskusstva', *Vestnik MGU*, No. 4, 1967, p.85.
23 See the discussion by Ia. S. Kapeliush and A. I. Prigozhin, 'Sobranie Sovetskoi Sotsiologicheskoi Assotsiatsii', *Vop Fil*, No. 6, 1966, pp.157-60, as well as 'Sessiia Sotsiologov', *Pravda*, 23 November 1967, p.6.
24 A. G. Zdravomyslov, *Metodologiia i Protsedura Sotsiologicheskikh Issledovanii*, Moscow, 1969, p.3.
25 V. S. Semenov, 'VI Vsemirnii Sotsiologicheskii Kongress', *Vop Fil*, No. 8, 1967, pp.121-32.
26 In addition to V. S. Semenov, the following have written about the VIth Congress: G. M. Andreeva, 'O VI Mezhdunarodnom Kongresse Sotsiologov', *Vestnik MGU*, No. 1, 1967, pp.65-72; M. T. Iovchuk, 'Mezhdunarodnyi Forum Sotsiologov', *Vestnik AN SSSR*, No. 2, 1967, pp.68-74; I. S. Kon and V. A. Iadov, 'Na VI Vsemirnom Sotsiologicheskom Kongresse', *Fil Nauki*, No. 1, 1967, pp.162-6.
27 Karel Makha and Iulius Strinka, 'Filosofskie Publikatsii v Chekhoslovakii v 1960-63 Godakh', *Vop Fil*, No. 1, 1965, pp.178-81, and K. Zagurskii, 'Pol'skaia Literature po Sotsiologii 1960-64 gg', *Vop Fil*, No. 4, pp.178-82.
28 V. V. Vodzinskaia and V. A. Iadov, 'U Pol'skikh Sotsiologov', *Fil Nauki*, No. 3, 1963, pp.133-7.
29 M. Kaleb, 'Pervaia Obshchegosudarstvennaia Konferentsiia Chekhoslovatskikh Sotsiologov', *Vop Fil*, No. 6, 1967, pp.149-52.
30 M. B. Belov, '*Voprosy Filosofii* na Cherepovetskom Metallurgicheskom Zavode', *Vop Fil*, No. 11, 1965, pp.161-2.
31 L. I. Seleskeridi, 'Chitatel'skaia Konferentsiia v Tbilisi', *Vop Fil*, No. 4, 1966, pp.172-4.

5
Areas of Research

Since the mid-1950s, the areas of Soviet sociological research expanded in number and scope. Subjects once thought to belong only in the realm of bourgeois sociology came under scrutiny, while more and more advanced methods were employed to study topics always considered acceptable.

This chapter singles out and surveys six areas of Soviet sociological research, namely: 1) labour; 2) social structure and stratification; 3) marriage, the family, *byt* (daily life, customs), divorce and the woman's role; 4) urban development, city planning and urban-rural relations; 5) criminology and juvenile delinquency; and 6) religion. Of these, the first two are examined in greater depth. The fields have been chosen because they appear to have been the areas of greatest activity, both from the theoretical and empirical points of view.* Beginning with a very brief chronological review of past work, the following accounts generalize about a field or highlight specific research findings.

A number of general points must be made about sociological research in the Soviet Union. In the first place, the sociologists were aware of the fact that theirs was a society sharply demarcated by urban-rural differences. While not always spelled out, the underlying processes, and effects, of industrialization and urbanization provided a broad background to specific research areas and problems. Second, references to 'survivals of the past', as *the* most prominent cause of certain types of social behaviour, occurred more often in the more theoretical discussions as opposed to actual research; that is, the gulf between official theory and actual

---

* Two detailed empirical case studies – one on public opinion and the other on time budget research – are treated separately, in depth, in Chapters 6 and 7. While not discussed below, a further area of increasing interest for Soviet sociologists was that of youth and their problems. The youth were frequently studied as separate components of the class structure. They are therefore subdivided into working class youth, collective farm youth, young intellectuals, students, etc. The topics of research undertaken by sociologists included the attitudes of working class youth towards labour, the cultural level of young workers and stimuli for getting an education or further education, life plans of youth, professional choice and motivation of rural youth, and problems of student life. Apart from this concern with the social location of youth and its consequences, the specialised sociologies often discussed their specific topic with reference to youth (for example, sociology of leisure and the problem of the use of leisure by the young). See, for example, B. G. Anan'ev and D. A. Kerimov (eds.) (1969), *Chelovek i Obshchestvo: Sotsial'nye Problemy Molodezhi*, Vol. 6, Leningrad; V. I. Dobrynina (ed.) (1970), *Molodezh' i Trud*, Moscow; S. N. Ikonnikova and V. T. Lisovskii, (1969), *Molodezh' o Sebe, o Svoikh Sverstnikakh*, Leningrad; L. N. Kogan (ed.) (1969), *Molodezh', ee Interesy, Stremleniia, Idealy*, Moscow.

research was conspicuous. Third, much of the research dealt, to a greater or lesser extent, with the creation of a new socialist form of social institution, for example, the city or the family. In this connection, for example, questions were raised regarding a 'Soviet' as distinct from a 'universal' city or family. Fourth, many research reports discussed what the various sub-divisions of sociology should study (for example, the sociology of religion). The research itself attempted to define specific fields of inquiry. At the same time a closer interaction between the various sociological sub-divisions was noticeable. For example, researches on urban planning and on the family, although carried out by different individuals, began to contribute to a better understanding of both. In many instances research published in one area told a great deal about another; using the same example, research on the family described work in urban affairs and vice-versa.

On the whole, the utilization of statistics was a problem shared by all of the researchers. Many were rather critical of the careless use and misuse of 'home-made' statistics. For example, researchers were admonished for presenting a table without stating the base number for their figures, for drawing 'statistical' conclusions from unrelated 'facts', or for assuming that correlation means causation. Equally crucial was the situation which referred to inaccurate statistics, a situation which applied to national statistics as well as to the 'home-made' variety. Here is one case reported by P. Fedoseev in a discussion of time budget research:

> What results had this research yielded? When scientific methods were used to determine losses of working time in production, it turned out that these were substantially greater than was apparent from the data of ordinary statistics. Ordinary statistics stated that losses of working time came to about one-tenth of one per cent for the country. But the results of the research showed that the figure was actually much higher – about ten to fifteen per cent for the annual total of working time. This means that the question of making effective use of working time in production is far more complex than could be assumed from the statistical data.[1]

The practice of withholding statistical material was also widely condemned by sociologists. As B. Grushin stated at a round-table discussion in 1966: 'The statisticians do not give us many data, being obviously captive to outdated considerations.' The other participants unanimously 'expressed the wish that the statistical administrations ... would be wise and sensible in separating those data that are indeed state secrets from those that are senselessly buried in the depths of statistical institutions because of someone's absurd over-caution or failure to understand true state interests'.[2] The absence of statistics in vital areas (for example, in crime), as well as the overall lack of data on the socio-demographic structure of the country, considerably hampered the work of the serious sociologist.

An enumeration of other suggestions for specifically improving research in their respective areas was a feature common to many researchers' reports. In writing up his/her research, the author usually described the project, reported the results and then concluded by expressing the need for the following: 1) improvement and expansion of demographic data available to the sociologist; 2) similar improvement of research methods and techniques, especially in regard to mathematical and statistical methods; 3) better training of sociologists; 4) more co-operation between sociologists as well as co-operation with other social scientists; 5) the publication of a sociology periodical; and 6) the translation and printing of sociological works published abroad, by both socialist and bourgeois sociologists.

Although not explicitly stated, the research described below is indicative of the diversification of views on any particular topic. Nonetheless, the unifying thread running through the research was the attempt (and the word attempt must be underlined) to answer or solve particular problems. For example, much labour research was concerned with the real problem of labour turnover and migration. In this and other fields, the desire to deal with particular problems produced an awareness of the lack of adequate social and sociological information and acted as a stimulus for the collection of basic data. Whether the information gathered was actually applied is a moot question.

Labour

Sociologists have been accused of trespassing on the territory of the economists, but with the increasingly successful application of the sociologists' findings, the criticism began to subside.[3] Be that as it may, it would appear that the economists were primarily interested in the economy at large – in production, distribution and the management of resources – whereas the sociologists concentrated on the individual in his relation to labour and production, and on labour in relation to society. The industrial sociologist specifically studied the organization of labour, labour relations, labour turnover, occupational structure, job qualifications (education and training), technological (and also societal) progress, automation and leisure.[4] But all Soviet sociologists were involved, albeit indirectly, with 'labour'. After all, in fundamental Marxist terms, 'the mental, physical and moral development of the working man is conditioned by the content and character of labour, by the rhythm and conditions of labour, and finally, by the socio-psychological life of the productive collective'.[5]

Sotsiologiia v SSSR stated that the basic task of sociological research on labour consisted of establishing what influence the production activities of different people had on the formation of socialist and communist relations (that is, the new society) and on the development of the individual (that is, the 'new man'). The functional requirements of the developing society, however, could diverge from the individual's requirements. It is at this point or, ideally, before this point that the sociologist must offer suggestions and/or warnings so that the objective requirements of society are fulfilled. His/her task involved manipulating two sets of factors. The first set, which refers to such things as the organization and conditions of labour, must be immediately altered: in other words, these factors, on account of their very nature, could and must, be made to coincide immediately with societal requirements. The second set of factors, which included, for example, the presence of unqualified types of labour and the low cultural and technical level of the individual, must also be modified; this process, however, is much slower than the first because it involves gradual change.

Thus the sociologist was to balance individual and societal requirements, with the latter taking precedence. Keeping this in mind, sociologists did a considerable amount of research into the relationship between the individual and labour and production. Part of this research concerned labour efficiency, that is, how workers utilize their working time. Such research – basically time budget and labour efficiency research – took into account the differences between various grades of workers and managers. Related research was carried out in connection with the ways and means of increasing production. This research examined workers' incentives – both material and moral – and workers' satisfaction or dissatisfaction with their jobs. Questions as to how best to utilize human resources and the causes of labour turnover – both within one sector of the economy and between different sectors of the economy – were also closely related to the basic problem of work satisfaction.

Another topic of research was the worker's relations with other workers. The working patterns of various groups were examined in an attempt to find out why some work groups function better together than others. Factory conditions and the impact of technology and automation were also studied for their effect on the work group, the individual and labour production.

A further area of research related to the education of workers. Education in this case referred primarily to raising labour skills and to additional training in one's own profession or re-training in another. But it did also encompass education in cultural and intellectual spheres. What one does during non-working time was seen as being closely related to labour performance: the more fully-rounded individual was the better worker. Taking non-working time into account, other sociologists studied the role of labour in the development of the individual and the methods of moulding the new personality.

Intensive work on many of the problems listed above was carried out in various parts of the country. The following account discusses some of the most important studies in labour sociology: these either initiated further research in some specific area, indicated changes in attitudes toward a specific research problem, or made suggestions for improving or coming to terms with a particular problem.

The Laboratory for Economic and Mathematical Research at Novosibirsk State University was among the leading research centres for labour sociology. Under the direction of V. N. Shubkin, the Laboratory concentrated on the related problems of education and occupation and on social mobility.[6] Accordingly, a major project sought to answer questions on the following:

> The social prestige and attractiveness of different occupations and types of work; the objective and subjective factors influencing the education, occupation inclinations, choice of occupation, job placement ... of various groups of young people; social, occupational and geographical mobility in choosing an occupation; the effectiveness of the system of production training in schools and some ways for improving the planning and preparation of qualified cadres; and improving the system of vocational guidance and counselling.[7]

The research, mainly by individual questionnaires, included a follow-up survey two years after the first (1962) trial survey of 300 secondary school graduates and an intermediate study of 9,000 secondary school children.

Concentrating on all aspects of job placement, the researchers discovered two gaps in vocational training and actual work. First, vocational training in secondary schools did not correlate with job placement: only 11 per cent of those interviewed entered the trade for which they were trained. Thus vocational training was relatively ineffective. Second, the individual's plans for higher education diverged from the actual placement both in industry and in education: while 80 per cent of the respondents wanted to continue their studies, only 44 per cent were actually able to do so. Demographic, social and material conditions were shown to affect the possibilities for further education. Like the Rutkevich research on the hereditary nature of the intelligentsia, the Shubkin team found that social origin affected educational opportunities and influenced the individual's evaluation of future jobs. According to the data, social differences manifested themselves in inequality of opportunities for continuing education among young people from urban professional families and the working class on the one hand, and rural youth on the other. The same occupations were found to have different degrees of 'prestige' among urban and rural young people and among children of workers' families and children of the intelligentsia. The latter point was discovered in the course of research on occupational preferences, done along sex-age and urban-rural lines.

The Novosibirsk study was one of the first to discuss these problems. In 1965, surveys employing techniques identical to those of the Novosibirsk study were conducted in Leningrad (by the Sociology Laboratory of Leningrad State University under the guidance of V. A. Iadov and V. Vodzinskaia), in the Buriat ASSR (by the Buriat Interdisciplinary Research Institute of the Siberian Branch of the USSR Academy of Sciences under D. Lubsanov), and in Poland (Institute of Philosophy and Sociology of the Polish Academy of Sciences and the Higher School of Economics under Professors A. Sarapata and A. Rajkewicz).

Workers' attitudes towards labour were the object of several studies by Soviet sociologists. The most advanced and comprehensive of these was conducted by the staff of the Sociological Research Laboratory of Leningrad State University (begun in 1964).[8] At twenty-five Leningrad enterprises, 2,665 workers under thirty years of age were selected 'by random, regional cross-section, according to the nature of their work'. In addition to gathering the usual objective data (on sex, age, occupation), the researchers attempted to characterize the worker's performance in the job by determining the degree or level of conscientiousness, discipline and initiative. They also studied subjective factors, namely, work satisfaction, satisfaction with wages and organization of labour, interest in work and motives for choosing the occupation.

Workers were ranked into six groups according to the degree of technical skill required by their occupation. 'Satisfaction with occupation' was found to vary from a negative attitude among heavy unskilled manual labour to a highly positive attitude among the most highly skilled group, panel operator setters. The factors in the work situation giving rise to satisfaction or dissatisfaction in work were ranked (index) as follows:[9]

Content of work (does it require ingenuity or not)	0.72
Pay	0.61
The possibility of improving skill	0.58
Variety of work	0.48
Organization of labour	0.38
Management's concern for workers	0.35
Physical effort	0.32

The authors of the study placed strong emphasis on the fact that the content of work emerged as the most significant factor determining job satisfaction. They argued that the content of work was the crucial determinant of whether or not material rewards furthered or hindered the formation of positive or negative attitudes towards work. In the case of workers engaged in occupations with a low (non-creative) content of labour, high wages acted as a form of compensation and furthered the establishment of attitudes which regarded work as a means of satisfying needs lying outside the work activity itself.

On the one hand, therefore, findings of the study in so far as they emphasized technology as a determinant of attitudes towards work were in agreement with a similar 'technological' perspective in Western industrial sociology.[10] On the other hand, the emphasis on material rewards as a compensating factor for intrinsically unsatisfying work gave support to a quite contrary position.[11] In this connection, it should be noted that Iadov and his colleagues have been criticized for underestimating the significance of material incentives as determinants of job satisfaction.[12]

It was an important contribution of the Leningrad study to recognize the need when carrying out research into job satisfaction to take into account occupational differences and the diversified attitudes of various groups. Problems of planning and management were seen to be soluble without identifying differentiated groups of people in terms of similarity of occupation, qualifications, needs and work motivation.

Sociological research on labour turnover, it is argued by Soviet sociologists, disproved the opinion widely held by economists that labour turnover is a purely economic phenomenon and that the means of controlling it should derive from improvement in economic circumstances, motivating a more efficient use and redistribution of manpower. This, for example, was the position of E. Antosenkov, head of a team of economists and sociologists affiliated with the Institute of Economic and Industrial Engineering of the Siberian Branch of the USSR Academy of Sciences and the Laboratory for Economic-Mathematical research of Novosibirsk University.[13] He and his team carried out studies in the years 1964-9 in Western and Eastern Siberia and showed that labour turnover is the result of the interaction of economic, social, socio-psychological, demographic and other factors.

Before the early 1960s, according to Antosenkov, the tendency was to subject all aspects of economic and cultural life to planning by directives. A corollary of this was the concept that labour turnover was a process not inherent in socialist economy. The reasoning was as follows:

> As the national economy plans reflect (or should reflect) all kinds of labour mobility necessary from the point of view of the national economy, any other labour force movement is inconsistent with the national economy interests. Hence, the above mentioned concept of the labour turnover followed [that] which was not represented (and could not even be so) in any plans. This situation was most clearly reflected in the *Short Economic Dictionary (1958)*, where an attempt was made to analyze the economic nature of this process. Two points were emphasized by the authors of the *Dictionary* in the first place: the uncontrollable character of labour turnover and its incompatibility with a planned system of socialist economy. They believed that labour turnover under socialism was not a consequence and a *sine qua non* of the existence and development of the socialist mode of production and of the social labour organization inherent to it. Hence they concluded that such a phenomenon could not be tolerated in socialist economy and should be fully eradicated by all possible means.[14]

With the help of sociological research into the effect on turnover of such factors as the level of organization and working conditions, the ways of recruiting and assigning personnel to jobs, the labour force shortage, especially in skilled trades, and living standards (among them housing and wages), the concept of labour turnover was altered. Antosenkov suggested that labour turnover can be defined as a result of the fact that the goals of certain working people, certain enterprises and the national economy as a whole do not coincide, that is, interests have not been satisfied.

Closely related to the above questions was research into the influence of population movement on the manpower problem. Studies by V. Perevedentsev, also from Novosibirsk, demonstrated regularities of population movement and also the fallacy of the idea that only planned migration existed or even predominated in the USSR.[15] (In particular, population movements were shown to be associated with the instability of the labour force.) Among the variety of reasons advanced for movement by migrants, economic factors were predominant. These included unsatisfactory wage levels and the actual character of work and living conditions. Further it became apparent that migration for supposedly different reasons (for example, personal motives, such as moving to relatives) was actually strongly influenced by economic considerations. A major consideration emerging from the work of Perevedentsev and his colleagues, much of whose work was concerned with migration on a regional basis, was the fact that population movement, and hence labour turnover, when viewed societally emerged as being very closely related to differences in living conditions and educational opportunities between the urban and rural population. Among the agricultural population in Siberia, for example, the move to the cities was shown to occur principally among the youngest and more highly skilled sections of the labour force. Other studies stressed that urban residents were better off than their rural counterparts on the same social level and that this had to be considered as one of the main reasons for the rural population deficit.[16]

As has been emphasized previously, a major source of Soviet sociological studies was the confrontation with practical problems. Evidence of this in the field of labour sociology concerns the influence of alterations in the length of the working week. It was found, for example, that approval of a reduction in the length of the working week – from six to five days – was positively correlated with residence in large, as opposed to small, cities. The basis for the greater approval in larger cities emerged as resting upon greater opportunities for utilization of the time made available in the form of leisure pursuits.[17]

A further example of the practical results of labour research is to be found in evidence available about the social consequences of the impact of research centres such as that at Novosibirsk. This evidence largely related to the presence and role of sociologists in Soviet factories. A report from the first Secretary of the Altai *kraikom*, for example, specifically linked the application of sociological surveys by the Novosibirsk department with the subsequent employment of sociologists in factories and to the establishment of a bureau of sociological research. As a result, it was claimed that labour turnover was reduced.[18]

Social Structure and Stratification

Since the beginning of the 1960s, previous theoretical work in the field of social structure and stratification was revitalized by concrete sociological research which, in its turn, produced modifications in the general concept of social structure. Sociological work in this field started from the general position that while the path towards social unity and a classless society was originally paved by the liquidation of an exploiting class, classes still exist, namely, the two non-antagonistic classes of workers and peasants. There is, in addition, one stratum, the intelligentsia. However, with the advent of more concrete sociological investigations, utilizing sociological and psychological variables, increasing stress was placed on examining intra-class, rather than inter-class, differences. In fact, it is in the area of intra-class study that one could find the most advanced research.

The first All-Union Conference on the 'Changes of the social structure of Soviet society' represented a turning point in research in this area.[19] Held in Minsk in January 1966, the conference was sponsored by the Social Sciences Branch of the USSR Academy of Sciences, the Institute of Philosophy and Law of the Bielorussian SSR Academy of Sciences and *Znanie*. More than three hundred scholars took part.

The opening paper at the conference was delivered by V. S. Semenov (Institute of Philosophy, USSR Academy of Sciences). His talk essentially said that the division of the population into working class, collective farm peasantry, and intelligentsia and employees was correct, but far too general. Within Soviet society there existed 'many social developments, degrees, and variants'.[20] He then outlined four basic trends of social class development on which writers on social structure have concentrated, namely:[21]

1) class differences between the working class and the kolkhoz (collective farm) peasantry, based on two forms of socialist *property*;

2) social differences between physical (workers and peasants) and mental (intelligentsia) *labour*;

3) socio-economic and cultural-*byt* differences between urban (urban workers and urban intelligentsia) and rural (peasants and agricultural workers and rural intelligentsia) *regions*;

4) social *differences within* the working class, kolkhoz peasantry, intelligentsia and employees. (Italics mine.)

The other conference participants filled in Semenov's four-fold scheme. Some, like Professor G. E. Glezerman, adhered to the position which stressed property relations as paramount. Others expanded the second proposition on labour: V. C. Podmarkov, for example, discussed occupational structure after stating that the most general principle of the professional structure was the division between mental and physical labour. The third argument was propounded by G. P. Davidiuk in his discussion of kolkhoz peasantry and the problem of shifts in population. And finally, many participants recounted their studies on the internal structure (hence, the intra-class differences) of the workers, the peasants and the intelligentsia.

In addition, new definitions of 'class' were proposed by some who said the term was no longer valid for socialist society. Iu. I. Shiriaev of Kiev said that the Leninist definition of class consists of two parts: a general definition, which is related to all classes (both the exploiting and working classes), and a particular definition, which is only related to the exploiting classes. Shiriaev complained that the general definition is upheld even though the social composition of classes under socialism is principally different from that under capitalism. Furthermore, he said that the particular definition is not applicable to socialist society since there are no exploiting classes. All in all, the term 'class' does not allow for the changes which occurred in socialist society. Another participant, N. A. Aitov, agreed that 'class' demands another definition. Since there is only one kind of relationship to the means of production, there are no classes; but since there are differences according to forms of property, there are classes. Therefore 'class' refers to class and non-class phenomena simultaneously. Hence, a redefinition was in order.

While a new definition was not accepted, it is clear that the participants went a long way from merely mouthing former concepts of class. Not only were inter- and intra-class differences elaborated in the discussions, but conclusions from concrete sociological research were cited as evidence. Therefore, it seems that modifications of the concept of class (both as property-based and antagonistic) were proposed.

Three participants at the Minsk conference were particularly noted for their work in the field of social structure. They are M. N. Rutkevich, Iu. V. Arutunian and O. I. Shkaratan. All concurred in the primary role of intra-class differences. Each specialized in one social group. Before reviewing their work individually, let us examine their more general comments on the study of social structure.[22]

There was agreement that a major task confronting Soviet students of social stratification was the development of a new theory which would make possible the analysis of a novel system of social relations. Progress towards the development of this theory was hindered by the neglect of intra- as opposed to inter-class relations. Such intra-class relations are, it was agreed, determined by the overall structure of class interrelations, but nevertheless have an independent significance with respect to the pace and direction of social change.

With regard to the question of relations between classes, the writers whose work is about to be examined in some detail made a number of discrete but complementary points. Arutunian, for example, emphasized the deficiencies of available data with respect to class composition. In particular he argued that the inclusion of the two anachronistic categories in the census returns (namely, private peasants and handicraftsmen not in producers' co-operatives and capitalists, landlords, merchants and kulaks) was a significant obstacle to progress in the analysis of class relations and their evolution. Paralleling this type of empirical criticism, Rutkevich pointed out the theoretical difficulties which arise from the fact that sociological literature, while emphasizing the novelty of class relations in the Soviet Union, at the same time underestimated the essential novelty of the social process and therefore of the groups involved in the stratification system. This position would appear to amount to an argument for the lack of any possibility of comparison between the social situation of the working class prior to 1917 and the social situation of the group referred to by the same concept subsequently. Such a position is not incompatible with that advanced by Shkaratan. With regard to the question of the influence of pre-Revolutionary social conditions, Shkaratan questioned the plausibility of treating class relations within the Soviet Union as being essentially homogeneous in character given the very wide variation in economic and socio-political circumstances of different regions at the time of the Revolution. Shkaratan's emphasis upon the need for a longitudinal historical dimension in the analysis of stratification was both novel and important. Of similar significance is the argument that he advanced for the impossibility of discussing changes in both class and professional profiles independently of a study of urbanization.

Professor Rutkevich of Sverdlovsk, engaged in identifying the intelligentsia,[23] divided mental workers into two groups – the employees or non-specialists (*sluzhashchii*) and the specialists. The former were defined as less qualified non-manual workers whose work did not require higher education; the latter were those people who received a secondary special or higher education and who were, by profession, engaged in mental labour. In other words, not all mental workers were included in his definition of intelligentsia. Much of Rutkevich's work was concerned with implementing this, as against the more official, definition.

Another phase of his research included an examination of the sources of recruitment of the intelligentsia. Although he did conclude that the main replacement of the intelligentsia came from the workers, the peasants and the non-specialist employees, he also indicated that the opportunities for further (i.e. high school) education – and thus entrance into the intelligentsia – were greater for urban families of 'comfortable circumstances' and of greater education themselves. On the basis of discovering the hereditary nature of the replenishment of the intelligentsia, Rutkevich suggested that the social composition of the students should conform more closely with the social composition of the population.

Extensive work on the social structure of the rural population was carried out by Iu. V. Arutunian of Moscow State University.[24] In his research on this subject, he maintained that the nature and quality of labour determined the nature of the social group within the class.* 'Differences in the quality of labour are linked with the social division of labour. Labour that is socially dissimilar in quality falls into two basic categories, physical and mental.' These categories, each of which appears in the state and collective sectors, were further sub-divided into skilled and unskilled labour. Once he had determined these divisions, Arutunian showed that variations between sectors (state and collective) and between classes (workers and collective farmers) were much less substantial than they were within them: the greatest differences were between people of skilled and unskilled labour.

Arutunian had three basic criticisms of the analysis of the social structure. First of all, he said the problems of the rural regions are reduced to problems of the peasantry and therefore the state sector is eliminated. Second:

> in considering the differences between the working class and the peasantry on the basis of the country as a whole, without regard for the kind of workers – urban or rural – the investigators are dealing with, ... it remains unclear to what degree the differences between workers and collective farmers are caused by different relations to property, and to what degree they are caused by the specific nature of city and countryside, of industry and agriculture.[25]

Arutunian saw the undervaluation of intra-class differences as the third and chief shortcoming of this research: 'it is inadequate for an analysis of social relations in a socialist society to base the division of society solely on the relationship of social groups to the ownership of the means of production.'

The study of intra-class structure was also stressed by O. I. Shkaratan of Leningrad.[26] In his research on the working class, defined by him as workers in the sphere of physical and mental labour, engaged in material production and employed in enterprises and institutions which are publicly owned, he saw differences in the 'complexity of labour' as the dominant factor in social differences. He sought to establish an index of 'complexity of labour' which would permit a measure not of the quality of labour itself, but of the differences between groups of people in different jobs. 'The fact that members of one and the same class belong to groups of workers with different skills, holding unequal positions in the system of social production, is decisive today in determining the social importance of the individual.'[27] Therefore, 'intra-class divisions into groups

---

* At Minsk, according to Arutunian, the speakers were virtually unanimous in choosing quality and character of labour as the criterion for the intra-class structure of the peasantry.

according to their socially heterogeneous labour determines the social cast of the individual and influences the possibility of advancement of those who come from these groups.'

Elsewhere Shkaratan set out to test and document the following theses:

- the development of a classless society will be accompanied by profound structural changes in the class units themselves, which will lose their class character and take on characteristics consonant with the character of the new society;
- the boundaries of the working class will expand to include those doing non-physical labour, including the technical intelligentsia;
- during the transitional period from capitalism to socialism, and during subsequent development, the working class (while unified by a common relationship to the means of production, by a leading role in the societal organization of labour, and by common sources of the basic means of existence) is still internally differentiated in many ways;
- intra-class structure is derivative not only from the type of overall social structure in the society, but also from the stage of development of social relationships;
- the social structure of both society as a whole and its components is stable within stages, given the same social order; this is connected with the level of development of social and economic relationships.[28]

In general, therefore, sociologists in the field of social stratification shifted their emphasis from a study of inter-class differences to one of intra-class differences. As a consequence, they stressed that, in order to achieve a homogeneous society, differences between as well as within classes must be removed.

However, there was no real consensus on how to differentiate or delineate classes, let alone differentiate within a class. For example, some defined the intelligentsia as all who are employed in mental labour; others defined them as a stratum between two classes, the workers and collective farm workers; others said there are two classes and each has its own intelligentsia. Nor was there agreement on differentiation within a class, be it in terms of qualifications (educational and cultural), character of labour (mental or physical), wages or place of work. However, once these intra-class differences were recognized as analyzable, other dimensions, such as nationality differences, family and living conditions and cultural variations, began to be considered.

Thus the sociologists began to paint a picture of a differentiated and stratified society in which different classes and different groups within the classes have varied attributes, interests, life styles. The painting was hampered, however, by brushes clogged with past theories and by a lack of new styles of composition.

Marriage, the Family, *Byt*, Divorce and the Woman's Role

The study of the development of marriage, the family and *byt* under socialism – that is, as social and interpersonal institutions which fulfil biological, economic and emotional functions – increasingly became an area of concern for Soviet sociologists. Supplementing the more general discussion of a socialist form of marriage and family, sociologists concentrated on the family because of the large increase in divorces, the falling birth rate and the large number of juvenile crimes.

A. G. Kharchev from Leningrad was the sociologist who broke the silence of the Stalinist era with his work on the family.[29] A most prolific writer in the field, his book *Brak i Sem'ia v SSSR* (*Marriage and the Family in the USSR*) represents the 'first contemporary attempt at a sociological study of this extensive problem (more accurately, not problem but rather sphere of social life)'. So wrote I. S. Kon in his review of Kharchev's 1964 book.[30] The volume looks at marriage and the family as objects of sociological research, at the social nature of these institutions and finally at the changes in, development of and differences between the family under capitalism, socialism and communism. In addition to his own research, Kharchev made extensive use of literature from other fields (e.g. ethnography, economics, jurisprudence).[31] He also relied on Western literature; in fact, according to reviewer Kon, 'it [the book] ... is free of that vulgar-nihilistic attitude to non-Marxist sociology which still sometimes rears its head in certain works and causes obvious damage to Soviet science'.[32] Another critic maintained that the 'sexual-psychological' aspect was a weak part of his research and that he did not offer enough recommendations from that research.[33] However, Kharchev was praised for his substantial contribution to sociology.

Kharchev's research was based on his 1962 survey of 500 couples who were getting married at the Leningrad City Registration Bureau (ZAGS) and also on an analysis of the data of these bureaux for the Uzbek SSR, the city of Kiev, the town of Tiumen and the Mga *raion* of Leningrad *oblast'*. The aims of the investigation were:

- to discover what those who intend to marry consider to be vital for a stable and happy family life, and how the choice of a future husband or wife is motivated;
- to find out the differences in the ages at marriage and the main trends of these differences;
- to establish the proportion, and importance, of marriages which involve the overcoming of certain prejudices and hence require a stronger subjective justification and greater personal responsibility for the decision. These include all marriages between people of different nationalities and, especially, of difference cultural, religious or ethnic groups;
- to obtain data on premarital acquaintance, including its duration.[34]

With these aims in mind, he gathered data on the social composition of the couples (age, family background), how long the couples knew each other, where they met and why they married. On the whole, Kharchev's research offered some answers to these relatively unstudied questions.

An overall survey of other areas of concentration of family sociology is simplified by the fact that in January 1967, the first All-Union symposium of sociologists working on the problems of marriage, the family and *byt* was held in Vil'nius.[35] Kharchev, who chaired the hundred-person symposium, opened the proceedings with a description of research in Leningrad where, he informed the symposium, researchers were concerned with three phases of research. The first focused on different aspects of marriage and family relations, the formation of the family, and the liquidation of conflict within the family so that the family might successfully carry out its role in educating the 'new man'. The second phase linked family research with urban and architectural problems (for example, a study of the composition of the family so as to ensure that housing met the needs of the population). And the third direction of research concerned the leisure of youth or, more specifically, the problem of leisure in relation to personality development, unregulated leisure and informal youth groups.

Many other topics, such as rural families, student marriages and the role of the family in socialization, were discussed at the symposium. The approach of bourgeois (in this case, American) and Polish sociologists to the subject was also examined. Problems of methodology and methods of research in this field were reviewed by participants from all over the Soviet Union. Particular emphasis was laid on the role of statistical (for example, tables of marriage and divorce rates) and ethnographical (for example, family histories) methods.

Divorce as a subject of social research – that is, the cause of divorce, including both subjective and objective factors – was also examined at the Vil'nius conference. Why study divorce? According to a *Nedelia* commentary on the conference: 'Everyone has long known the aphorism that all happy families are alike, but each unhappy one is unhappy in its own particular way. But it has also been established that the path to family disintegration has its own laws and causes. It is essential to study them.'[36]

In documenting the causes of divorce, the researchers stated that divorce itself was not indicative of the decay of the institution of marriage: 'The individual is not running away from family life in general, and destruction does not at all threaten the family nucleus in our society.'[37] The best proof of this, they said, is the large number of repeated or second marriages. Noting that research findings were relatively constant throughout the country, the researchers stated that intellectual and moral differences were the main causes of the disruption of a marriage. Drunkenness, the pet source of many social evils, and a 'lightminded approach to marriage', a trait often manifest in the young, were also cited as causes of divorce. Directly related to the latter was the feeling among some sociologists that physical maturity proceeded more rapidly than emotional or economic maturity. Some suggested programmes for sex education and special pedagogical or family consultation services to help remedy this situation. Others suggested that the state make financial provisions to cover the expense of setting up a home. This last proposal was echoed a few years later in 1970 in some Bielorussian research on the family: long-term, interest-free credit from the state to help newly-weds set up home was recommended.[38] At the symposium, proposals to enlist sociologists in the courts to work on cases involving 'violations' of family life and juvenile delinquency were put forward. Also voiced was the hope of studying separately urban and rural families as well as families from various sized cities (for example, large, average and small).

The role of the woman – as wife, mother and worker in production – was another major topic at the Vil'nius conference. The basic contradiction between the professional and family roles for women was discussed. Z. A. Iankova, for example, told of research she had conducted with the Section of Sociological Research of the Institute of Philosophy (USSR Academy of Sciences) in 1965-7 and the Institute of Concrete Social Research of the USSR Academy of Sciences in 1969 in Moscow, Penze and Leningrad on the structure of the domestic role of women and its influence on the process of overcoming residues of inequality between the sexes. She concluded that the structure of the domestic role depends in many instances on: the content and character of labour in social production and therefore is connected with the woman's professional preparation and orientation; the structure of the family (is it nuclear or extended?); and the models of domestic roles (for example, does dusting have any prestige?).[39]

As indicated in Iankova's study, sociologists were concerned about the woman's role as housewife. The excessive burden of housework and the resulting 'retardation' due to the consequent absence of free time were causes of concern. Time budget research did show that women do more than their fair share of housework. 'The patriarchal tradition of "household bondage" lives – and flourishes! The age-old division of labour that takes over on the thresholds of our homes is dying hard.'[40] Mixed with criticism of household duties and the consequent loss of free time was a plea for time and labour-saving services.

Sociologists also examined the woman's role in production. In 1966, A. I. Pimenova discussed those factors which define and limit a woman's participation in socially productive work and sought to discover those conditions which would extend her participation.[41] Factors such as income and education were found to have a direct bearing on women's professional activities. Economic as well as 'moral' stimuli were cited as motives prompting women to work: economic stimuli included the desire to receive additional means for the maintenance of the family, while the moral reasons included contact with people and the desire to be of some use to society. The research yielded three practical suggestions:

- take additional measures to raise the professional qualifications of women, especially among the middle-aged and the housewives, and increase average earnings;
- establish places to take care of the children of working mothers;
- organize special commissions on the problems of women's labour.

In general, research in this field invariably produced suggestions for solving or alleviating some of the problems which initiated the research: not surprisingly, most of the plans were linked with state aid or intervention, as in the case of living accommodation or services.   The research also inadvertently indicated contradictions between theory and reality. In theory, the socialist family, a new type of institution, was a happy one, but at the same time divorce must be explained; similarly, women were theoretically supposed to be equal to men, but in reality women were doubly burdened with career and family and home obligations.

Urban Development, City Planning and Urban-Rural Relations

The overall task of sociologists studying the social problems of the city and the village was to examine the interdependence between the new forms of social relations in labour and everyday life (that is, the communist forms of social relations) and the existing or planned forms of urban and rural life.[42] They were meant to investigate the *zakonomernosti* of the development of different forms of urban and rural life, the paths and means for most quickly eliminating the differences between urban and rural areas, and the ways of creating relatively similar conditions in these regions.   This all meant concentrating on urban planning.

The main debate on urban development centred around the problem of the size of the city. Adherents of the officially sanctioned group favoured the theory of 'optimal cities'. According to this theory, a city should be limited to that size at which life in the city is at the optimum: criteria for determining this optimum range from health and public safety factors to retail facilities and educational opportunities. Consequently, regulating the growth of large cities, intensifying industrial development in medium-size cities and invigorating smaller ones were all encouraged. Adherents of this school of thought stressed that regulation of the growth of large cities was not an end in itself: 'without such regulation it is impossible to site production forces in the country rationally and economically, and it is impossible to strengthen the industrial role of medium-size and small cities.'[43] In other words, city growth should be planned – and not planned in isolation from long-term schema for development of entire economic regions.

The other group maintained that large cities will not and should not perish as had been both assumed and suggested. On the contrary, new cities, as well as existing cities, would and should grow even larger. Adherents of this plan maintained that a 'new, higher, social-spatial form, based on an unconstrained layout of extensive areas, on specialization and on the spatial separation of functional zones, contrasts with the old urban form and constitutes a means for overcoming and resolving its [the old urban forms'] contradictions'.[44] According to these people, the concept of extensive zones of intensive development had two advantages over the opposing notion of optimal size cities: first, it envisaged a territorial linkage between industry and agriculture, thereby providing the necessary condition for the elimination of the difference between town and country, and second, it resolved the problem of the rational utilization of inter-city space. Other critics of the 'theory of the optimal city' stressed that the criteria of optimality or effective growth were absent: they maintained that there was no evidence to prove that city growth had to be restricted or that smaller cities were more functional than larger cities (that is, optimal size cities display no special advantages over other cities). V. Perevedentsev pointed out that 'the productivity of labour in large cities is many times higher than in the small ones, and in the super large cities it is many times higher than in the large cities.'[45] If the productivity of social labour is generally considered to be the chief criterion for effectiveness in distributing productive forces, the author suggested that the case for large cities was obvious.

While the debate continued, most sociologists concurred that knowledge about the economic, social, demographic, public health and other aspects of the growth of cities was inadequate. One had gone so far as to say that 'our present knowledge in the area of the sociology of the city is such that it does not qualify for attention in a serious discussion'.[46] L. N. Kogan and V. I. Loktev also complained of the lack of research on the influence of social factors on the construction of urban plans. They suggested that a city 'portrait', consisting of the state of social resources, contacts between inhabitants, type and structure of neighbourhood units and the possibilities for cultural development, become a subject of sociological research.[47]

Plans for social development of a different order were also made by sociologists. N. Aitov, for example, discussed plans which were drawn up at the request of the city party committees and the executive committees of their Soviets in two cities in Bashkiria, namely, Neftekamsk and Sterlitamak.[48] His study uncovered, for example, an adequate number of cinemas in these cities but an inadequate number of children's institutions. Lack of co-ordination between the local authorities, departmental agencies and the various ministries was blamed. Aitov then suggested that a city social development plan include a demographic forecast and on this basis provide for growth of the city economy and long-range development of all service, cultural, educational, athletic and sports facilities. Aitov advocated that the city Soviets themselves should develop this social plan for a five- to ten-year period. This somewhat veiled request for more city autonomy ran parallel to similar requests by other sociologists.[49]

It would thus appear from this brief look at urban sociology that one of the main problems considered was how to balance planning and non-planning in the urban context. Planned intervention in the formation of an urban environment was not entirely successful: the failure of the *mikroraiony* (neighbourhood units) to develop tightly knit communities within the larger city environment is a case in point.[50]

Criminology and Juvenile Delinquency

The revival of criminology began in 1957 when the first articles advocating a renewal of the study of the causes and prevention of crime appeared.[51] While these articles expanded and eventually developed into monographs, surveys and texts, research was transferred from governmental institutions to the universities where, in 1964, courses in the study of crime were introduced into all legal institutes and law faculties; by 1965-6, certain institutes of pedagogy and psychology had initiated similar courses. Concurrently, the case was argued for studying crime not only as a juridical but also as a social and/or sociological phenomenon. Within the latter context, how was crime defined for research? Why did crime exist? And what indeed were its causes?

'The *backwardness of social consciousness* relative to the objective conditions of life in socialist society contains the possibility of the violation of the principles of socialism, and it is the violation of these principles that leads to the existence of crime.'[52] Socialist society *per se* lacked inherent social causes of crime, but 'there are objective causes which, although they do not derive from the nature of socialist society, *still do objectively exist*.'[53] Socialist society had two kinds of crimes: 1) crimes caused by the existence of capitalist countries; and 2) crimes derived from vestiges of capitalism in people's minds and behaviour. Although these two interact, the first were insignificant in number, while the second indicated the 'lag in social consciousness behind social existence'.

Since subjective and objective factors caused crime, both must be studied. Different theorists stressed one or other of these factors, the more official line being that the objective factors are the most prominent. But opinion seemed to be turning to the view expressed in 1965 by S. S. Ostroumov and V. E. Chugunov: 'a number of objective conditions influence the manifestation of anti-social views and habits ... . Yet it is not the conditions of material life which drive [people] to crime. Everything rests on the level of the consciousness and culture of these individuals.'[54] Like the theorists, the majority of the researchers focused on the objective aspects of crime, while the minority concentrated on subjective factors such as the psychology, temperament and character of the offender. Increasing emphasis, however, was placed on the latter.

This is easily illustrated by research on juvenile delinquency. The purely juridical approach to the problem of crime in the past was one which consisted of merely listing those objective factors which correlated with crime, in this case, with juvenile delinquency.[55] For example, a direct relation was discovered between criminality and a low education, poor upbringing, drunkenness, etc.[56] However, the trend was towards an approach which combined an analysis of objective and subjective factors. Thus, in a paper entitled, 'Typical mistakes in the family upbringing of adolescent lawbreakers' delivered at the Vil'nius conference on the family, Z. Baeriunas discussed the 'mistakes' as follows: 'In some families, more significance is attached to social factors, while in others, to psychological [factors].' Parents' employment (or unemployment), an incomplete family and low material security were cited as 'social factors'. 'Psychological factors' included: 1) pedagogical neglect of the child from a very early age and then a hasty attempt to re-educate him/her; 2) strict authority over the child from infancy, but the inability to sustain this influence in adolescence; and 3) independence from an early age which the child did not know how to handle.[57]

Others looking at the motives of crime debated the relative importance of the social and the biological in the criminal act. In 1969, for example, B. D. Ovchinnikov discussed both sides of the question and concluded by pleading for an investigation of both aspects.[58]

In general, the discussions admitted that Soviet society, for a variety of reasons, had crime and it must be studied. Motives for crime were more or less connected with the 'moral formation' of the individual and with the concrete living situation, with the subjective and the objective. On the whole, the individual, and not society, was at fault. On the other hand, society was expected to solve the problem of crime.

What, then, were the measures suggested for the prevention and cure of crime in general and juvenile delinquency in particular? Almost all commentators would have agreed that, in the first instance, an analysis of crime requires research to help discover, understand and subsequently eliminate those causes of anti-social behaviour which society can influence. Such research, they said, should include the reasons for the fluctuations in the incidence and nature of crime and in the personal characteristics of the law breakers.[59] The desirability of predicting overall indices of the state of criminal activity throughout the country and then of drafting measures to eliminate those negative influences which stem from unfavourable conditions were readily acknowledged.[60] For example, to combat drunkenness and its effects, economic measures (raising the price of vodka), educational measures (publicity) and administrative measures (forbidding the sale of liquor) have been advocated.[61] Plans against 'boredom' included building sports facilities and other amenities for helping to broaden leisure pursuits as opposed to anti-social acts.[62] Greatly favoured were measures to help in the 'moral formation' of the individual, that is, before he or she performs an anti-social act. In addition, it was argued that crime prevention research should examine and determine the effectiveness of the methods of 'curing' this social ill (for example, the forms of punishment) and should include a programme for re-educating the people connected with offenders (for example, the family members as well as the offenders themselves). It should also list specialists, such as psychologists and sociologists, in the agencies engaged in crime prevention or in institutions for corrective labour as was done in Poland.[63] Finally, statistics on crime should be made available.

Religion

Like so many other fields, the sociology of religion and atheism lay rather dormant during the cult of personality. This dormancy was most noticeable because in the preceding years empirical investigations into religious sectarianism, investigations of a local, regional, historical and ethnographic nature, were of special importance.[64] Research all but ceased at such institutes as the Academy of Sciences, the Communist Academy and the Union of Militant Atheists. But research on religion was resumed, mainly by scholars at institutes of philosophy, history and ethnography attached to the USSR Academy of Sciences, the academic institutes of the Ukraine, Bielorussia, Kazakhstan, Moscow, Leningrad and Kiev universities, and others. The Institute of Scientific Atheism of the Academy of Social Sciences, along with its institutional network in the republics and *oblasti*, also took part in this type of research.

According to the Soviets, the sociologist of religion should have been concerned with the following.[65] First, he/she should explain the extent of the practice of religion by different social groups in Soviet society and in different regions of the country. Once the believer was identified, the researcher should define the degree and character of religious observance among different groups of believers (for example, different sects) and consider the motives for performing religious rites, the psychology of the believer and the causes of the vitality of religious survivals.[66] He/she should have analysed the relationship between consciousness and behaviour – namely, the correlation between the consciousness of religious and non-religious elements, the transformation of religious ideas under the influence of socialism and the relationship of the intellectual, emotional and spiritual in the believer.

Another aspect of the sociology of religion involved education in atheism. Sociologists were supposed to continue the struggle with religious ideology – and its defendants; they were to help prepare cadres of Marxists familiar with problems of religion and atheism. Various research teams in fact included party workers and propagandists of atheism. Hence the sociology of religion might best be retitled as the problems of scientific atheism and eradication of religion.

Questions on anti-religious training, the history of religion and atheism, sociological research, and philosophical criticism of religion came under detailed scrutiny in a review of fifty years of research.[67] In addition to stressing that one of the decisive conditions for the success of anti-religious training is a *sociological* analysis of the causes of the existence of religion in socialist society, the authors of the article stated that a new philosophical criticism of religion is feasible at the junction of the (Marxist) study of religion, on the one hand, and sociology, ethics, aesthetics, demography, ethnography, archaeology, anthropology, social psychology and other sciences, on the other. In other words, a more concrete analysis of the *social* nature and roots of religion could and should be attempted by applying both philosophy and sociology. Instead of merely emphasizing the ideological side of religion, the philosophical, historical and sociological aspects were studied jointly: this fact did not preclude independent research on the essence and value of man, ethical and cultural ideas, and modernist tendencies in religion – all of which were still fields of concern for the philosophers. Religious beliefs and the moral doctrines of religion, including the class character of religious beliefs and morals, the incompatibility of religion with communist morals and the teachings of the Bible, the Koran and other books of this nature, were examined and criticized. But the *sociology* of religion was emphasized more and more.

A study done in 1963 by the Institute of Sociological Research in Leningrad is a good example of sociological research in this area.[68] The aim of the research was to discover the causes of the vitality of the baptism ceremony and the motives for baptism. A positive correlation was found between baptism and less skilled workers and between the influence of religious ritual and the believers' level of education. Particular emphasis was placed on the influence of 'survivals of the past' and on the role that relatives played in preserving religious ritual. In some cases, the performance of religious ceremonies was associated with nationality. The main conclusion drawn from the data was that the 'reason for baptising children in the majority of cases is not the religious beliefs on the part of the parents, but their indifference, their conciliatory attitude towards religion combined with the influence of incidental factors.' To remedy this situation the author suggested the development of new rituals based on folk traditions and customs, permeated with elements of the new socialist culture. Another study of religious observance was undertaken by the members of the Department of History and Theory of Atheism at Moscow State University.[69] The research was carried out during a number of years: the department periodically sent expeditions to different regions of the country (for example, to Orenburg *oblast'* in 1962, to Krasnoiarsk *krai* in 1963, to Leninsk *raion* of Moscow in 1966). In order to direct atheist upbringing, said the researchers, we must know the social, professional, age and sex composition of the believers, their specific and unique religious conceptions and sentiments and the fluctuation(s) in their beliefs in response to contemporary conditions. On this basis, the researchers proceeded. Like the previously cited research, these researchers found that a large part of the believers had low or few occupational qualifications and a low level of education; a large part of the believers were women and were elderly (in the fifty-six to sixty-five age bracket or over sixty-five). These findings coincided with similar studies of various sects throughout the country.[70]

These researchers from Moscow State University concluded by noting that concrete research in the sphere of religion was not organized throughout the country, that the degree and character of religious observance in all social groups was not studied and that comparative data about the dynamics of such observance in different regions of the country were not sought. They suggested organizing instruction in atheism among different groups of the population (including the various groups of believers) and advocated the improvement and co-ordination of concrete sociological research on religion.

The application of some research on the effectiveness of atheist upbringing was reported in *Pravda* by N. Andrianov, Rector of the Pskov City Party Committee's Public Institute for Social Research.[71] Having investigated the believers and finding that they were predominantly old, with neither a higher education nor specialised occupational skills, the researchers suggested that the system of atheist education be reconstructed, improved and diversified. Hence the sociological research led to changes. Propagandists became more informed about the basic trends in the re-orientation of the church's ideological positions. According to Andrianov, their training began to focus not only on an historical criticism of religion, but also on questions of deepening the social bonds, linking the individual with society, developing new forms of human spiritual and cultural life, etc.

In sum, the sociology of religion aimed to unearth and explain various aspects of religious observance and stressed the weakening of religion, and suggested ways either to eradicate religious beliefs or provide some form of substitute. A by-product of the research was the collection of material of an ethnographic nature on various religious groups situated throughout the country.

1 P. Fedeseev, 'Marksistskaia Sotsiologiia i Konkretnye Sotsiologicheskie Issledovaniia', *Partiinaia Zhizn'*, No. 20, 1967, p.37.

2 B. A. Grushin, quoted in 'Sila i Slabosti Molodoi Nauki', *Literaturnaia Gazeta*, 6 August 1966, p.2. The participants' quote is also from this source.

3 L. Leont'ev, 'Sotsiologiia i Ekonomicheskaia Nauka', *Literaturnaia Gazeta*, 26 May 1966, p.2.

4 See the comprehensive section V entitled 'Sotsial'nye Problemy Truda i Dosuga' in *Sotsiologiia v SSSR*, Vol. 2, G. V. Osipov (ed.), Moscow, 1966, pp.5-267. Many of these essays are translated in G. V. Osipov (ed.), *Industry and Labour in the USSR*, London, 1966. See almost any issue of *Chevlovek i Obshchestvo* and *Sotsial'nye Issledovaniia*, as well as any of the collections on sociology in general.

5 Osipov (ed.), *Sotsiologiia v SSSR*, Vol. 2, p.9.

6 V. N. Shubkin, 'Molodezh' Vstupaet v Zhizn'', *Vop Fil*, No. 5, 1965, pp.57-70; article in N. V. Novikov *et al.* (eds.), *Sotsial'nye Issledovaniia*, Vol. 1, Moscow, 1965, pp.118-39; 'Kolichestvennye Metody v Sotsiologicheskikh Issledovaniiakh Problem Trudoustroistva i Vybora Professii', *Kolichestvennye Metody v Sotsiologii*, A. G. Aganbegian, G. V. Osipov and V. N. Shubkin (eds.), Moscow, 1966, pp.168-231; 'Ob Ustoichivosti Otsenok Privlekatel'nosti Professii', *Sotsiologicheskie Issledovaniia:Voprosy Metodologii i Metodiki*, R. V. Ryvkina (ed.), Novosibirsk, 1966, pp.247-67; and *Sotsiologicheskie Opyty*, Moscow, 1970, pp.151-251.

7 Shubkin, *Vop Fil*, No. 5, 1965, pp.57-8.

8 A. G. Zdravomyslov and V. A. Iadov, 'Opyt Konkretnogo Issledovaniia Otnosheniia k Trudu', *Vop Fil*, No. 4, 1964, pp.72-84; article by the same authors in *Sotsiologiia v SSSR*, Vol. 2, G. V. Osipov (ed.), Moscow, 1966, pp.187-207. The book with all of the results of the research was published as A. G. Zdravomyslov, V. P. Rozhin and V. A. Iadov (eds.), *Chelovek i Ego Rabota*, Moscow, 1967. See also two Soviet reviews of the book: T. Zaslavskaia, V. Shliapentokh and V. Shubkin, 'Sotsiolog i Ego Rabota', *Izvestiia*, 10 October 1967, p.4, and N. F. Naumova, 'Sotsiologiia Truda, ee Uspekhi i Problemy', *Vop Fil*, No. 7, 1968, pp.130-3.

9 A. G. Zdravomyslov and V. A. Iadov, 'Effect of Vocational Distinctions on the Attitude to Work', *Industry and Labour in the USSR*, G. V. Osipov (ed.), London, 1966, p.114.

10 Joan Woodward, *Management and Technology*, HMSO, London, 1958.

11 See, for example, the John H Goldthorpe *et al.* thesis in volume 1 of *The Affluent Worker: Industrial Attitudes and Behaviour*, Cambridge, 1968.

12 See, for example, Zaslavskaia, Shliapentokh and Shubkin, *Izvestiia*, 10 October 1967, p.4.

13 E. Antosenkov (ed.), *Opyt Issledovaniia Peremeny Truda v Promyshlennosti: Po Rezul'tatam Ekonomicheskogo i Sotsiologicheskogo Obsledovaniia Tekuchesti Rabochikh Kadrov*, Novosibirsk, 1969, and E. Antosenkov, *Labour Turnover in USSR National Economy: Socio-Economic Nature and Principles of Control*, Novosibirsk, 1970, 15 pp.

14 *Ibid.* pp.5-6.

15 See his *Migratsiia Naseleniia i Trudovye Problemy Sibiri*, Novosibirsk, 1966; *Narodonaselenie i Ekonomika*, Moscow, 1967; and 'Migratsiia Naseleniia i Ispol'zovanie Trudovykh Resursov', *Voprosy Ekonomiki*, No. 9, 1970, pp.35-43.

16 T. I. Zaslavakaia, *Migratsiia Sel'skogo Naseleniia*, Moscow, 1970, 348 pp.

17 L. Gordon and B. Levin, 'Nekotorye Sotsial'no-Bytovye Posledstviia Piatidnevki v Bol'shikh i Malykh Gorodakh', *Voprosy Ekonomiki*, No. 4, 1968, pp.138-42.

18 G. Sviridov, 'Iz Praktiki Konkretnykh Sotsiologicheskikh Issledovanii', *Partiinaia Zhizn'*, No. 16, 1970, pp.35-8.

19 I. I. Kravchenko and E. T. Faddeev, 'O Sotsial'noi Strukture Sovetskogo Obshchestva', *Vop Fil*, No. 5, 1966, pp.143-54, and K. L. Potaenko and M. L. Tsegoeva, 'Izmeneniia Sotsial'noi Struktury Sovetskogo Obshchestva', *Fil Nauki*, No. 3, 1966, pp.133-8. Some Soviet writers traced this back to a statement first seen in an article by F. Konstantinov and V. Kelle, 'Istoricheskii Materialism-Marksistskaia Sotsiologiia', *Kommunist*, No. 1, 1965, p.17.

20 V. S. Semenov, Moscow Home Service, 31 May 1966.

21 *Ibid.*

22 For references, see the authors listed individually below.

23 See his 'O Poniatii Intelligentsii kak Sotsial'nogo Sloia Sotsialisticheskogo Obshchestva', *Fil Nauki*, No. 4, 1966, pp.20-8; 'Izmenenie Sotsial'noi Struktury Sovetskogo Obshchestva i Intelligentsiia', *Sotsiologiia v SSSR*, Vol. 1, G. V. Osipov (ed.), Moscow, 1966, pp.391-413; *Izmenenie Sotsial'noi Struktury Sovetskogo Obshchestva*, Moscow, 1966;'Sotsial'nye Istochniki Popolneniia Sovetskoi Intelligentsii, *Vop Fil*, No. 6, 1967, pp.15-23; 'O Kriteriakh Sotsial'nykh Razlichii i Ikh Primenenii k Intelligentsii', in *Protsessy Izmeneniia Sotsial'noi Struktury v Sovetskom Obshchestve*, M. N. Rutkevich (ed.), Sverdlovsk, 1967, pp.76-88; 'Problemu Izmeneniia Sotsial'noi Struktury Sovetskogo Obshchestva', *Fil Nauki*, No. 3, 1968, pp.44-52; 'V. I. Lenin i Problemy Razvitiia Intelligentsii', in *Doklady k VII Mezhdunarodnomy Sotsiologicheskomu Kongressu*, O. N. Zhemanov (ed.), Sverdlovsk, 1970, pp.3-13; 'Protsessy Sotsial'nykh Peremeshchenii i Poniatie "Sotsial'noi Mobil'nosti"', *Fil Nauki*, No. 5, 1970, pp.14-21.

24 Iu. V. Arutunian: 'Sotsial'naia Struktura Sel'skogo Naseleniia', *Vop Fil*, No. 5, 1966, pp.51-61; 'Konkretno-sotsial'noe Issledovanie Sela', *Vop Fil*, No. 10, 1966, pp.166-9; Sotsial'nye Aspekty Kul'turnogo Rosta Sel'skogo Naseleniia', *Vop Fil*, No. 9, 1968, pp.114-31; *Opyt Sotsiologicheskogo Izucheniia Sela*, Moscow, 1968; 'Rural Sociology' and 'Rural Social Structure' in *Town, Country and People*, G. V. Osipov (ed.), London, 1969, pp.218-48; *Sotsial'naia Struktura Sel'sel'skogo Naseleniia*, Moscow, 1971.

25 Arutunian, *Vop Fil*, No. 5, 1966, p.52. Also in 'Rural Social Structure', in *Town, Country and People*, p.235.

26 O. I. Shkaratan: 'Sotsial'naia Struktura Sovetskogo Rabochego Klassa' *Vop Fil*, No. 1, 1967, pp.28-39; 'Rabochii Klass Sotsialisticheskogo Obshchestva v Epokhu Nauchnotekhnicheskii Revoliutsii', *Vop Fil*, No. 11, 1968. pp.14-25; 'Problemy Sotsial'noi Struktury Sovetskogo Goroda', *Fil Nauki*, No. 5, 1970, pp.22-31; *Problemy Sotsial'noi Struktury Rabochego Klassa*, Moscow, 1970. For Arutunian and Shkaratan, see also V. A. Provotorov, 'Obsuzhdenie Problem Sotsial'noi Strukury Obshchestva', *Fil Nauki*, No. 1, 1966, pp.145-8, and O. V. Belykh *et al.*, 'Ob Opyte Konkretnykh Sotsial'nykh Issledovanii', *Fil Nauki*, No. 3, 1966, pp.139-48.

27 Shkaratan, *Vop Fil*, No. 1, 1967, p.33.

28 Shkaratan, *Problemy Sotsial'noi ...*, p.4.

29 A. G. Kharchev, *Brak i Sem'ia v SSSR*, Moscow, 1964. p.325.

30 I. S. Kon, 'Tsennoe Issledovanie', *Fil Nauki*, No. 1, 1965, p.120.

31 Some of the findings which appear in this book were previously published in an article entitled, 'O Nekotorykh Rezul'tatakh Issledovaniia Motivov Braka v SSSR', *Fil Nauki*, No. 4, 1963, pp.47-58.

32 Kon, *Fil Nauki*, No. 1, 1965, p.120.

33 I. Mindlin also reviewed the book. See 'Staroe v Novom', *Novyi Mir*, No. 12, 1964, pp.260-2.

34 A. G. Kharchev, 'Marriage Motivation Studies' in *Town, Country and People*, G V Osipov (ed.), London, 1969, p.73.

35 See N. V. Ustinovich, 'Sotsializm i Sem'ia', *Vop Fil*, No. 7, 1967, pp.137-40 and M. A. Kirillova and M. G. Pantratova, 'Simpozium Sotsiologov po Issledovaniiu Problem Sem'i Byta', *Fil Nauki*, No. 4, 1967, pp.198-9. Also N. Solov'ev, Iu. Lazauskas and Z. Iankova (eds.), *Problemy Byta, Braka i Sem'i*, Vil'nius, 1970, 247 pp.

36 I. Kasiukov and A. Mendeleev, 'Nuzhen li Talant Sem'ianinu?', *Nedelia*, No. 12, 1967, p.18.

37 *Ibid.*

38 See the conclusion in N. G. Iurkevich, *Sovetskaia Sem'ia: Funktsii i Usloviia Stabil'nosti*, Minsk, 1970.

39 Z. Iankova, 'O Bytovykh Roliakh Rabotaiushchei Zhenshchiny (k Probleme Osyshchestvleniia Fakticheskogo Ravenstva Zhenshchiny s Muzhchinoi) in *Problemy Byta, Braka i sem'i* by N. Solov'ev, Iu. Lazauskas and Z. Iankova (eds.), Vil'nius, 1970, pp.44-9.

40 V. Besedina and T. Mamonova, 'Sprosim Nashikh Muzhchin', *Komsomol'skaia Pravda*, 27 May 1966, p.2.

41 A. I. Pimenova, 'Sem'ia i Perspektivy Razvitiia Obschestvennogo Truda Zhenshchin pri Sotsializme', *Fil Nauki*, No. 3, 1966, pp.35-44.

42 See the section devoted to social problems of the city and village in the second volume of *Sotsiologiia v SSSR*, G. V. Osipov (ed.), Moscow, 1966, pp.267-337. For a bibliography on studies of urbanization see D N Pevzner, *Sotsiologicheskie Issledovaniia Goroda*, Moscow, 1967 mimeographed.

43 B. Khorev, 'Kakoi Gorod Nuzhen?', *Literaturnaia Gazeta*, 2 April 1969, p.12.

44 O. S. Pchelintsev, 'Problemy Razvitiia Bol'shikh Gorodov', *Sotsiologiia v SSSR*, Vol. 2, G. V. Osipov (ed.), Moscow, 1966, p.284.

45 V. Perevedentsev, 'Spornoe Mnenie: Goroda i Gody', *Literaturnaia Gazeta*, 26 February 1969, p.12.

46 Khorev, *Literaturnaia Gazeta*, 2 April 1969, p.12.

47 L. N. Kogan and V. I. Loktev, 'Sociological Aspects of the Modelling of Towns', *Town, Country and People*, G. V. Osipov (ed.), London, 1969, pp.107-8.

48 N. Aitov, 'Na Perekrestke Mnenii: Gorod-Proportsii Razvitiia', *Izvestiia*, 17 February 1972, p.5.

49 See B. Michael Frolic, 'The Soviet Study of Soviet Cities', *Journal of Politics*, Vol. 32, No. 3, 1970, pp.675-95.

50 *Ibid.* For one example, see E. Levina and E. Syrkina, 'Razmyshleniia o Mikroraione', *Zvezda*, No. 10, 1966, pp.150-6.

51 I have used the unpublished master's thesis of Peter H. Solomon, Jnr., for the background of this discussion. See his 'Soviet Criminology: The Effects of Post-Stalin Politics on a Social Science', Columbia University, 1967.

52 M. D. Shagorodskii, 'Prichiny i Profilaktika Prestupnosti', *Voprosy Marksistskoi Sotsiologii*, V. P. Rozhin (ed.), Leningrad, 1962, p.96. (Italics mine.)

53 *Ibid.* (Italics by Shagorodskii.)

54 S. S. Ostroumov and V. E. Chugunov, 'Izuchenie Lichnosti Prestupnika po Materialam Kriminologicheskikh Issledovanii', *Sovetskoe Gosudarstvo i Pravo*, No. 9, 1965, p.101.

55 See the discussion (and disapproval) of this by B. S. Utevskii, 'Sotsiologicheskie Issledovaniia i Kriminologiia, *Vop Fil*, No. 2, 1964, pp.46-51.

56 One commentator criticised those who first correlate an insufficiently high level of education with crime and then complain that the absence of higher or secondary education is a negative phenomenon. V. N. Kudriavtsev, *Prichinnost' v Kriminologii*, Moscow, 1968, p.80.

57 Ustinovich, *Vop Fil*, No. 7, 1967, p.139.

58 B. D. Ovchinnikov, 'Sostnoshenie Sotsial'nogo i Biologicheskogo v Sviazi s Problemoi Prestupnosti', *Vestnik LGU*, No. 12, 1969, pp.142-50. For a classification of motives for crime, see P. S. Dagel, 'Klassifikatsiia Motivov Prestupleniia i ee Kriminologicheskoe Znachenie', *Nekotorye Voprosy Sotsiologii i Prava*, L. A. Petrov (ed.), Irkutsk, 1967, pp.265-74.
59 V. Kudriavtsev, 'Analiz Plius Tekhnika', *Izvestiia*, 30 September 1966, p.3.
60 G. M. Minkovskii, 'Nekotorye Prichiny Prestupnosti Nesovershennoletnikh v SSSR i Mery ee Preduprezhdeniia', *Sovetskoe Gosudarstvo i Pravo*, No. 5, 1966, pp.84-93.
61 'Antiobshchestvennye Iavleniia, Ikh Prichiny i Sredstva Bor'by s Nimi', *Kommunist*, No. 12, 1966, pp.58-68.
62 See V. N. Kudriavtsev, 'Problemy Prichinnosti v Kriminologii', *Vop Fil*, No. 10, 1971, pp.76-87.
63 V. Kudriavtsev, 'Prestupnost': Sootnoshenie Sotsial'nogo i Biologicheskogo: Dana li pri Rozhdenii', *Literaturnaia Gazeta*, 29 November 1967, p.12.
64 A. I. Klibanov, 'Piat'desiat let Nauchnogo Issledovannia Religioznogo Sektantstva', *Voprosy Nauchnogo Ateizma*, No. 4, 1967, pp.349-84.
65 A good review of the literature on this subject may be found in E. G. Filimonov, 'Problemy Konkretno-Sotsiologicheskikh Issledovanii Religioznosti v Sovetskoi Literature (1961-66)', *Konkretnye Issledovaniia Sovremennykh Religioznykh Verovanii*, A. I. Klibanov et al. (eds.), Moscow, 1967, pp.217-42.
66 See the first conference on the psychology of religion as reported by P. A. Lopatkin and M. A. Popova, 'Problemy Psikhologiia Religii', *Vop Fil*, No. 7, 1969, pp.150-5.
67 G. L. Andreev et al., 'Nauchnyi Ateizm za 50 Let', *Vop Fil*, No. 13, 1967, pp.37-47.
68 D. M. Aptekman, 'Prichiny Zhivuchesti Religioznogo Obriada Kreshcheniia v Sovremennykh Usloviiakh', *Vop Fil*, No. 3, 1965, pp.83-9.
69 I. N. Iablokov, 'Ob Opyte Konkretnogo Issledovaniia Religioznosti', *Vestnik MGU*, No. 4, 1967, pp.27-35.
70 L. N. Mitrokhin, 'Methods of Research into Religion', *Town, Country and People*, G. V. Osipov (ed.), London, 1969, pp.182-201.
71 N. Andrianov, 'Puti k Istine: Zametki ob Ateisticheskoi Propagande', *Pravda*, 7 September 1970, p.2.

6
Public Opinion Research

Public opinion research in the Soviet Union underwent many changes in both theory and methodology. The expansion and improvement of this form of research reflected the increasingly pragmatic trend in sociology, the growing belief among decision-makers in the functional value of such research, and the greater acceptance of sociological research by the country at large. A survey of public opinion research affords an excellent opportunity of chronologically tracing changes in the field of social research in general.

According to Soviet theory, a public opinion poll in and of itself constituted a means of activating opinion by focusing attention on important social problems. The educational importance of polling is further advanced by publishing the most characteristic answers to the questionnaires in the periodical press, thus exposing the collective opinion, evoking 'nation-wide' discussion and giving the Soviet people the further possibility of replying through the newspaper. In answering questions, it is argued, people speak about themselves and describe their needs and desires. Thus envisioned, public opinion polling was a learning and educating process for the party, the researchers and the public.

The theory underlying the alleged function of Soviet public opinion research underwent substantial changes. In the beginning, a distinction was made between socialist and bourgeois public opinion. Bourgeois public opinion research was characterized by the fact that it: 1) seeks to explain how effective bourgeois propaganda is; 2) interferes in the actual formation of opinions; and 3) maintains the illusion of the democratic character of the administration and management of capitalism.[1] The essential difference between this bourgeois public opinion and socialist public opinion was that in the latter only one opinion existed. Later on, however, it was admitted that public opinion in socialist societies was not unanimous on all subjects. 'It is foolish when some critics arrogate to themselves the exclusive right to speak in the name of the people ... The people are not a faceless mass with identical tastes.'[2] Or more strongly stated in a Soviet review of a book entitled *Obshchestvennoe Mnenie Sovetskogo Obshehestva* (*Public Opinion in Soviet Society*):

> The political and ideological unity of our people does by no means signify a full unity of opinions of all of the Soviet people on the questions of social life – moral, legal, aesthetic, etc. We have arguments about taste, norms of behaviour, morality, art, literature, etc. As a result of such discussions there is a serious polarization of opinions in the course of which there arise significantly diverging and even mutually exclusive opinions.[3]

The gradual recognition of these 'significantly diverging and mutually exclusive opinions' demonstrably altered the scope and value of this type of research.

The announcement on 19 May 1960 by *Komsomol'skaia Pravda* of the opening of its Public Opinion Institute – the first of its kind in the Soviet Union – marked the turning point in the study of public opinion. Soviet development in the field of public opinion research closely followed, albeit at a lag of several years, the Polish example. In both countries the communications media initiated the surveys – in the Soviet Union, the komsomol newspaper, and in Poland, radio and television. In the early attempts of both countries, the sampling and representativeness of the surveys were poor; the answers to the questionnaires merely suggested the existence of certain phenomena but permitted no evaluation of their scope and generality. But as Polish sociologists suggest, these scientifically questionable efforts on the part of the press broke the ice for more strictly controlled surveys by making the idea palatable to the public. In fact, according to some Soviets, the popularization of the public opinion poll was too successful: questionnaires as such were used indiscriminately by many unqualified people. In many such cases, the questionnaire was hastily and poorly constructed, and the generalizations or conclusions drawn from it therefore appeared unfounded. Such flimsy research impeded the work of the more competent and serious professional sociologists by sullying their research. But even with this 'notorious questionnaire mania', public opinion polling became an accepted method of research. *Komsomol'skaia Pravda's* Public Opinion Institute initiated this by institutionalizing public opinion research.

From May 1960 until the end of 1967 when the department closed, the Institute conducted two polls separately and fourteen polls through the newspaper: several of the latter were also conducted simultaneously by interviews. The number of respondents per poll varied from a few thousand to 46,000. The duration of the polls' press coverage lasted from one month to three years, although some of the results from the polls were unreported.

The usual procedure was to print a questionnaire, with closed- and open-ended questions, in *Komsomol'skaia Pravda* and ask the reader to reply; in some cases, however, people were interviewed directly. After an indefinite time, some 'typical' replies were printed and further requests for the newspaper readers to participate were made. Subsequent presentation of the poll either involved quotations from the respondents' replies, interspersed with or without much editorial comment, or lectures from 'responsible' individuals on the subject, or a polemic on one isolated area of the poll. The final coverage was usually written by a staff member of the Institute who summarized and tabulated, sometimes with charts and graphs, the results of the poll, and offered comment and criticism on the topic.

The topics of the polls ranged from 'How has your standard of living changed?' and 'How can you best spend your holidays?' to 'In the name of what are you studying?' Some of these subjects, such as 'What is your opinion of the young family?', emphasized accepted attitudes towards the subject and their findings revealed the extent to which the assumptions of a formal morality dominated Soviet thinking on such matters. A more sophisticated variety was the poll entitled 'How do you rate our service industries?', a poll which permitted government and party representatives to present changes to be introduced since the fall of Khrushchev. Other polls took the form of consumer research, eliciting the demands and complaints of the consuming public and, at the same time, offering gifts to those readers who supplied the most valuable suggestions. Another poll was a type of audience research by which the newspaper attempted to ascertain the character, preferences and reading habits of its readers. And the 'free time' poll corresponded to an intensive study of the same subject by other social researchers, namely time budget researchers.

Since the beginning of the Institute's endeavours, many changes – in method, presentation and results – occurred. Developments occurring within and between the various polls are now examined and evaluated, chronologically by topic.*

The *Komsomol'skaia Pravda* Polls

A poll on averting war was the first carried out by the Public Opinion Institute. Ten localities along the thirtieth meridian, which runs through four Union Republics, were chosen on the basis of the social and occupational diversity of the respondents. Of the 1,000 people chosen at random, the sex ratio was sixty-forty in favour of men. About 50 per cent of the respondents were workers, 12 per cent collective farmers, 12 per cent office employees, 10 per cent students, 10 per cent servicemen, and 5 per cent pensioners and housewives. Thus the proportions in the sample for the sex and occupation categories did not follow those of the population as a whole. The same applies to the last two of the four age groups, namely, the sample's thirty-three to forty-five bracket and the over forty-five group did not correspond with the proportion of the Soviet population as a whole, whereas the fourteen to twenty-five and the twenty-six to thirty-two categories did.

'*Komsomol'skaia Pravda* sees in the result of the poll a complete vindication and support of the Soviet government's foreign policy. Judging by the replies that are printed, this is not an unfair interpretation since many of them are written in the familiar formulae used by Soviet propaganda.'[4] *But not all.* The range of differences was interesting. Some respondents replied that war will be averted because 'war is not a means of settling international disputes – the history of the last two world wars proves this'. A collective farmer in the same region suggested that 'the people do not want war, and since the people do not want it, they will have their way'. A student at the S. M. Kirov Pedagogical Institute at Vitebsk pointed to the tragedies of Hiroshima and the German concentration camps as 'facts which live in people's minds; therefore people will not permit a war'. The majority, in affirming that mankind will succeed in averting war, gave as their

---

* The *Komsomol'skaia Pravda* public opinion polls are listed in chronological order, by topic, in the Bibliography. The questionnaires themselves are in Appendix I.

reasons either the downfall or the 'senility' of capitalism, Soviet rocketry, her technological and scientific strength, or the staunch policy of the CPSU and the government.

Five months later in October 1960 the second poll – 'How has your standard of living changed?' – was conducted. The questionnaire was distributed by railroad conductors to the occupants of a single carriage on each of sixty-five trains leaving Moscow on one day, canvassing a total of 1,600 people in all. As Soviet critics have pointed out, the poll poorly represented the kolkhoz workers while it over-represented those people travelling 'under orders' or on holiday. Once again, the proportion of men to women (three to two) and the occupational categories did not coincide with the population as a whole. Moreover, the poll did not include a question on the respondent's level of education, an important factor in improving one's standard of living.

The poll showed that while the standard of living did not change for 20 per cent of the respondents, it did increase for 73 per cent; this rise occurred for all strata throughout the country. The replies from the 7 per cent of the sample whose standard of living had declined were discussed in connection with suggestions for improving the standard of living. The Soviet pollsters concluded that the Soviet people link the standard of living with the policies of the CPSU and wholeheartedly support these policies. They also noted that, with the exception of fifty-nine people, every respondent made suggestions as to how standards might be raised. This was interpreted to mean that the broadest strata of the public are objectively interested in nationwide social development.*

The third poll, begun in January 1961 and tabulated by July, was on a subject of great contemporary interest – Soviet youth. At the end of twenty days the Institute had received 19,000 responses, 1,500 of which were disqualified for sundry reasons. The respondents were the youth aged fifteen to thirty who read *Komsomol'skaia Pravda*. *Komsomol'skaia Pravda's* circulation was 3,400,000 in 1960. Therefore half of 1 per cent of its readers answered the poll, and of these, only 11 per cent (1,933 out of 17,446) were from the countryside. The overwhelming majority of answers came from city 'activists'. Like the first two polls, this poll proved that the overwhelming majority of Soviet youth enthusiastically supported the regime. But the open-ended questions allowed for valuable (self-) criticism. In fact, the editors themselves said that the 'young generation cannot be accused of lacking self-criticism; they speak out boldly about their shortcomings'.

The request to name the strong traits of the Soviet youth yielded predictable responses: love of homeland, patriotism, resoluteness, heroism and collectivism made up the list. The answers to the question 'Are there any negative characteristics common among young people?' were more varied. The number one target was drunkenness. The second was the *stiliagi* (the teddy boys) – their

---

* The day after the results of the poll were published, *Komsomol'skaia Pravda* printed comments by various state ministers praising the findings and discussing the suggestions.

worship of foreign fashions, music and dancing. Then came the complaints about time-wasters, the passive people, the parasites and those totally occupied with sex. A 29-year-old chauffeur considered the desire to 'stand out', to 'make a better appearance than others', a negative trait. A negative characteristic was one which distinguished the individual's behaviour and beliefs from the norms set by the group or the society as a whole.

There was one notable exception to the favourable appraisal of the young generation. A 19-year-old female worker from Moscow wrote the following:

> The fact is that life is not very interesting. And this is not only my opinion but the opinion of the people I go around with. ... One feels a lack of discipline and culture in the behaviour of young people. ... Money is everything. Luxury and well-being, love and happiness. You condemn those who do not work, who do nothing. Why, they are only to be envied, because they are enjoying life. We only live once!

Her letter sparked off many denunciations from other youth, but some agreement with her views was carefully interspersed with the criticism.

The fourth poll, conducted through the newspaper in the middle of August 1961, was entitled, 'What do you think about the scouts of the future?' The questionnaire attempted to elicit answers on readers' attitudes toward work-production teams, such as the brigades of labour, the competition for labour and the acquisition of honorary titles. The respondents were asked to indicate the shortcomings in the competition for communist labour and any necessary changes in the system of receiving honorary titles. In addition to stating occupation, age, education and residence, the respondent was also asked, 'Are you taking part in the movement for communist labour? If not, why not?' Then if he/she wished, the respondent could indicate his/her name. The questionnaire was first published on 16 August. Additional replies were requested on 23 August and 30 August, when responses from brigade leaders and other foremost communist workers were published.

The Public Opinion Institute also directly interviewed some members of collectives of communist labour. The Institute retained six of the seven questions from the questionnaire originally published in the newspaper and added four others to it. The additions focused on the distinguishing features and benefits of a collective of communist labour but provided no room for negative replies.

One year later, the results were tabulated and printed in the newspaper. Curiously enough, the number of participants from the two parts of the poll was not specified. Instead, the entire group – 1,662 in all – was divided according to the participant's relation to the movement: about one-half of the participants were not taking part in the movement, a little more than one-quarter were working for honorary titles, and a little less than one-quarter were members of a collective of communist labour. All of the replies to the questions were tallied according to these three groups. The authors concluded that although the principles of communist labour were clear, the best experience had not become the norm for everybody. In order to attain this end, they suggested a further study of the weak and strong aspects of the movement.

The fifth poll – 'What do you think of the young family?' – was published on 10 December 1961; readers were requested to reply by 31 December. The first replies were published on 17 December and a second batch on 6 January 1962. In both cases, no editorial comment appeared. Such comment was only published when the results of the questionnaire were tabulated in July 1964 – three years after the first questionnaire on this topic appeared. Earlier, in February 1964, *Moscow News* published an English version of the results. Here, emphasis was placed on 'building' a Soviet marriage and a Soviet family. Failures did occur, but 'money worshipping, petty selfishness, disloyalty and jealousy' were to blame. But by the end of the article the basic reason for success or failure in married life had become the presence or absence of love with true ideals, moral integrity and moral respect.

The *Komsomol'skaia Pravda* presentation interspersed quotations from the respondents' replies with much editorial comment. This report was based on replies from 12,104 participants, whereas *Moscow News* cited 14,000. Moreover, the author of the *Komsomol'skaia Pravda* article concentrated on the question, 'In your opinion, how prepared are the young people who are entering marriage to create a family?', whereas the other report surveyed the entire twelve-question questionnaire. On the basis of the data, the *Komsomol'skaia Pravda* author concluded that opinion on this question is basically negative. 'Public opinion considers that the youngsters are far from always prepared to create a family, first and foremost, morally. Almost one-half of those who answered negatively spoke of this.' Thus the two presentations differed in their emphasis, although both may be said to be connected with the moral code set forth in the 1961 Party programme.

Between the poll about the young family and the lengthy sixth poll on the study of free time, *Komsomol'skaia Pravda* printed questions it had asked 1,000 students at Moscow State University in the spring of 1962. Neither a discussion of the sampling method nor the results of the poll were published: instead, ten replies appeared without any comment. The most interesting question was the first: 'Which of the motives below induced you to devote yourselves to your chosen speciality?'

- tradition of your family
- romanticism of the profession
- the relative ease of the job
- the desire to gain popularity and glory
- sense of mission
- high pay for the given profession
- striving to move in cultured circles
- impossibility to study your choice
- not thought of it
- if possible, what other kind of motive?

The ten respondents concurred on the force of tradition and romanticism, while they also favoured the sense of calling or mission. Commenting on this question in his book *Sila Obshchesvennogo Mneniia* (*The Force of Public Opinion*), B. A. Erunov, obviously with more access to material than the readers of the newspaper, stated that almost no one had included as a motive the relative ease of a job, high pay or the impossibility of studying a chosen vocation.[5] On the contrary, he wrote, everyone discussed romanticism and love of profession. The only conclusion to be drawn from the ten replies printed in the newspaper is that everyone was deeply dedicated to his profession-to-be, to knowledge and to learning; the only thing that hindered one's goal was war, illness or an unhappy marriage.

Soviet youth were thus given another plus rating. The next task of the researchers was to see how the youth were spending their free time. Inaugurated on 4 January 1963, the free time poll was to appear sporadically on the pages of the newspaper until February 1966. It was a model of Soviet public opinion polling and, at the same time, the boundary between the early and later forms of polling.

The questionnaire's six questions covered the following points: How much time, on the average, do you spend each day on the following (work, housework, physical needs, going to and from work, etc.)? What do you do with the remaining time? What do you do on your day off? What would you like to do with your free time? What prevents you from spending your free time as you would wish? What are the most important ways you see for making better use of leisure time? Thus, half of the questionnaire was designed to elicit specific answers; the other half permitted the respondent to express his/her opinion on how to improve the given situation. This division seems doubly beneficial for the researchers who could thus amass such data on actual time use and then could suggest, on the basis of the respondents' replies, ways of remedying a poor situation or controlling an already valuable one.

The presentation of the replies at first followed the format of previous polls. A week after the poll's first appearance, the questionnaire was re-published along with four responses from Moscovites and people from Moscow province. The same procedure was used the following week. Then, after a week's time, five replies were printed in response to a letter (printed in *Komsomol'skaia Pravda* on 11 January) from a girl who said she had no goal in life; she could find no interesting way to use her time and she had to 'compel' herself to study. She 'simply lives'. She was advised to develop a speciality, go to school and love her work.

The next discussion of the free time poll appeared in mid-February. This time the readers were subjected to a discussion of 'collectivism' and public spiritedness (*obshchestvennost'*), including civic acts. In March, a member of the research team discussed young people's hopes and plans for using leisure. T. Gromova was specifically concerned with criticising the practice of aimlessly wasting free time and she ended with 'to spend time waiting is to waste life'. Several months later the questionnaire was discussed by a teacher who reviewed answers received from other teachers. She came to the conclusion that teachers do not have sufficient free time, a fact which she found especially appalling since a teacher must develop his/her personality not only for himself/herself but for the *kollektiv.* In the June write-up, a Moscow architect linked the use of free time with the housing problem and suggested a new 'complex' which would unite housing with social and productive activities. A similar discussion took place in August when the first secretary of the Orskii city committee spoke about youth dormitories.

  The November commentary shifted from an instructive and authoritative tone to one of ridicule. People who did not indicate their addresses on the questionnaire forms were compared with Goncharov's nineteenth-century character, Oblomov. With tongue in check, the author painted a picture of the modern Oblomovs. For example, asked 'What do you do on your day off?' they replied, 'The devil knows what!' 'What do you like to do with your free time?' elicited 'Lie on the sofa', 'Sometimes read – but not more than a book a month', or 'Nothing!' 'If you wish, indicate your name.' ... 'What for?' The main difference between the original Oblomov and the present day Oblomov was that the former would not have had enough energy to fill out the questionnaire or spend four kopeks for postage. Continuing with jabs at parasites and praise for komsomol workers, the author ended the article by hoping 'first and foremost to infuriate Il'ia Il'ich [Oblomov] and force him to pick up the gauntlet thrown in his face. Of course', he cautioned, 'this act requires definite moral strength. But – we shall hope'.

  By the end of December 1963, the Institute had received 12,000 replies to the published questionnaire. A separate questionnaire 'by a specially worked out model' was then used when people at forty points throughout the country were interviewed; these points were supposed to represent the main geographic regions of the country. The results obtained from one point, Ust-Kamenogorsk (situated in the heart of the Altai mining region), were then printed.* The authors of the article turned to the theme of social or civic work, specifically complaining that not only was there a lack of civic work in Ust-Kamenogorsk, but also that the use of the term 'civic work' was often inconsistent. Here was one of the first acknowledgments of the crucial role that semantics play in obtaining data. Also discussed were the cultural attractions and detractions of the city.

  Two further communications with *Komsomol'skaia Pravda's* readers appeared exactly a year after the first publication of the questionnaire, that is, in January 1964. Imitating the youth poll of 1961, the editors of the newspaper turned to the people who are 'prominent [among] and popular' with the youth to explain their views on problems of interest to the youth. A separate questionnaire asked these older representatives to describe how they spend their leisure time and how they integrate it into their busy lives. The replies, printed on two days, gave advice to the *Komsomol'skaia Pravda* readers from Heroes of Socialist Labour, a

---

* From the figures supplied, it was impossible to determine the exact composition of the 103 respondents: about one-quarter were students, two-fifths workers, and perhaps the remainder were intelligentsia and white-collar workers.

CPSU member since 1896, a composer, the USSR Minister of Defence, a people's artist and an academician.

A year and half later, in June 1965, 450 ninth-grade and 550 eleventh-grade pupils – a difference not mentioned again in the results – filled out the free-time questionnaire in Smolensk. Combining the replies for a school day and a Sunday, the pollsters concluded that most free time was spent on passive activities such as reading and watching television. Those activities which required 'active intellectual output and bore the beginnings of creativity' ranged from tenth to twentieth place. However, the replies to 'How would you like to spend your free time?' reversed this order. Obstacles to spending free time as one wishes, listed by the 700 pupils who were not completely satisfied with the way they spent their spare time, were, in order of frequency: the amount of school work, personal laziness, unfavourable home conditions, parental interference and limited material means. Only the last reason – limited material means – was mentioned again in the final tabulation of the entire poll. Complaints were also voiced about the high price of tickets, the lack of sports facilities, and the 'lack of a place to meet without adult chaperonage, a place to converse and make declarations of love, and a place to dance.'

Six months later, in February 1966, the conclusions from the two-part free-time poll were given a three-day spread in the newspaper. Some 2,730 people participated in research conducted in thirty cities which, according to the researchers, sufficiently represented the main geographic areas of the Soviet Union (with the exception of the Baltic and the Trans-Caucasian regions). These cities were then classified according to the size of their populations; the proportion of people in each of the four designated population groups (up to 10,000; 10,000 to 100,000; 100,000 to 500,000; more than 500,000) was then compared with the proportion of people in comparable cities throughout the USSR, according to the 1959 census. This comparison forced the researchers to conclude that the poll was weighted on the side of the larger cities. Here, for the first time, the collected characteristics of the sample population were revealed and discussed in terms of the overall population, a fact which should subsequently allow independent researchers to evaluate and validate the data. In the poll, the proportion of people in the seven listed occupation groups compared favourably with the proportion of the Soviet population: the group of pensioners and housewives (who received 3 to 5 per cent more representation in the poll) was the exception. The sex ratio of the participants very closely resembled the ratio in the Soviet population at large. As for age, there was a 'dislocation' in favour of the young adults. Least analogous to the population at large were the proportions of the different levels of education of the sample population: the questionnaire's respondents had more education.

Some 10,392 people participated in the newspaper variety of the poll. They mailed their responses to the questions, indicating at the same time – as did the participants of other polls – their sex, age, occupation, education, family status, living conditions (for example, separate flat, communal flat, hall of residence) and city of domicile. As could be expected from a self-selecting sample population it deviated from the proportions of the entire Soviet population. The respondents were more educated (37 per cent of the sample had a secondary education and 14.3

per cent higher education) and younger (82 per cent were sixteen to twenty-nine years old) than the population of the Soviet Union; 61.1 per cent were male. Residence differences, so carefully distinguished in the other half of the poll and so significant in the discussion of free-time use, were not described.

For the first time, the *Komsomol'skaia Pravda* researchers discussed the representativeness of a poll in comparison with the total Soviet population. On this basis, they cautioned the readers to bear in mind that the poll was weighted in certain directions. Second, in regard to the newspaper poll, the pollsters did not claim that the replies represented the entire Soviet youth. On the contrary, they stressed that the participants were active, young and educated. This was a strong indication of the composition of former poll participants.

The significance of the free-time poll lay not only in its greater size in comparison with its predecessors, but also in the fact that subsequent discussion revealed greater sensitivity to the methodological problems involved. For the first time, the pollsters included a chart which outlined the respondents' proposals for ways of improving leisure. Increasing free time, expanding the facilities for leisure, increasing the income of the population, improving organizational work, improving housing and amenities, and cultivating and improving the quality of free time were the six alternatives, listed here in descending order of general popularity.

The poll uncovered two basic problems – one, of increasing the amount of free time, and the other, of developing its structure (makeup). The former, it was argued, should be tackled by decreasing non-working, rather than working, time (for example, time spent on housework and travel to work) and the latter by studying and then remedying the inequality in the distribution and utilization of leisure time. The poll found that inequality in the distribution of leisure existed because different social groups used their time differently and because various ways existed for enjoying leisure. Hence leisure time was structured unequally, according to the following factors: 1) 'biological factors', for example, students spend less time with children; the young, more time on tourism; 2) the process of 'abolishing problems', for example, workers study more than the intelligentsia because they need to raise their educational level; 3) 'neutral factors', for example, men attend sports events more frequently than women; 4) 'clearly developed social character', for example, the intelligentsia and students have a more developed or 'progressive' structure of free time than housewives or pensioners. Left unmentioned was a correlation between the uses of free time and the participants' desires for using their free time.

The question of subjective and objective factors also entered this discussion. Subjective factors, based on the 'low culture' of free-time use, played a secondary role. Objective factors, which included (in order of importance) the shortage of free time, the insufficient development of the material and technical base of leisure, the shortage of personal means, and the deficiency in the organization of leisure, were first in importance.

The conclusions from the poll were in no way startling. The pollsters were quick to point out that their basic findings coincided with those reached by G. A. Prudenskii and his *kollektiv* at the Siberian branch of the Academy of

Sciences in 1958-60. However, they emphasized the fact that the size of the urban population was a main factor in time use, disuse or misuse.

A year after the results of the poll appeared in *Komsomol'skaia Pravda*, B. A. Grushin published a lengthy book in which he described and analyzed the poll and simultaneously examined the problem of free time.[6] He was primarily concerned with trying to determine the size, structure and content of free time. His overall conclusion was that the way to increase free time is not to decrease working time but rather to change the structure of non-working time. Moreover, objective, not subjective, factors were the main cause of the insufficient development of free-time elements. Of special interest here is Grushin's reference to income: groups possessing large material means have the possibility of increasing their free time as a result of decreasing time spent on labour connected with their occupation, transport and, especially, daily needs. He therefore concluded that a further increase in the working person's income will enable more extensive development of all elements of free time. Grushin also refuted the misconception that everyone takes equal advantage of facilities provided by the state: the fact that the Soviet Union had so many thousands of theatres does not mean that all Soviets took equal or similar advantage of them.

Furthermore, Grushin's discussion of the content of free time is unique because he examined the issue of quality as well as quantity. The quantitative factor encompassed: 1) the subject of the action (doing *what*); 2) the character of the action (*how*, in what form); 3) the number of activities (*how many* different ones); and 4) the proportional time spent on each action (*how important* is each activity to the individual). The qualitative aspect included: the difference between an active and passive activity; the attitude of the individual toward a given type of activity; the relations between different types of activities; and the presence of contradictions between different types of activities and between different population groups. The study of both the quantitative and the qualitative sides of the free time problem should have added a further dimension to this form of research.

Of much less consequence is the seventh questionnaire, entitled 'To Mars, with what?' Given twenty-five days to complete the questionnaire, the reader was asked which fifteen items – the best representatives of twentieth-century civilization – should be included in a rocket to be sent to Mars. The newspaper published several replies in March, April and June 1963; the last consisted of answers received from foreign countries. Then, in October, the results were tabulated over a four-day period.

Some 6,425 people contributed to the *Komsomol'skaia Pravda* search for the best expressions of (Soviet) achievements in the arts and sciences. They identified the most important document of the century (the CPSU Programme), the great man of the epoch (Lenin by 98.2 per cent) and the person whose exploit had glorified the twentieth century (Iuri Gagarin). Answers to other parts of the poll, concerning *the* technological invention, work of literature, score of music and reproduction of a painting or sculpture, were more varied. Those that fell outside the generally accepted responses were used to illustrate a point. For example, the question about which musical score to send to Mars elicited thirty-three responses in favour of jazz. Commenting on this, the editors single out this 'insignificant in size, but extremely eloquent, figure of 0.5 per cent'.

> We do not in the least have a malicious feeling of 'victory' over jazz, which has become all but the symbol of moral decay in the eyes of some of our bigoted culture-bearers. No! We are glad of something else, and we have our own interpretation of this figure. It is simply pleasant to be made aware that our youth, while by no means adverse to jazz or to light music in general, do not make a shibboleth of the saxophone.

The next two polls, which appeared in the middle of 1964, introduced material incentives. The first was carried out jointly with the All-Union Scientific Research Institute of Technical Aesthetics. In the introduction to the poll, the Institute said that the time had passed when a consumer bought everything that a store offered for sale and traced the problem to a question of taste. To test this view, the poll was conducted. To ensure a large response, the editors of the Public Opinion Institute promised three prizes – two transistor receivers and one receiver – and 'stimulatory bonuses' for the most valuable suggestion on the construction and improvement of television, radios and record-players. One-third of the questions were designed to elicit the readers' preference in style(s). Another third queried the need for remote control and automatic record-changers. The last part of the questionnaire requested the participant to name the brand of equipment he/she had and then to discuss the pros and cons of the said instrument. Suggestions for changes were welcomed. Some 14,000 people, mainly with engineering backgrounds (if we can judge from the composition of the winners), participated in the month-long contest. The three winners' answers were published in *Komsomol'skaia Pravda*, along with the minutes and official statements of the judges; those who received 'stimulatory bonuses' were named and their occupation and place of residence noted.

This poll, the first of its kind in *Komsomol'skaia Pravda*, was basically a form of consumer research. Using the *Komsomol'skaia Pravda* readers as the chosen population, the researchers were able to elicit the demands and complaints of the consuming public. The poll was set up in such a way that mere praise of the existing services was of no benefit to the participant. Since deficiencies were already stated as the cause of the diminution of sales, prizes were given for concrete suggestions and not for praise. It may be presumed that the pollsters did obtain thoughtful and useful suggestions from the consuming public.

The second contest, entitled 'An Innovation demands a Name', began with the publication of the results of the first contest. Lasting for about a month, this poll requested the participants to name seven types of communications equipment. Ten prizes for the best names were offered by the Administration of the Radio-Electronic Industry of the *Sovnarkhoz* (Regional Economic Council) of the USSR. A year later the results were announced. 46,000 people participated! This was by far the greatest response to any poll conducted by the Public Opinion Institute. Unlike the previous contest, the only 'information' obtained was a suggestion for a name. The names, however, were to be recommended to the specific industries involved. These contests seemed to demonstrate at least one advantage of offering a material incentive, namely, the probability of obtaining a large number of replies. They certainly indicated the willingness of the public to offer suggestions in the field of consumer goods.

At the beginning of August 1964, the paper printed some replies to a questionnaire which the Institute had conducted among nine- and ten-year-old schoolchildren. The purpose of this poll, conducted in well-known Komsomolsk-na-Amur and little-known Komsomolsk in the Ivanovskaia *oblast'*, was to determine the meaning of fifty words relating to phenomena of the past. The researchers stated that they had a control group as well as a group of older children. They were also concerned with distinguishing replies from city and country children: 500 from the city and 500 from the rural regions were interviewed. The poll was intended to show the withering away of 'survivals of the past', bad habits and Old Testament ideas. Words describing religion, the kulaks and the class struggle had lost their original meaning. 'The Virgin', for example, was defined as 'a woman who works in a vegetable garden'.* 'But', added one commentator, 'ask them what *blat* [string-pulling, "fixing"] and *nakhlebnik* [parasite] mean. It would be better if they were less informed on these questions'. Another pollster stated that although the children did not have first-hand experience with the words in the questionnaire, their understanding 'reflects the subjective perception of the adults in their family'. 'Bureaucrat', for example, was defined as 'Father wanted to go on holiday but they did not allow him to do so'. On 'bribe', 'this is when money is given on the sly so that no one sees'. Over half of the participants knew what a 'speculator' was.

Like the earlier poll taken at Moscow State University, the pollsters failed to indicate the composition of the sample or to tally the results: the control group and the rural-urban differences were not discussed. While it is obvious that the schoolchildren were unable to correctly identify the meaning of such terms as 'dowerless girl' or 'house spirit', their knowledge of more current evils (for example, bureaucracy) or 'survivals of the past' (for example, private property) seemed to indicate the presence of the same in the society.

The tenth poll conducted by the Institute began in November 1964 and by the end of 1967 had not been given final coverage in the press. The topic was designed to increase the researchers' knowledge about the conditions of, complaints about, and suggestions for the service industries; thus, 'How do you rate the service industries?' Included in service industries were trade, communal eating, transport, medical facilities, combines (*kombinaty*) of everyday services, cultural institutions, sports centres and communications enterprises. These industries, in turn, were to be rated according to the following conditions: unnecessary expenditures of time, inconvenient hours of service, unsatisfactory organization of supplies, poor fulfilment of orders and low standards of personnel.

---

* The children were obviously confusing *Bogoroditsa* (the Virgin) with *ogorodnitsa* (market-gardener).

When judging the quality of the services, the respondents were asked to state the basic reasons for the shortcomings and to propose improvements. Positive comments were also solicited.

The first few press reports concentrated on one aspect or another of the poll. On 7 January 1965, a L'vov-and-Moscow based reporter discussed the problems associated with commercial advertising. The function of advertising, he asserted, was to inform consumers, describe the qualities and properties of the goods, and educate people's tastes. He complained that there was an advertising paradox, namely, that while windows and neon were abundant, they were almost completely useless and unused.

The next month's report revolved around the relations between consumers and salespeople. It was compiled from the responses of those readers who replied 'Poorly!' to the question, 'How do you rate the service industries?' The author condemned the rudeness of the salespeople, some of whom did not even bother to respond to enquiries, and the inexperience of the salespeople, most of whom appeared to be young. She also stated that stores closed too early and did not open promptly at nine o'clock; moreover, the consumer was often not sure that the salesgirl would eventually come and open the shop. Finally, the author arrived at the heart of the matter: buyers were many and goods were few.

A week later some letters from specialists in various service departments were introduced by the editors as follows:

> Judging by the answers of the service workers, they are united in their sincere interest in their work, in their warm striving to satisfy (as much as possible) the enquiries of the people, and in their feeling of resentment towards and annoyance with the shortage of equipment and materials for work, and with the stagnation, inefficiency and carelessness in the organization of their labour.

Two letter writers from the Central Mechanical Computing Station (run by the Central Statistical Board) suggested the use of a state network of electronic computer centres to solve the ever-growing problem of serving the nation. They proposed using computers to determine sales and demands and to allocate and distribute goods.

The subject for March included the reasons why enterprises did not work to their full capacity (for example, there was only one shift or the hours of opening were unsuitable). This topic was followed by a discussion of the relation of profit and pricing. Then complaints about repairs and orders which are not filled on time were aired. Answers to these and other complaints were supplied by the author, a former *Gosplan* (State Planning Commission) expert; the system of payment and incorrect organization of production were blamed.

In April, 346 visitors to Detskii Mir (a Moscow department store for children) were interviewed. The majority of them complained about the impossibility of procuring children's goods. Why can't children's articles be bought? 'Deficit' was the cry. 'But look at the shelves. There is a surplus of impractical stock.' Another answer was offered: children's goods are not produced because they are unprofitable. A third reply referred to the disdain for studying consumer demands. 'Specialists ... do not know how to and do not want to distinguish consumer demands ... . Today nowhere and no one studies (with the exception of the firm of Detskii Mir) the demand for children's goods. No one knows the existing demand.' The plea for consumer research was most explicit.

The fact that the poll data could be utilized with the explicit intention of bringing about policy changes was made clear eight months later when *Komsomol'skaia Pravda* discontinued its previous practice of asking relatively unknown authors to discuss specific service problems. Instead, three ministers of trade were interviewed. The interviewers, furnished with the answers from the 6,127 respondents, seemed to assume that the respondents' answers to the questionnaire were the correct ones. For example, 'One-quarter of the respondents said this ... How can *you* explain this?' 'Well, *you* said this – they say that. How can *you* justify the difference?'

The first to be interviewed was A. I. Struev, Minister of Trade. During the interview he admitted that the demand for goods was greater than the supply; his solution for studying consumer demand was the establishment of branches of the already existing All-Union Scientific Research Institute. Then he partially attributed dissatisfaction with the way in which goods were distributed throughout the country to the lack of stores. He further agreed with the poll participants that store hours were not convenient for factory workers. Finally, he concurred with the participants that salespeople were neither professionally trained nor given enough authority: he also considered changing the system of payment to salespeople.

N. N. Tarasov, the Minister of Light Industry, was the second to be interviewed. Agreeing with the poll participants that there was both an insufficient quantity of and poor quality of goods, Tarasov noted future plans to remedy the situation, plans which included the creation of a ministerial sub-branch of the Ministry of Light and Foodstuffs Industries. Responding to a question on the study of current and prospective consumer demand, he cited the ties between industrial and trade enterprises (for example, the Bol'shevik experiment). He was enthusiastic about the practice of sending the inventory ticket from purchased articles back to the factory which had produced them so that the factory would know which items were most popular. He further suggested raising the material incentive of workers so that, for example, samples demonstrated in the House of Models and at exhibitions could appear more quickly as consumer goods on the shelves.

The last to be interviewed was the RSFSR Minister of Automobile Transport and Highways, S. P. Artem'ev. Unlike the previous interviewees, he seemed hesitant to recognize the problems which the respondents raised about the general malfunctioning of the transportation system. A particularly large number of critical letters on this topic came from people in the countryside, but city inhabitants also supplied complaints.

These three ministers were thus presenting some solutions to the problems which beset the service industries. As government or party representatives, they also indicated to *Komsomol'skaia Pravda* readers changes to be introduced since the fall of Khrushchev. Since the press presentation was not completed, no further conclusion is possible.

Such is also the case with the next (and last) three polls which first appeared in April, June and October, respectively, of 1966. Coinciding with and conducted at the Fifteenth Congress of the Komsomol, the first of these, 'Komsomol members about the Komsomol', focused on problems connected with the life and activity of the komsomol. The three-fold questionnaire explored the main tasks of the komsomol, the relations between the komsomol member and his/her local organization, and the most pressing questions in the life of the komsomol organization. At this first stage of research, 3,000 city and country komsomol members, aged fourteen to twenty-eight, were queried; attention was given to their demographic, social, professional, educational and komsomol characteristics. The researchers stated that at a second stage of interviewing non-komsomol members of the corresponding age group would be questioned. In the meantime, the newspaper readers were asked to fill in a shortened version of the questionnaire.

This poll received only two notices in the newspaper. The extremely short May 1966 article, which concentrated on question four from the original poll ('How has the komsomol helped in the fulfilment of life plans?'), aired the views of five respondents. The September 1966 article centred on the principle of 'free and open discussion' (*glasnost'*) or, in this case, on the absence of an 'upward' and downward' flow of information between the rank-and-file and the local komsomol leadership. This striking situation, however, seemed to be of little concern to the komsomol committee workers who, according to the author of the article, did not at that time see this as a problem.

The twelfth questionnaire, begun in June 1966, continued the more and more pragmatic pattern of the Institute's research. This particular research, as increasingly was the case with much other sociological work, was performed by the Institute in conjunction with other research bodies. And here again, different state agencies had the opportunity of ascertaining opinions, suggestions and criticisms, and then applying their knowledge to the problem at hand, namely, 'How do you best spend your holidays?' and 'How do you wish to spend your holidays?' In fact, the poll seemed to be an outgrowth of the polls on free time and the service industries. This link should have further enabled the researchers to evaluate the results and the accuracy of these previous polls and, at the same time, continue to amass data – some overlapping and some completely new – on the structure and organization of the annual holiday.

Although there was no indication at the time of its introduction that the poll would consist of more than one questionnaire, the two parts of the poll – the first concentrating on the present and the second on the future – were published within a month of each other. Three of the twelve questions of the first questionnaire considered the pros and cons of the organization of the annual holiday. Then came questions on the most valuable type of holiday, the location and timing of such a holiday, the problems involved in co-ordinating parents' and children's holidays, and ways of furthering mass tourism. Another question, most unusual in approach, asked the participants to indicate which categories of people –

distinguished by age, occupation, social position, etc. – have the best organized leisure and which have the worst; manifestations of these differences were requested. Finally, a question which duplicates one from the free-time poll asked for proposals for improving leisure. Two of the six suggested replies from the free-time poll were omitted, but they were either previously covered or irrelevant here. The remaining four suggested answers were listed as follows: expand the material base of leisure, increase the income of the population, raise the 'culture' of leisure, and increase the length of the holiday.

A week after the printing of the first part of the poll, the questionnaire was reprinted with several questions omitted. Once again, the editors stressed that the information obtained from the questionnaires would help the Soviet, trade union and komsomol organizations and the organs of public health to find an optimal solution to many holiday problems. At the same time, they emphasized that the questionnaire should also turn the readers' attention to their own attitudes towards leisure, for example, 'Is it always sufficiently creative?' Then several replies were published. Within a week four more replies appeared on the pages of *Komsomol'skaia Pravda*; after another two weeks, several letters were printed.

With the announcement at the end of July that the Institute had received 600 replies, the second part of the questionnaire appeared. Two of the poll's ten questions were related to the material base of leisure. Two others focused on the development of tourism, another on the relation between mass tourism and transportation facilities, and another two on the effect of different sources of information on the choice of location and type of holiday. Another question sought to discover the reader's preference first for a holiday with or without a free travel warrant,* and then a holiday in one or in several places. Additional questions tried to discern the purpose of a holiday and then to discover ways of achieving it (for example, by material means or whatever). The last query sought to answer the question, 'Holiday with whom? – family? friends? colleagues? professional colleagues? unknown company? alone?'

Two months later, the question of winter as opposed to summer holidays was discussed. The number of advocates of a summer holiday was considerable; their battle cry was 'sea, sun, cheap fruit and cucumbers'. At the same time, the defenders of winter holidays lauded winter sports and stressed the possibilities of taking advantage of big city attractions. (Theatres, for example, are closed in the summer.) Explaining that many of the respondents were in favour of a change, the author of the article complained that winter holidays were poorly organized and under-publicized; winter facilities, moreover, were clearly inadequate. And, as in the case of many of the other polls, the author directed the attention of organizers and planners to further developing and exploring the possibilities of winter holidays.

---

* A free travel warrant (*putevka*) was authorization for officially sponsored (recreational) travel, accommodation or remedial treatment.

Within five days, the head of a department in the Central Scientific Research Institute of Experimental Planning stated that no sphere was as weakly studied or as poorly planned as leisure. Candidate of Architecture, N. Shelomov, saw leisure as a rich source of income and, in this connection, suggested the creation of an independent section of the economy devoted to leisure, a section which would completely centralize the 'industry of leisure'. He subsequently touched on the problems of protecting natural areas such as the Caucasus and the Baltic regions and developing additional areas.

The last write-up reverted to the favourite Institute practice of relying on known and popular people of the older generation to explain their views on the given topic. Offered here were eight letters on leisure, leisure and work, and leisure and youth. Unlike the Shelomov report, this November 1966 article did not concentrate on the existing deficiencies in the organization of leisure, but instead turned to the absence of a 'culture' of leisure and to the problem of the people's 'inability' to rest. The youth, in particular, had these problems. Hence, the lessons from their elders.

The very last *Komsomol'skaia Pravda* poll studied marked the beginning of an approximately two-year study on 'The reader about himself and about the newspaper'. The Institute was to study the newspaper's audience in the hopes of determining readers' thoughts about and proposals for the newspaper. The first part of the research attempted to discover subscription practices, content preferences,* satisfaction and dissatisfaction with this newspaper in comparison with others, and length of time spent reading. Judging from this form, it would seem that *Komsomol'skaia Pravda* would have been able to ascertain the composition of its audience.

Critiquing Public Opinion Research

It will already have become clear from the preceding survey that public opinion polls were on the whole characterized by an increasing concern with methodological questions, such as with the representativeness of the sample in relation to the population at large. Indeed, one significant contribution of public opinion research was its stimulation of debate about survey methods. Almost from the outset, the *Komsomol'skaia Pravda* polls came under direct attack. Thus, in June 1961, after the results of the first three polls had been published, a conference was held to consider public opinion polling.[7] At this conference, the main concerns were the use of open and closed questions, sampling methods and the role of statistics. A debate developed between B. Grushin of the Public Opinion Institute, who defended open questions, and F. D. Livshits, Candidate of Economic Science, who spoke in favour of closed questions. Stressing the importance of the

---

* Out of the forty-nine headings for the different types of articles, the Institute's articles ranked in sixteenth place.

choice of the subjects to be investigated, Livshits condemned the second poll on the standard of living because, he stated, the Central Statistical Administration already conducted research on this very question. The other participants did not criticize the topics of the investigations but they did attack the general sampling procedures. A. G. Volkov of the Scientific Research Institute of Labour said that the respondents were not selected at random. V. D. Mirkin from the RSFSR Central Statistical Administration added that all population groups were not represented. All the conference participants stressed the need to use statistics and statistical methods in doing public opinion research.

By June of 1963 comment on the third poll was available.[8] Candidate M. Kh. Igitkhanian said that although the organizers of the youth poll had not been able to 'typify' the composition of the sample population in advance, the poll was nonetheless representative and characteristic of Soviet youth.[9] This, however, was as far as his praise went. He said that Soviet researchers did not know how to conduct public opinion polls; they were ignorant of general statistical principles, concrete methods of typology and tests for the reliability of the polls' results. He then stated that polls conducted through the newspapers ascertained the opinion of isolated individuals rather than collective opinion. Finally, he warned that neither a detailed elaboration of the methods of opinion polling nor an improvement in the techniques of analysis could by themselves ensure accuracy: the results of a poll could reflect true public opinion only if, along with provisions for representation in sampling and objectivity in analysis, the very subject of the poll was of interest to the respondents.

In 1965, a major contribution to the debate over public opinion research was made by B. A. Grushin in an article which examined and weighed the past efforts and outlined future possibilities of this type of research.[10] The material from the first seven polls formed the basis of his discussion. Grushin stated that most often a public opinion poll proceeded from a study of a part to a generalization about the whole. In other words, the researcher received a picture of a particular phenomenon and then 'enlarged' it to generalize about the whole. Therefore, 'if we want to form an opinion about a social object on the whole, it is necessary that the sample – in whatever form and to whatever degree – reflects all of the existing features of the structure of the studied object.' He argued that the sample must be large enough so that one may generalize about society in general and separate social groups in particular; furthermore, it must be objectively proportional to different groups in the social structure. Another factor which played a very important part in the definition of these groups was those objective and subjective 'possibilities' which the researcher has at his/her disposal. As far as the Public Opinion Institute was concerned, noted Grushin, it 'continually had to take into consideration the absence of the necessary number of workers who would be fully qualified to study programming, conduct questionnaires and analyze the received material'.[11]

Grushin then turned to the problem of sampling, namely, selective sampling as opposed to random sampling or a combination of the two. The pros and cons of these methods were discussed. The treatment and recognition of the 'errors' of spontaneous research (that is, the method most frequently used at the beginning of the Institute's work) received special note. Such errors referred to the (possible) distortion due to readers' self-selection. For example, kolkhozniks, the less educated, women and the more passive youth were minimally represented in the *Komsomol'skaia Pravda* questionnaires. Or more positively, the most conscious, active and literate part of the population, the 'foremost' youth, responded to the newspaper questionnaires. One of Grushin's several suggestions for remedying this situation – and here he echoed Igitkhanian's remarks – was to construct a questionnaire on topics which directly involve the respondent.

Grushin saw the problem of representation (and hence, of participation) of certain groups as follows:

> The essence of the problem is that people do not want to express their opinion. Thus unwillingness can be expressed in the complete refusal of a person to answer the questionnaire, as well as when he/she gives answers which do not correspond with his/her genuine views. The cause of such reluctance – fear, feeling of protest, bashfulness, inconvenience, not understanding the aim of the questionnaire, etc. – can vary to a great extent. ... The extreme expression of this is the refusal of a person to participate in a questionnaire. At first glance, there is nothing strange about such a refusal ('don't want to – *ne nado*!'), all the more so as there is always the possibility of finding another person, characterized by the same socio-demographic parameters, who agrees to answer the questionnaire with pleasure. However, in actuality such an 'avoidance' is a great danger, especially if it has some kind of definite trend or mass character.[12]

These revealing problems had not, to my knowledge, been examined before Grushin's penetrating essay. Nor had any indication of the degree of the wish for anonymity in such research been previously given: according to Grushin, up to 25 per cent do not sign their name or they list their name saying, 'I wish you not to expose my name.' This problem was further associated with the role of the interviewer. While acknowledging that an interview is the most effective method for guaranteeing the 'minimum loss' of material, Grushin said that the interviewer might either constrain, embarrass or rush the interviewee so that, as a result, the researcher obtained the opinions of the interviewer rather than those of the interviewee.

On the whole, Grushin was able to use the material from the first seven polls – polls already tried and worked out on Soviet soil – and then instruct public opinion pollsters on ways of further improving and validating this type of research. There can be little doubt that much of his advice was heard and digested by the Public Opinion Institute as well as by other public opinion researchers.

To Grushin's criticisms of the polls can be added other Soviet criticism of public opinion research in general. Some of the defects noted by the Soviets arising from the 'notorious questionnaire mania' – notably the fact that the work of serious sociologists was impeded by the shoddy work produced as a result of this craze – have already been mentioned. Another outcome of this popular fascination with public opinion research was the huge quantity of material gathered. Critics complained that isolated facts from the mass of material were chosen to fit pre-conceived notions: since there was too much to process, the original hypothesis of the research was easily proven by merely eliminating those elements which did not support it. But, at the same time, the results from the research may have also be interpreted too broadly; for example, if fifty people supported one idea, the pollsters concluded that all of the people in the USSR followed suit.

If the pollsters have been criticized for their interpretations of the polls' results, they were also attacked for the poor construction of the questionnaire, inadequate and inaccurate sampling methods and their polling in general.[13]   Such a fundamental task as pre-testing the questionnaires was often omitted; the sample was often merely a haphazard or purposely structured collection of individuals from which further generalizations about the country at large or about a specific social group were invalid. In the final analysis, the poll was neither reliable nor sound.

In addition to the deficiencies in the actual research method, attention focused on that which was common to most other forms of sociological research in the Soviet Union. Consider, for example the absence of socio-demographic data. In 1966, Kantorovich argued that 'the leaning towards questionnaire methods has come about, I believe, largely because of the scarcity of published statistical data.'[14]   These sentiments were voiced many many times. Then there was the lack of co-operation between researchers in the same, or in a related, field working on similar problems. Finally, the results of many of the polls were not applied: 'solutions' may have been offered, but they fell on deaf ears.   Grushin, for example, reported that nothing was done about the free-time questionnaire because of the lack of co-ordination between interested institutes. But he also indicated that some research findings were put into practice: the *Komsomol'skaia Pravda* questionnaire about industrial design led a light industry firm to make special designs for radios and electrical equipment, and the questionnaire on holidays was being used by the trade unions.

Early dogmatic rejection of public opinion research in general was modified. Although the original anti-public opinion research pronouncements were still mouthed, albeit less and less frequently, new creative public opinion polling was carried out. By the 1970s it was permissible and advisable to study opinions about the concrete 'thing' (the objective) and the more abstract 'idea' (the subjective). What is more, what began in the non-academic sphere spread to the academic. By accustoming the public to such research, the *Komsomol'skaia Pravda* Institute served the best interests of academic sociologists. (It was suggested that an Institute of Public Opinion, along with a number of branches in different parts of the country, be established to collate and process information and train researchers.)[15]   In addition, the publication and popularization of public opinion polls and the subsequent criticism of them, greatly improved the effectiveness of this research.

What did the growth of this type of sociological research indicate? May we not rightly draw the parallel between the expansion, improvement and acceptance of public opinion research in particular and the development of Soviet sociological research in general? Such was the case in Poland where the first public opinion institute in the socialist world was established during the renaissance of Polish sociology.[16]   While the development of sociology in these two socialist countries was not parallel (for example, sociology was more institutionalized in Poland), the Poles indeed set an instructive example for the Soviets and enabled the Soviets to borrow from socialist friends.

The head of the Polish Public Opinion Poll Centre, Anna Pawelczynska, noted in 1966 that her centre fulfilled two parallel socio-political functions:

- as a channel of information on objective and subjective facts important to public life, thus supplying public, political and governmental institutions with the premises essential for practical decision-making, and
- as an expression of the democratization of public life, constituting a scientific instrument for the communication of public opinion to institutions responsible for socio-political and economic activity in various spheres.[17]

If Soviet sociological research did not reach this two-fold stage, it was cognizant of the successful and 'freer' work the Poles were doing. Moreover, it was certainly influenced by their research. As early as 1963, A. Kharchev, the Leningrad sociologist noted for his work on the family, described Polish progress as follows:

> In Polish sociological research, one meets numerous problems which would be of interest to party and government leaders as well as to science, but which in the Soviet Union are still under taboo. The subjects studied range from people's motives for joining the party, mutual relations between young and old party members, the role and functions of the political staff, the role of traditions in army life and army education, young people's motives for entering army schools, right down to divorce and family relations. Moreover, in publishing the results of their research, the Polish sociologists present them in a comparatively (untailored) form, regardless of any political unpleasantness for the party leaders. Thus data on the prevalence of a negative attitude to Marxism or to the restriction of civic liberties, which emerged from a 1961 poll of Warsaw students, were published in their entirety in the specialized press, something which would be inconceivable for the Soviet Union at present.[18]

The following year, the Polish Centre was praised for conducting extensive polls on fifteen to twenty subjects, the results of which were printed and sent to the appropriate party and state agencies. All in all, Polish research methods (and topics?) were first praised and then are gradually adopted.

There is no doubt that public opinion research in the Soviet Union underwent a remarkable metamorphosis. The above study of the work of the *Komsomol'skaia Pravda* Public Opinion Institute easily confirms this diagnosis. But aside from the limitations imposed by research techniques, this type of research was restricted to certain areas of enquiry at the expense of others. The topics studied were more or less 'safe' topics. They had the dual function of supplying information to researchers and other interested parties (for example, the party) and permitting a channel of expression (for example, to 'let off steam'). But to the dismay of some Soviet sociologists, this branch of sociological enquiry did not study how public opinion was shaped nor who or what shaped public opinion.[19]

1 A. K. Uledov, 'O Filosofskoi Metodologii i Konkretnykh Metodikh Sotsial'no-Psikhologicheskogo Issledovaniia', *Metodologicheskie Voprosy Obshchestvennykh Nauk*, D. I. Chesnokov *et al.* (eds.), Moscow, 1966, pp.66-7.

2 V. N. Shubkin, 'O Konkretnykh Issledovaniiakh Sotsial'nykh Protsessov', *Kommunist*, No. 3, 1965, p.55.

3 Iu. A. Sherkovin, 'Obshchestvennoe Mnenie v Sovetskom Obshchestve', *Vop Fil*, No. 11, 1964, p.175.

4 Hugh Lunghi, 'Opinion Probe in Russia', European Service General News Talk, 26 May 1960, p.4.

5 B. A. Erunov, *Sila Obshchestvennogo Mneniia*, Leningrad, 1964, pp.31 and 53.

6 B. A. Grushin, *Svobodnoe Vremia: Aktual'nye Problemy*, Moscow, 1967, 174 pp.

7 See a report of the conference by Iu. K., 'V Statisticheskoi Sektsii Moskovskogo Doma Uchenykh', *Vestnik Statistiki*, No. 6, 1961, pp.82-4. The third poll was omitted from the discussion.

8 The results of the third poll were presented in a lengthy book in 1962. See B. A. Grushin and V. Chikin, *Ispoved' Pokoleniia*, Moscow, 1962, pp.249.

9 M. Kh Igitkhanian, 'Dukhovnyi Oblik Sovetskoi Molodezhi', *Vop Fil*, No. 6, 1963, pp.75-85.

10 B. A. Grushin, 'K Probleme Kachestvennoi Reprezentatsii v Vyborochnom Oprose', *Opyt i Metodika Konkretnykh Sotsiologicheskikh Issledovanii*, G. E. Glezerman and V. G. Afanas'eva (eds.), Moscow, 1965, pp.61-107.

11 *Ibid.* p.77.

12 *Ibid.* p.99.

13 See the discussion by A. G. Zdravomyslov in *Metodologiia i Protsedura Sotsiologicheskikh Issledovanii*, Moscow, 1969, pp.114-37.

14 V. Kantorovich, 'Rodstvennaia Nam Nauka', *Literaturnaia Gazeta*, 5 May 1966, pp.1-2 and 14 May 1966, pp.1-2.

15 A. I. Prigozhin, 'Metodologicheskie Problemy Issledovaniia Obshchestvennogo Mneniia', *Vop Fil*, No. 2, 1969, p.73. A section of public opinion was opened in the Academy of Sciences' Institute of Concrete Social Research.

16 For a discussion of Polish public opinion research, see the *Polish Sociological Bulletin* (Semi-Annual of the Polish Sociological Association), especially work by Z. Gostowski (No. 1[13], 1966; No. 2[20], 1969; No. 2[22], 1970), W. Wisniewski (No. 2[14], 1966), and K. Lutynska (No. 2[20], 1969; No. 2[22], 1970).

17 Anna Pawelcznyska, 'Principles and Problems of Public Opinion Research in Poland', *Empirical Sociology in Poland*, Warsaw, 1966, p.14.

18 A. Kharchev, 'Sotsiologicheskie Issledevaniia v Pol'she', *Vop Fil*, No. 6, 1963, p.149.

19 Prigozhin, *Vop Fil*, No. 2, 1969, p.70.

7

Time Budget Research

Time budget research, like public opinion research, played an historical role in the growth of Soviet sociology. In fact, time budget studies were the first empirical investigations to be made after the Twentieth Party Congress. Such research, with emphasis on the methodology of the studies and the results of working peoples' and kolkhozniks' use of time, is here examined.

A Critique of Time Budget Studies

Soviet time budget research – that is, research on how people spend their time – was a sequel to earlier Soviet research in this area. Initiated by Academician Strumilin and others in the 1920s, this research was designed to show the important changes in the lives of the workers in the first years of Soviet power. The second stage of research was the result of the transition to the seven-hour work day at the end of the 1920s and beginning of the 1930s. Time budget research since the beginning of the 1930s, according to one of the foremost researchers, G. A. Prudenskii, was of minimal value: 'Aside from individual and insignificant efforts to work out time budgets for students and for some groups of social workers in 1930, and two or three selected studies of time budgets for workers and kolkhozniks in 1934-35, our statisticians did not do any research on time budgets of working people'.[1] Then, in the late 1950s and early 1960s, the third wave of time budget research began: it coincided with the 'building of communism' and with the shortening of the work day. Since that time, a considerable number of studies were conducted in the USSR.

Researchers stated that the fundamental task of the investigations was to establish the dependence of the development of different processes (such as the all-round development of the personality) on the presence of non-working time and to discover the uses of non-working time. The presence and use of non-working time were considered to be positively (or negatively) connected with the development of the mental and physical capabilities of the individual. Another idea behind time budget studies was the importance of non-working time as a period in which the individual 'reproduces' energy which is then utilized during working time. Thus society, as well as the individual, profits from non-working time. At the same time, non-working time was viewed as one of the indices of the level of development of the individual, of a definite social group, and of society as a whole. And finally, the research sought to answer the question, Does the individual have sufficient non-working time to satisfy his/her intellectual and physical needs?

Using the methods outlined in the following section, the time budget researchers described and charted the variables which influence the amount and use of non-working time. Two types of charts appeared in the research write-ups. The first involved the composition of the sample. For example, age variables were charted against sex, or educational level against age. The second type – by far the more common – compared the given variable (e.g. sex, age, or occupation) with different times of time expenditures (e.g. time on housework or leisure time). In only a few instances were more than two variables correlated.[2] In other cases, some data said to be collected were not tabulated or discussed. As shall soon be apparent, different researchers concentrated on different variables and omitted others.

The basic unit of the time budget studies was the type of work: each study was billed as the non-working time of workers, engineering, and technical personnel (ITRs), office workers, or kolkhozniks.[3] The difficulty with these classifications, however, is that either they were not held constant or they were not precise enough. The problem is particularly acute with the classification of the ITRs – the engineers and technical personnel 'with a higher or secondary education engaged in technical management or industry or transport'.[4] This category, like the others, encompassed a wide range of working people; at times, it also included the term *sluzhashchii* – white collar or office worker. Many studies combined the two groups so that the distinction was blurred or overlooked. One study, the Baikova study, sometimes called the group 'engineering and technical *workers*', while at other times 'engineering and technical *intelligentsia*'.[5]

A further problem relating to the classification of working people involved the samples. In most cases, we did not know how the sample was chosen nor how representative it was of the population. Only in the *Komsomol'skaia Pravda* poll (see Chapter 6) was the sample said to be weighted in certain areas. One might assume that the sample was representative of a certain factory and of its workers, but surely this was not so in all cases. For example, the Leningrad sample had (proportionally) too many well-educated workers.[6] Thus it appears that the time budget studies were reports of specific workers in specific types of factories. Moreover, regional characteristics were but briefly indicated in the studies. But even if they were more fully explained, the combination of worker classification and regional classification would still have limited the possibility of generalizing about the entire Soviet Union. Perhaps this concern is unwarranted since the main divisions of time expenditures (e.g. working time, time on housework, and free time) were relatively constant, and the use of time followed certain trends. Variations did occur, but many of them may be explained by an examination of working and/or regional conditions.

Comparison with the European Coordination Centre for Research and Documentation in Social Sciences' multi-national research work indicates other problems in Soviet time budget research.[7] In the first place, there was no allocation in the Soviet research for activities which occurred simultaneously. For example, if a person was reading on the way home from work, how was the time to be classified? In most cases, the Soviets would define this as time spent returning from work: the reading time was therefore ignored. In the second place, questions about with whom or in the presence of whom a given activity occurred – and where it took place –

were lacking. Soviet time budget studies merely listed the amount of time spent on an activity. Finally, the significance of the specific weekday in determining use of time was not considered. It is true that Soviet research considered the work day and the day off, or sometimes the work day, a Saturday and Sunday, but it did not differentiate (as did the Szalai team) between a Monday and a Tuesday.[8]

Some other factors were also neglected. In the first place, there was little cross-tabulation, comparing multiple variables against each other or controlling several variables at a time to check others. Moreover, the findings from the separate studies were rarely compared with each other. Most of the studies did compare their data with the earlier findings of Strumilin,[9] but they often failed to mention that the 1924 Strumilin study interviewed 624 people of whom nine per cent came from Moscow, six per cent from Leningrad, and the remaining eighty-five per cent from the provinces; they were people who lived near the factories and the large towns, and hence can be classified as urban. The tendency to compare studies with those in the past seemed, however, to be diminishing. In its place was cross-national or cross-socialist comparative research.

With the above reservations in mind, we will now examine the methods of the time budget studies.

Time Budget Methods

The Siberian Research Institute of Labour and Wages and the Siberian Branch of the USSR Academy of Sciences initiated a series of time budget studies throughout the Soviet Union when, in 1952, they launched a two-year programme on how workers in Siberia and the Urals spent their non-working time. The fifteen investigations of the more than 25,000 time budgets of workers, engineering and technical personnel (ITRs) and white-collar workers in a number of industrial enterprises were collected and presented in one volume.[10] The editors stated in the introduction that the fundamental task of their investigation was to work out recommendations for methodological practices in the study of non-working time. They warned that it was necessary to regard the collection only as a preparatory stage to the publication of further scientific works on the problem of non-working time.

Each of the fifteen studies was conducted by different *kollektivy* of workers. The authors were not only colleagues and teachers from the economic cadres of higher educational institutions of Siberia, but were also workers in the party, trade union, komsomol and other organizations. Students in the higher party schools sometimes aided researchers. In some instances, the urban committee of the party guided the work. Whatever the case, the research was a joint effort between practical workers from industry and social (public) organizations and members of the Siberian institute. This kind of alliance was typical of most time budget research.

The survey method was used to investigate the workers' use of time over a twenty-four hour period. Interviewing was conducted at the enterprise during non-working time – before the beginning and/or after the end of work, or during the lunch break – or at home. The general information filled out by the registrar and the informant included the following: residence, location of work, age, sex, education, type of worker, wage category, fulfilment of norms, length of service, marital status, number of children, living conditions, and what appliances (and similar things) the family owned. The informant also kept a diary of his/her time use for the twenty-four hours: non-working time was divided into four categories (see Prudenskii's categories in Table 7.1) and was examined for a workday, a day off, and a holiday. He/she was aided by the registrar as follows:

> On the day of the preliminary talks with the person who is to be surveyed the registrar must complete the general (information) part of the time budget form. On the next day the registrar questions (in detail) the interviewee about the allocation of his time for the last twenty-four hours; by these directed questions, the registrar makes the separate use of time distinct. Writing down the amended answers of the respondent on a separate piece of paper and amending the auxiliary notes which were taken by the respondent himself, the registrar transfers them to a clean time budget blank, placing these answers in the corresponding boxes and lines.[11]

The commentary on the data usually explained some peculiarities of the region or the enterprise under investigation, presented the tables with explanatory notes, and discussed with criticisms and suggestions (which sometimes were direct party programme questions) the particular misuse or waste of time. Mention was usually made of the changes in the structure of non-working time: the changes were measured in terms of the findings of S. G. Strumilin's earlier research in the 1920s. No statement was made as to how respondents were chosen. Although these respondents could not remain anonymous, the authors pointed to the need for conducting the sample on a strictly voluntary basis.

By the end of 1960, the Institute of Economics and Organization of Industrial Production of the Siberian Branch of the Academy of Sciences held the first conference on the problem of non-working time of working people, entitled the 'Free time of working people under the conditions of the reduction of the working day.' The three hundred people who attended the conference were workers at scientific institutions and higher education establishments, representatives of the party, trade union and komsomol organs, leading workers from the *sovkhozy*,[12] directors and head engineers of industrial enterprises, etc. The topic under discussion was divided in two: 1) the rational use of non-working (including free) time, and the improvement of cultural and *byt* amenities; and 2) the methods of studying non-working time of the workers. The conference participants offered several suggestions. Firstly, they noted that time budget research, which was conducted by scientific institutions or trade unions, must be co-ordinated with party and statistical organs. Then, they recommended polling – either by a registrar or by self-registration – as *the* method for observation. The poll could either be conducted on the basis of enterprise or territorial classifications. The period of observation could vary: the most complete study would cover a week's time, but if this was impossible, then a three-day survey – including a weekday, a day preceding a day off (e.g. a Saturday), and a day off – would be acceptable. A time budget for a weekday and a day off was also possible. Finally, the two seasons suggested were winter and summer.

The recommendations from this conference and the proposals and methods from the Siberian study have been the bases for further time budget research. Other studies have not published actual questionnaire and information blanks, nor have they been as comprehensive in interviewing instructions.[13] On the whole relatively few changes were introduced in the time budget procedure, but certain variations did occur.

G. A. Prudenskii, who headed the 1959 Siberian studies, was joined in 1964 by B. Kolpakov in a detailed discussion of the methodological problems of time budget research. In an article entitled, 'The experience of measuring the non-working time of workers',[14] they reiterated the need for answering those ninety-five to one hundred questions on the distribution of time which had been established in the 1959 Siberian study. They did, however, allow for additional questions about the respondent, questions which were to depend on the aims of the research. The *best* method, stated the authors, was the questionnaire conducted by the 'registrars, specially selected and carefully instructed. It was also possible to alter the method of self-registration, especially among the engineering and technical personnel (ITRs), the office workers, and the scientific workers. However, for them as well, a *control* was necessary for guaranteeing the authenticity of the data'.[15] The merits of self-registration, considered here for the first time, consist in the ability of the workers themselves to introduce concrete suggestions for the best use of non-working time. The authors further suggested that the statistical organizations work out a single method for time budget research.[16]

Prudenskii and Kolpakov did not favour either the daily or weekly method at the expense of one or the other. But they did take into account the seasonal differences and hence advocated summer and winter research. Unlike the previous studies, however, they discussed the question of representativeness:

> As practices shows, satisfactory representativeness – about the size and structure of non-working time of the participants – in conformity with the enterprise, the *raion* or the *oblast'*, is guaranteed by investigating 0.5 per cent - 1.0 per cent of the workers or the inhabitants. The sampling must then include approximately eight to ten per cent of the workers or inhabitants of the categories under study.[17]

Finally, they remarked that the statistical groupings must describe the structure of non-working time completely and must guarantee the possibility of revealing the factors which influence the level of the various time expenditures.

In 1964-1965, Prudenskii, writing in *Vremia i Trud* (*Time and Labour*), further examined time budget research.[18] He reiterated the Prudenskii-Kolpakov proposal for studying the workers' recommendations, and this time illustrated his point by using the 1963 Krasnoiarsk data. Of the entire number of workers' suggestions, about 18 per cent were related to intra-city transportation, 23.9 per cent to the trade network and the organization of communal food catering, 14.1 per cent to the rationalization of housework and the work of *byt* institutions, and 7 per cent to children's pre-school institutions.

This later report by Prudenskii also took a firmer stand on the best length for a time budget study: the weekly time budget was preferred to the daily one. In addition, Prudenskii altered his view since the 1959 pilot study in which he suggested that the time budget should begin from the moment of rising and continue until the following day's moment of rising. He recommended that the respondent begin with a given hour and end after twenty-four hours; thus, a 'general balance of the twenty-four hour budget' may be developed. Furthermore, he stated that a study of the whole twenty-four hour period was not necessary. He was, in fact, going back on his 1960 suggestions about the possibility of 'target research' in which only certain individual expenditures of time were investigated.[19] Finally, he thought it desirable to repeat studies at intervals of not less but not more than once every two or three years.

Although Prudenskii was the most prolific writer on time budget methodology, he was not the only commentator. G. S. Petrosian of the Institute of Economics of the Academy of Sciences of the Armenian SSR was another notable writer on the subject; he was a former participant at the 1960 conference and at the Krasnoiarsk, Novokuznets, and Noril'sk discussions of methodological problems. Petrosian investigated the time use of workers, office and white-collar workers, and engineering and technical personnel in Novosibirsk and Erevan; he studied a weekday, a Saturday, and a Sunday.[20] The basic methodological problems to be tackled were: 1) the method of the questionnaire; 2) the representativeness of the sample; 3) the period of coverage; 4) the grouping of the data; 5) the classification of the types of time expenditures; and 6) the choice of the subject for observation.

Petrosian noted that four methods have been used in gathering time budget data, namely:

- questionnaire by special registrars for a twenty-four hour period;
- questionnaire for a twenty-four hour period, combined with self-registration by the participant and with a supplementary list of time expenditures which was to be corrected under questioning;
- direct investigation of separate elements or groups of time expenditures;
- registration of non-working time – by means of a questionnaire combined with partial registering of the working day – with the aim of elucidating casual links between working and non-working time (for example, as regards the brigades of communist labour).[21]

The method most often used, he stated, was that of the questionnaire for a given twenty-four hour period. The role of the pre-instructed registrar was to question the interviewee; if the interviewee performed two or more actions simultaneously, then the entry was only recorded for one fundamental expenditure.[22] He also commented on the third method which was used only for determining time spent on shopping and city transportation. However, Petrosian suggested that such a method might be used on a wider scale, particularly for studying the use of communal and municipal services.[23]

His brief discussion of the representativeness of the sample did not coincide with Prudenskii's, but Petrosian did reaffirm the importance of a representative sample.

In determining the representativeness of the sample, we considered the relative importance of each trait *vis-à-vis* the total population. In a number of cases, it is proved sufficient to examine only between 5 and 10 per cent of the total universe.[24]

In other words, at times the time budget authors considered that five to ten per cent of the population were representative of the entire population, but the criteria for such an assumption were never mentioned.

Like Prudenskii, Petrosian discussed the acceptable length of a study and the influence of seasonal variations. He also mentioned the differences in examining a separate worker's time expenditure and an entire family's time expenditures. A study with the family as the base unit was defined as one which included those members of a family who reside in one location and those other people who are living with the family on the day of the investigation.

The next methodological question Petrosian discussed was that of grouping. Like the majority of time budget researchers, he included age, sex, marital status, composition of family, education, income, length of work and qualifications, size of living quarters, etc., as classifying factors. What was unique was his inclusion of social group as a category. Furthermore, unlike other researchers, Petrosian considered the influence of national and ethnographic peculiarities on use of time.

The classification of time use led to a debate between time budget researchers: each of the authors had found his own way of classifying time, and had, in turn, attacked the other systems. Petrosian prepared the following outline of the competing positions (see Table 7.1).

Table 7.1 Classification of time budgets of workers (24-hr period)[25]

S. Strumilin: 1961
I.   Necessary time
        A. Obligatory labour
            1. Productive labour:
                a. in political economy
                b. in personal economy
            2. Housework
                a. preparation of food
                b. care of children
                c. other expenditures
            3. Time losses
                a. walking to and from work
                b. shopping
        B. Unavoidable demands of life
            1. Eating (at work and at home)
            2. Sleeping (day and night)
II.   Free time
        A. Physical developments
        B. Cultural amateur activity (public or social obligations, study, reading, amateur art)

    C. Cultural leisure (cinema, theatre, house games)
    D. Other entertainment (guests, etc.)
    E. Inactive leisure

Scientific Research Institute (Moscow): 1962

I.   Time at production and time connected with production
    A. Working time
    B. Lunch break
    C. Start and finish of shift
    D. Going to work
II.   Time not connected with work at production
    A. Housework
    B. Social work
    C. Work on personal affairs
    D. Moving
    E. Leisure, including sleep in the day
    F. Nightly sleep
    G. Eating
    H. Care of self (including medical treatment)

N. A. Klimov (Moscow): 1961

I.   Working time
II.   Free time
III.   Time for looking after oneself
IV.   Additional time expenditures

V. Patrushev (Krasnoiarsk): 1961

I. Production time
    A. Time on productive labour
      1. On production
      2. Housekeeping (knitting, sewing, making household articles)
      3. Personal subsidiary plot
    B. Additional work expenditures
      1. Idle time
      2. Transportation to and from work
      3. Care of self before and after the shift
      4. Lunch rest (without time on eating)
II.   Time for re-producing working strength
    A. Time on housework
      1. Shopping
      2. Preparation of food
      3. Care of house, clothing, shoes, laundry
      4. Care of children
      5. Other expenditures (receiving information, permits, walking to savings bank)
    B. Time on satisfying natural, physiological needs

1. Eating
2. Care of self
3. Sleeping
4. Time to satisfy physical, intellectual, and social needs (free time)

Institute of Economics and Organizations of Industrial Production of the Siberian Branch of the Academy of Sciences: 1959-1961 (G. A. Prudenskii)

I.   Working time
II.   Non-working time
    A.   Time expenditures connected with the stay at production
    B.   Housework and care of self
    C.   Sleeping and eating
    D.   Free time

P. Maslov: 1961

I.   Working time
II.   Non-working time
    A.   Time on day-to-day affairs
    B.   Free time
        1.   Useful leisure
        2.   Active leisure
        3.   Entertainment
        4.   Inactivity

Petrosian's own conclusion was that not one opinion on the classification question existed. This fact hinders a comparison of the data from the different studies.[26] Nevertheless Section III explores the variables used and studied by the researchers who concentrated on workers, ITRs, and office workers. Petrosian's own study, which had the greatest number of tables with the largest number of determining variables, is taken as the model. Other studies are subsequently compared with it. Section IV looks at the time budgets of kolkhozniks. Sections III and IV thus describe and analyze the different types of research on the use of non-working time.[27]

Workers, Office Workers, and Engineers and Technical Personnel: Factors Influencing the Use of Time

The Petrosian book, based on 10,089 twenty-four hour budgets from 3363 workers, office workers, and ITRs in Erevan (Armenia), is a well-structured model of Soviet time budget research. It starts with a discussion of the division of time expenditures, the methodology and the sample. The second chapter begins with a discussion of the socialist character of the *zakonomernosti* and tendencies of the use of non-working time under socialism. The five general laws are stated as follows: 1) the absence of antagonistic contradictions in the structure and character of the use of non-working time by different social groups; 2) the harmonious unity between working and non-working time and the tendency of non-working time to increase; 3) the harmonious unity of free and other non-working time in view of the tendency of the constant growth of free time; 4) the *socialist* character of the use of non-working time which is a result of such things as the freedom of the individual under socialism; and 5) the growing rationality and improvement of the use of non-working time.

The body of the second chapter, however, presents and illustrates the different factors which influence the use of non-working time. Here, Petrosian explains, lists and illustrates how non-working time is structured; certain categories, such as the time spent on housework and free time, are stressed. In the concluding chapter, Petrosian enumerates suggestions for further rationalizing time use. But let us first turn to those factors which influence the structure of non-working time.

The first category is *conditions of employment*. Petrosian divides this four ways. The first variable is the sector of the economy (e.g. construction or transport). The second involves the character and level of organization of production: the former refers to where the individual works (e.g. whether he is out in the open or down a mine) and the latter to such factors as the status of production discipline, cooperation between shops, and fulfillment of production plans. The third variable is the working conditions (e.g. fire prevention facilities) and the last is the level of cultural and *byt* services at the factory.

Although Petrosian set out to show how important the four subdivisions of the conditions-of-employment category are in determining how non-working time is structured, he did not exactly accomplish this. Because the other two authors were more successful, we must interrupt the Petrosian report to examine their findings.

G. V. Osipov and S. F. Frolov in *Sotsiologiia v SSSR* discuss a 1962 study conducted at a number of large-scale enterprises in Gor'kovskaia *oblast*.[28] They divided time use into five categories: work and time connected with work, sleeping and eating, housework and care of self, leisure, and raising cultural and professional levels. They then investigated three factors which determined the distribution of time:

- the character and content of *labour*, determined by the technical level of production and by what position the worker is placed in in relation to technology;
- individual characteristics, namely: age, sex, education, party membership, length of service, income, etc.;
- family and *byt* circumstances, including family position, number of children, household conditions, distance from place of work to home, etc.[29]

These factors were said to interact, coincide and even neutralize each other, forming in the aggregate a concrete 'social situation'.

Using these time divisions and time distribution determinants, Osipov and Frolov attempted to show that the 'character and content of labour' is *the* factor which determines the use of time. This dependence was established first by examining the relationship between the time use of workers and ITRs in different factories and the nature of production at these factories, and secondly, by determining a positive relationship between the structure of time use and the character and content of work. The data also indicated that the structure of workers' and ITRs' time budgets strongly depended upon the type of factory where they were employed. This was illustrated in a few tables correlating the structure of time with the type of technical level of production at different factories. In general, the authors found a positive correlation between active, varied, and complex *working* time, and active, varied, and complex *non-working* time.

Finally, Osipov and Frolov describe a model with which, they state, it is possible to analyze and foresee changes in the time budgets of groups of people with different individual and social parameters. As a consequence, a 'differential approach to various groups of society in the planning of social change(s) and in determining measures for regulating social development in the interests of such individual' is feasible. Especially important, according to Osipov and Frolov, is the fact that this formula permits one to take into account the individual's personal characteristics and, at the same time, to 'prepare the conditions which further [the individual's] harmonious development'.[30]

V. A. Artemov proposed another alternative to the purely statistical method of grouping (that is, selecting and identifying characteristics of statistical groups) used in time budget research – namely, correlation analysis and model building.[31] Like Osipov and Frolov, Artemov wanted to create a model of time that would describe the structure of time, indicate how to redistribute working time as non-working increases and permit predictions of behaviour. In building this model, he advised analyzing possible connections between the following: 1) time expenditures; 2) personal characteristics (e.g. age and sex) and living conditions (e.g. housing arrangements); and 3) the personal characteristics and living conditions themselves. His schema for the first two, found in Appendix II, are the first stages of the model he hoped to develop and utilize.

But let us return to Petrosian's study where the *calendar day* is the second category influencing the structure of non-working time. Petrosian's two charts are divided into workday and day off for Novokuznets and Erasnoiarsk; a three-fold division was established for Erevan – namely, a workday, a Saturday, and a Sunday. Free time on the days off increased or stayed the same in all cases because working time was parcelled out in varying proportions to free time activities. Thus men's free time increased significantly more than the women's on the free days. The most significant change in all cases occurred in the amount of time women spent on housework.

Another factor which alters the structure of non-working time is the *season of the year*. Petrosian's general arguments are numerous: the season could change participation in sports, the time it takes to go shopping, the amount of television viewed, etc. But his point cannot be completely substantiated because he used September and December as examples. (The samples, moreover, were not comparable.) The difficulty in trying to support the logical argument with data from other time budget studies is compounded by the absence of all but a few follow-up studies which, in point of fact, did not examine the respondents at different times of the year.

Petrosian spends the least amount of space on the next category – *the type of occupation of the individual*. While he says that differences in labour – mental and physical – condition the structure of working and non-working time, he offers little further comment or any tables. He does differentiate between three types of occupation, namely, workers, office workers, and ITRs. Of the three, the office workers are said to have the most free time and the ITRs the least (see Table 7.2).

Table 7.2   Per cent of total time expenditures[32]

Category of personnel	Working time	Non-working time connected with job	Housework and care of self	Physio-logical needs	Free time
Workers	24.6	7.0	6.2	35.6	26.4
	(25.2)[a]	(6.0)	(10.2)	(38.7)[b]	(19.5)
ITRs	27.3	5.0	10.1	36.5	21.1
	(24.4)	(4.4)	(10.8)	(40.6)[b]	(19.8)[b]

[a] Figures in parentheses are the Kiev figures; the other figures are from the Leningrad study.

[b] Under physiological needs, the figures in parentheses include care of self. By the same token, the category of housework for the figures in parentheses does not include care of self.

A few other studies did specifically differentiate and compare the time expenditures of these groups. Few, however, gave separate figures for office workers and ITRs; instead, they combined them in one classification. The Laboratory of Sociological Studies of the Department of Philosophy of the Leningrad State University studied the time budgets of one hundred workers and office personnel of the Kirov plant in Leningrad in 1961.[33] The results from this study may be compared with the 1962 study of 342 workers, office workers and ITRs conducted by the Kiev Laboratory of Concrete Social Research.[34]

These studies, in which the working time is relatively constant for both types of workers, do not fully support Petrosian's generalizations: free time for both categories of personnel is almost identical in Kiev, whereas there is a 5.3 percentage points difference in Leningrad.[35]

Petrosian continues by considering the role of *age and sex*. 'No other factor shows such a strong influence on the structure of free time (and housework) as do age and sex'.[36] Table 7.3 is Petrosian's age table comparing men and women up to twenty-five, twenty-six to fifty, and over fifty in various free-time activities. The chart is accompanied by the following generalizations:

- youth spend more time on sleeping and eating than older people;
- youth has more free time at its disposal than the middle-aged, but the older people have the most free time;
- men of all ages have more free time and time connected with their work than the women;
- women of all ages spend more time on housework and looking after themselves than the men;
- on the whole, working women of all ages are always more occupied than men.

Almost every time budget study similarly discusses the significance of age and sex.[37]

The sixth category – *marital status and composition of the family* – indicates whether or not a man or woman has a family and how many and how old are the children. The Erevan figures show that people with families had considerably less free time than unmarried people; they also spent it differently (see Table 7.4).

Table 7.3 Structure of non-working time, depending on sex and age[38] (in hours and minutes per day)

	Up to 25		26-50		Over 50	
	Men	Women	Men	Women	Men	Women
Time connected with work at production	1-44	1-41	1-45	1-40	1-13	1-10
Housework and care of self	1-46	2-39	2-30	5-14	1-26	4-17
Sleeping and eating	8-35	8-21	8-28	7-35	8-37	8-58
Total free time of which:	4-31	3-52	3-37	2-13	5-17	2-02
Study and raise qualifications	1-16	1-22	0-15	0-08	-	-
Self-education	0-21	0-33	0-11	0-07	1-02	0-28
Social work	0-04	0-02	0-03	0-01	0-02	0-28
Physical education and sport	0-14	0-11	0-02	0-01	0-03	0-01
Entertainment	1-38	1-09	1-54	0-42	3-21	0-35
Bringing up children	0-05	0-13	0-23	0-48	0-18	0-41
Amateur activities	0-21	0-12	0-24	0-12	0-13	0-05
Remaining time	0-32	0-10	0-25	0-14	0-18	0-11
Other time	0-25	0-16	0-26	0-14	0-13	0-11
Total non-working time	17-05	16-49	16-46	16-56	16-51	16-38

Table 7.4   Changes of expenditure of free time, depending upon family status[39] (in hours and minutes)

	No family		Family with children	
	On a day	%*	On a day	%
Study and raising qualifications	1-13	24.3	0-08	5.7
Self-education	0-21	7.7	0-09	6.4
Social work	0-09	3.1	0-02	1.4
Physical education and sport	0-18	6.1	0-02	1.4
Entertainment	2-38	53.7	1-01	43.3
Bringing up children	-	-	0-18	12.8
Amateur activities	0-04	1.4	0-14	9.9
Other	0-03	3.7	0-27	19.1
Total free time	4-46	100.0	2-21	100.0

* Petrosian's percentages are not correct. For example, the figure for studying for the 'no family' category is 25.5 per cent (and not 24.3 per cent as listed) and for entertainment, 55.2 per cent (and not 53.7 per cent as listed). No explanation is offered.

Petrosian's conclusions are backed up by the Kiev study. Single men had six hours and forty-five minutes of free time per day, whereas those with children had six hours and four minutes. The difference was greater for women: single women, four hours and thirty-four minutes, and married women with children, three hours and thirty-five minutes. Although the amount of free time for both sexes in Kiev is greater than that in Erevan, the percentage of time spent on study and raising qualifications – the category which shows the greatest amount of change in the Erevan study – are parallel to the Erevan figures (see Table 7.5):

Table 7.5   Per cent of free time spent on study and raising qualifications[40]

	Men	Women
Single	28.4	24.8
Married, with children	6.8	3.7

Similar findings on the use of free time were found when Petrosian examined the influence of the number and age of children in the family.

Petrosian's next classification concerns the *size and character of the dwelling and the presence of public (communal) conveniences* (e.g. utilities, facilities). Better housing conditions meant less time on housework and care of self, and more free time and time for sleep. The greater the number of public facilities, the greater was the amount of free time. Like most of the other discussions, Petrosian points out that the increase of time spent on housework (due to housing conditions, etc.) signified a corresponding decrease of free time. No further details were given here.

A factor closely related to the above is the *presence in the family of household equipment and cultural articles*. This category includes washing machines, refrigerators, televisions, bicycles, etc. As might be expected, the family which owns a large number of equipment spent less time on housework and had more free time.

Petrosian next turns his attention to *income* and time use. He found that the higher the income, the greater the amount of free time. The accompanying table shows that the difference in actual free time between the lowest and highest paid workers was two hours, while the percentage of total non-working time varied from 18.1 per cent to 29.4 per cent (see Table 7.6).

The Petrosian data coincided with the 1960s Siberian studies which, for the first time, had compared free time with income. Subsequent research in 1963 also indicated a positive relation between increased income and increased free time. One researcher concluded:

> The shortening of the general amount of non-working time spent on material and everyday needs, the strengthening of the role of the public sphere of everyday (byt) services in satisfying needs, and the reduction of time spent fulfilling the most laborious functions of housework occur with the growth of income.[41]

The plotting of income and time came under heavy criticism from the advocates of models. Artemov stated that it was possible to calculate free time by income, but this gives a distorted and isolated picture of reality and necessitates a neutralization of other main factors, such as age and family status. Needless to say, his criticism, although specifically directed at the problem of income, would apply to all factors.

Table 7.6   Changes of expenditures of non-working time depending upon the income per month for one member of the family (in hours and minutes)[42]

	Up to 30 Rubles	31-50 Rubles	51-75 Rubles	76-100 Rubles	Over 100 Rubles
Time of simple re-production of working strength (occupied time):	13-25 (79.9)*	13-14 (78.4)	12-41 (73.9)	11-49 (70.5)	12-04 (70.6)
Time connected with work at production	1-32 (9.1)	1-41 (10.0)	1-31 (8.8)	1.02 (6.2)	1-26 (8.7)
Housework and care of self	4-11 (24.9)	3-51 (22.8)	2-48 (16.2)	2-10 (12.9)	2-52 (10.9)
Eating and sleeping	7-42 (45.9)	7-42 (45.6)	8-22 (48.9)	8-37 (51.4)	8-46 (51.0)
Time of extended re-production of working strength (free time)	3-02 (18.1)	3-14 (19.2)	3-58 (23.1)	4-45 (28.4)	5-02 (29.4)
Other	0-02 (2.0)	0-24 (2.4)	0-31 (3.0)	0-11 (1.1)	- -
Total non-working time	16-37	16-52	17-10	16-45	17-06

* Figures in parentheses are in %.

Educational level and commitment to studies is Petrosian's next category. Of all the categories so far mentioned, this one is accompanied by the greatest number of tables. In fact, most of the other time budget studies increasingly concentrated on education and further study; they included in their presentations comprehensive tables linking studies and educational levels with income, age, sex, length of work, and educational level. They usually pointed out that the person who was more educated understands the significance of time and values his/her time; he/she endeavours to use his/her time for more elevated and rational activities and for greater satisfaction of his/her intellectual and cultural needs.

Raising the level of the cultural and occupational preparation of the worker is also postulated as a necessary condition for raising productive work. In this respect, Baikova showed that for the ITRs there was: 1) an increase in time spent on education as the general level of education rises;[43] 2) a distinct relationship between age and further studies; 3) a definite shortcoming in the educational system, especially in evening and correspondence courses; and 4) a correlation between education level and 'technical creativity,' a term which remained undefined.[44]

At this juncture we must again interrupt the Petrosian discussion to examine the only study which was particularly concerned with the difference that institutionalized evening study made in the use of time. Such a study was carried out in Kostroma by the Institute of Economics of the Academy of Sciences and the Kostroma Textile Institute.[45] The first part of the study (March, 1960) involved full-time workers and white-collar workers who studied in evening schools and *tekhnikumy*. The second study, which re-interviewed two-thirds of the 1960 sample in March-April 1961, involved workers and office workers who also combined work with study. The purpose of the follow-up investigation was to determine the effect of shortening the work day from eight to seven hours.

The comparison of evening students' time budgets on the different days of the week – this study distinguished four types of days, namely, a work and a study day, a pre-holiday, and a day off – revealed that during the week all of the time expenditures underwent essential changes, but in different directions and at a different rate[46] (see Table 7.12). Lamkov, the author of the article, carefully explained the table:

> Thus, on the day off, all of the non-working time grew in comparison with the weekdays by 41.5 per cent, and free time increased in comparison with the weekdays by 87.8 per cent. The situation was different on the pre-holiday: although all of the non-working time (thanks to the shortening of the working day) increased in comparison with the weekdays, the free time decreased. The reason for this is that other elements of non-working time – which, in their turn, are determined by different needs of the people – influence the size of free time (e.g. housework).[47]

Lamkov was quick to point out that the differences between the two years were more significant than those between the four types of days. This was not unexpected since the aim of the research was to discover the consequences of the shorter workday and work week (see Table 7.7).

Table 7.7   Expenditures of time (in hours and minutes) of evening students for 25 hours on various days of the week (according to 235 budgets)

Expenditures of time by type	Week study day	Week non-study day	Pre day-off day	Day off	Week study day as basis for comparison	% of week study day		
						Week non-study day	Pre day-off day	Day off
I. Working time	7-03	7-07	6-10	-	100.0	100.9	87.5	-
II. All non-working time	16-57	16-53	17-50	24-00	100.0	99.6	105.2	141.6
a) Connected with work	1-36	1-34	0-53	-	100.0	97.9	55.2	-
b) Housework	0-29	0-54	1-32	1-50	100.0	186.2	317.0	379.3
c) Necessary requirements (sleeping, eating, caring for self)	8-28	8-26	9-37	10-09	100.0	99.6	113.6	119.9
d) Free time, including	6-24	5-59	5-48	12-01	100.0	93.5	90.6	187.8
study	5-18	2-51	2-12	6-08	100.0	58.8	41.5	115.7
Total for day (I and II)	24-00	24-00	24-00	24-00	-	-	-	-

Like all of the other time budget researchers, Lamkov reiterated that free time may be increased not only by shortening the working day, but also by reducing time spent on housework and other 'irrational' time expenditures. Consequently he found it is helpful to discover which time had been freed from which sources and then to analyse new uses of this 'liberated' time. But, unlike other time budget researchers, he graphically showed the redistribution of time (from 1960 to 1961) as follows (see Table 7.8):[48]

Table 7.8   Redistribution of time (from 1960 to 1961)

Time freed on account of shortening of time on: (in % of total time freed)		Redistribution and increase of time on: (in % of total redistributed time)	
		Non-working time,	
Working time	43.8	connected with work	13.7
Housework	17.9	Eating	6.1
Taking care of self	7.6	Sleeping	31.2
		Housework, projects,	
Social work	11.6	preparation for lessons	20.4
		Studies at	
Leisure and relaxation	4.4	educational institutions	21.9
Time losses			
(undistributed time)	14.7	Other expenditures	6.7
Total	100.0*		100.0*

* 100.0% = 7 hours and 55 minutes

Lamkov offered his approach as an experimental way of showing the redistribution of time, an approach which he hoped would be imitated. Clarification of the sources of released time and the individual's primary needs, he explained, may help in studying the growing needs of the population, in securing conditions for the cultural growth of the Soviet people, and partially, in obtaining conditions for the preparation of specialists through part-time study.

But let us return to Petrosian. *Form of work in one's speciality and one's qualifications* is another factor which determines how one uses time. Without a table or other specific data, Petrosian first acknowledges that because age is closely related to one's length of service, this category is a conditional one. Nonetheless, he says that those workers who have considerable responsibility in production spent more time at the factories while they, for example, conduct courses so that other workers may learn necessary skills. Their free time, however, grew at the expense of time on housework and care of self. Petrosian does not add much more detail here, nor are other discussions on this topic to be found in other time studies.

Petrosian briefly notes the influence of the *brigades of labour* on using time. He indicates that members of the labour brigades use time more rationally than other workers. This, he says, is the result of the high level of labour organization and the production process. Once again, time devoted to study, raising productive qualifications and self-education – the categories which show the greatest differential – were singled out for special comment. The men in the brigades of labour are described as the foremost and most conscientious vanguard of workers. Their high level of consciousness (which is partially determined by the amount of time they spend reading literature and attending meetings at the factories) 'promotes the rational use of working time as well as the most effective use of non-working time'.[49]

Except for his statement on the importance of age and sex, Petrosian does not seem to weigh the other factors discussed above. He merely shows that they should be considered because they do alter – to a greater or lesser extent – the structures of free time. And he comes to the conclusion that 'the analysis of time budgets in a number of cities in our country shows that non-working time is in fact used unequally by individual members of society and by individual categories of workers; [non-working time] depends on the influence of different objective and subjective factors'.[50]

Unfortunately, Petrosian does not cover all of the factors so far studied which influence the use of time. For example, he excludes the vital role of *party membership*. While mentioned in the Osipov and Frolov sample, this factor was only included in the Leningrad and Kiev presentations. The Leningrad study indicated that party members spent almost twice as much time on study, social and political reading, and social work as non-members. Non-members, on the other hand, spent considerably more time reading *belles lettres* and participating in amateur art activity, sports and table games. Both groups participated to a fairly equal extent in the other listed activities – walking, having guests, listening to the radio and watching television, inactive leisure, etc. It should be noted, however, that party members had four hours and two minutes of free time, while the non-party members had three hours and forty-six minutes.[51] Similar findings come from the Kiev study where major differences occurred in the time spent reading newspapers and magazines and studying. The party members in Kiev had five hours and four minutes of free time, whereas the non-party members had four hours and fifteen minutes.[52] Both studies lead to the conclusion that party members spent more free time on 'constructive' activities than non-party members who, in turn, were more concerned with private and individual matters.

One other factor which may determine the structure and amount of time is the *length of the working day*. Patrushev, a Candidate of Economic Science and a participant in the UNESCO research, examined this problem in the last chapter of his book, *Intensivnost' Truda pri Sotsializme (Intensity of Labour under Socialism)*.[53] He discovered that the amount of free time for men and women was relatively constant for people in Krasnoiarsk *krai*[54] who worked six, seven, or eight hours a day in 1959. Men who worked for seven hours a day had only slightly more free time than those who worked eight hours; there was no difference, however, between workers who had a six and seven-hour day.[55] Women who worked for seven hours had only eighteen minutes more free time than eight-hour workers, whereas those who worked for six hours had the same amount of free time as eight-hour workers! From these figures Patrushev concluded that 'the size of free time depends not only on the length of the working day, but also on the additional time expenditures on labour and housework'. (The preceding figures applied to Krasnoiasrsk *krai*.) Here, the free time of seven-hour male workers was about an hour more than the eight-hour workers', but the six-hour workers' free time was only about half an hour less than that of the seven-hour workers'. (This was still about half an hour more free time than the eight-hour workers.) The women who worked seven hours, on the other hand, had an hour less free time than the eight-hour workers and about two hours less than the six hour workers. Increased non-working time for women meant, in most cases, increased time on housework.

Patrushev was unable to end his study by saying that the length of working time is not a significant variable in the amount and use of non-working time. If he had, the original intention of the time budget research – namely, to see what difference shortening the working day to six or seven hours makes in time use – would be totally negated. He therefore concluded that the shortening of the working day 'alters the size of free time and its use'.[56]

Workers, Office Workers, and Engineers and Technical Personnel: Factors Altering Time Use

The last chapter in the Petrosian book is concerned with the basic ways of *rationalizing the use of non-working time*. Rational use of time applies to time spent on 'necessities', such as sleep, as well as to free time. Time is considered 'rational' if it positively affects the intellectual and physical development of the individual and 'irrational' if it has a negative effect. For example, time spent on housework and on work connected with production is considered irrational. Thus it is important and essential first to shorten time on these activities and then to ensure that this time is spent more rationally.

Petrosian first suggests equalizing or smoothing the effects that *territorial differences* have on workers' living conditions. The basic reason for irrationally using non-working time, he says, is the fact that a number of cities are inadequately provided with adequate living conditions (including trade, medical, transport and household services) and cultural facilities. His point is illustrated in a table examining the non-working time of men and women in ten cities in the country (see Table 7.9).[57] He comes to the overall conclusion that the non-working time of workers living in these cities is significantly different in general and in detail.[58]

The basic cause of these differences, he continues, is the *shortcomings in planning*. Every time budget researchers concurred on this point and specifically pointed to the lack of cordination in planning. While most of these researchers recognized that data from the time budgets offered the possibility of correctly planning a network of institutions and services, they merely offered vague suggestions. Petrosian, on the other hand, drew up a form for ascertaining workers' material and economic conditions which includes detailed questions on the presence, number, condition and size of the following: trade, public catering, city transport and communications, available housing, communal services, domestic (and welfare) services, education, culture, health, physical culture and sport, and legal services.[59] The form, which is an attempt to work out 'norms' and establish planning indices, was not accepted or tried.[60]

Another of Petrosian's suggestions refers to improving the level of the *organization of byt*. Here the key word is organization. The working day must be shortened, but better use of the remaining non-working time must also be made through 'organization'. Organization consists of two components. The first concerns the organization of facilities and services – or 'things' – whereas the second concerns the organization of the people using these facilities or services. It is in the latter that party, komsomol and trade union organizations play a vital role because 'the workers sometimes do not know how to use their free time'.[61]

Direct organization and planning of non-working time must, he said, occur in two stages. The first requires a 'scientific definition of minimal and/or maximal norms of time expenditure'. Then planned budgets of non-working time could be drawn up. Initial plans would be determined by sex and later ones by age, family position, social groups, etc. Petrosian conceptualized a schema to show the planned approximate use of free time for a week (see Table 7.10).[62]

Table 7.9   Non-working time for a weekday (on the average, in hours and minutes)

City (number of time budgets)	Time of simple reproduction of working strength (occupied time)				Time of extended reproduction of working strength (free time)	Other	Total
	Time connected with work at production	House-work and care of self	Sleeping and eating	Total			
Moscow (1241)							
Men (876)	1-45	2-03	7-20	11-08	4-18	0-35	16-01
Women (365)	1-36	4-46	7-10	13-32	2-38	0-19	16-29
Kolomna (237)							
Men (107)	1-40	1-42	8-38	12-00	4-57	-	16-01
Women (130)	1-27	3-55	8-53	14-15	2-50	-	17-05
Erevan (10089)							
Men (4035)	1-20	2-16	8-28	12-04	4-10	0-36	16-50
Women (6054)	1-41	4-34	7-54	14-09	2-24	0-21	16-54
Tiblisi (53)							
Women (53)	1-40	3-20	7-40	12-40	2-00	1-20	16-00
Sverdlovsk (5271)							
Men (3235)	1-02	2-32	8-40	12-23	4-24	-	16-47
Women (2036)	1-02	4-22	8-30	13-54	2-53	-	16-47
Novosibirsk (396)							
Men (130)	0-53	2-43	8-58	12-34	3-09	-	16-43
Women (266)	0-47	5-10	8-11	14-08	1-43	-	15-51
Krasnoiarsk (1092)							
Men (826)	1-55	2-30	8-39	13-04	3-10	0-25	16-39
Women (266)	1-38	4-55	7-58	14-31	2-17	-	16-48
Norilsk (7651)							
Men (5082)	1-28	1-36	8-42	11-46	3-40	0-40	16-06
Women (2569)	1-10	4-05	8-06	13-21	2-00	0-55	16-16
Novokuznets (1000)							
Men (681)	2-44	2-41	7-32	12-57	4-03	-	17-00
Women (319)	3-01	5-02	7-17	15-30	1-20	-	17-00
Omsk (1030)							
Women (1030)	1-27	5-12	7-42	14-21	1-27	0-29	16-17

Table 7.10   Personal budget of free time of workers for a week

Structure of expenditures (free time)	USE 1961 (estimated) hours and minutes			Approximate changes for planned period (multiplied by...)			Scheme (projected) in hours		
	Men	Women	Average	Men	Women	Average	Men	Women	Average
Study and raising qualifications	3-13	2-01	2-13	2.8	3.5	3.4	9	7	8
Self-education	4-33	3-33	3-57	2.2	4.0	3.0	10	14	12
Social work	1-30	0-48	1-00	2.0	3.7	3.0	3	3	3
Physical education and sport	1-54	0-42	0-48	4.2	10.2	10.0	8	8	8
Entertainment	14-50	9-26	12-50	0.2	0.5	0.3	16	14	15
Bringing up children	2-33	2-39	2-38	2.4	2.2	2.3	6	6	6
Amateur activities	2-00	1-30	1-37	-	0.2	0.2	3	2	3
Remaining expenditures	1-04	0-22	0-46	-	-	-	-	-	-
Balance	31-37	21-01	25-49	1.6	2.6	2.0	55	54	55

a. Average weekly time spent on activities = 25-49
b. Additional time, from decrease on:
   1. Time on housework: 17-50
   2. Time connected with work on production: 2-24
   3. Other time expenditures: 2-54
   4. Working time (12-48) minus the increase of time on sleeping and eating (6-45): 6-03
c. Future total: 55-00 (combination of A and B)
   Chart explains how this 55-00 is divided up

It is clear from this table that Petrosian considers that certain activities deserve additional time: physical education and sports – ten times the present amount of time; study and raising qualifications – 3.4 times; self-education – three times; and social work – three times. Time on these activities should especially increase for women. Needless to say, other time budget authors stressed slightly different categories.

Petrosian's final concern with rationalizing the use of non-working time is related to the fact that the length and limits of working time for individual categories of workers are ill-defined. He illustrates this by pointing out that the workday load varies in type and time according to the categories of working people, type of industry, sectors of the economy, and regions of the country. He recommends a clearer definition and a more precise delimitation of working time.

Kolkhoz Time Budget Studies

A review of time budget research of kolkhozniks is simplified by the fact that only two studies have been conducted since the first two in the early 1960s.[63] The first 1964 study, like its predecessors, compared its data primarily with the 1924 and 1934 kolkhoz studies. The main difference, however, lies in the depth and scope of this work.[64] The second 1964 kolkhoz study criticized the first for not sufficiently analyzing the qualitative differences of several types of free time, that is, for not comparing the free time of kolkhozniks living in central homesteads and in remote villages. The aim of the last piece of research was to remedy this defect.[65] The two 1964 studies are similar in most aspects (unless otherwise noted in the discussion below), but the bulk of this section is devoted to the first 1964 study, the more detailed of the two.

A. S. Duchal headed the March 1964 research which was sponsored by the Department of Scientific Communism of the Academy of Social Sciences attached to the Central Committee of the CPSU and by the Department of Philosophy of the Stavropol Agricultural Institute. The kolkhoz 'Rossiia' in the Novo-Aleksandrovsk *raion* of the Stravropol'skii *krai* was the subject of the research; it was chosen as a typical kolkhoz because of its 'economic position and cultural level'. Data from analogous research conducted at three other kolkhozes were combined with the results from the 'Rossiia' and, while Duchal generalized from all four kolkhozes, she actually took specific examples from the 'Rossiia.' Each family, assisted by teachers from the schools, *tekhnikumy* and institutions for the mechanization of agriculture, received a questionnaire blank (which was not shown in the published report) and subsidiary blanks for time distribution.

The data that Duchal requested from the respondents differed from that of the previous kolkhoz studies. The first, the Lenkova study in 1960, stated that such factors as age, education, and sex were recorded, but these data were not published. Moreover, the Lenkova study only described the types of time expenditures for four occupational categories of kolkhoz workers, subdivided into summer and winter work. This study, however, was the only one to mention party membership as a separate category, but this information was not printed. The 1960 Bibik study specified the occupation, age, sex, marital status, and number of children of the respondents. Time use was then plotted – by sex – for a weekday and a free day. Thus the biggest change in the write-up was the sex division. The data about the respondents in the Duchal (1964) study were much more substantial and comprehensive. The emphasis, moreover, had shifted to the kolkhozniks' educational level as a main determinant of how they spent their time. The last study is less comprehensive than Duchal's because it only concentrated on the differences that residence – central or remote village – made in the structure of free time.

If the discussion and presentation of the composition of the sample was altered, so was the discussion on the method of research. The 1960 Lenkova study made no mention of sampling technique, nor of how the kolkhoz population was studied. The Bibik study, however, specifically stated that the purpose of the study was to compare a progressive and a backward kolkhoz from each of two provinces; the hope was to determine the influence of the kolkhoz's prosperity (e.g. determine the presence of cultural and service institutions) on the structure of time use. The researchers then described how the data were collected. On the other hand, the two 1964 studies barely discussed how data were gathered, but they did state that self-registration was used. Both also indicated that the kolkhozes were chosen for their 'typicalness', but the criteria were hardly specified.

All of the kolkhoz studies considered the role of such factors as the seasons, electrification and mechanization, transportation facilities, scientific discoveries, etc., in the use of time. Comparisons were often made with time expenditures of kolkhozniks and peasants of the past. Unrelated statistics, such as the number of tractors in the USSR from 19— to 19—, were often inserted in the text. Pronouncements from the CPSU Programme and a smattering of Lenin quotations were also interspersed with these figures.[66]

Instead of quantitatively comparing Duchal's findings with those from the other studies – a task made most difficult by the fact that there is no common base (e.g. the Duchal study describes time [by sex] for summer and winter, while the Bibik study, for example, describes time [by sex] for a weekday and a free day) – let us examine some salient features of Duchal's research.

Her discussion of the time spent on social work (*obshchestvenniia rabota*) is a most unusual one. The previous kolkhoz studies merely listed the amount of time spent on this category for their particular study and for Strumilin's 1934 study: no attempt was made to explain the marked decrease of time. Comparing her work with the 1934 study, Duchal, however, stated 'This [decline] is evidence of the fact that social work is basically carried out by a narrow circle of activists... and at the same time that the basic mass of kolkhozniks are not involved in active social work'.[67] Duchal listed three reasons for the reduction:

- a change in the concept of 'social work': in 1964 it was frequently intertwined with production and mass cultural work, and kolkhoz members simply did not distinguish the two in research interviews;

- the fact that social activity of agitators, lecturers, etc., was now undertaken only during periods of election campaigns;
- a drop in social work now occurred when there were frequent instances of a neglectful attitude towards the opinion of the rank and file of workers.[68]

Data from the last study coincided almost entirely with Duchal's, but the authors suggested that social work itself had changed. In other words, many types of social work which formerly demanded special time expenditures were now carried out by mechanized means (e.g. the press and television). Nevertheless, both 1964 studies showed considerable concern for this topic.

The Duchal study also spent a considerable amount of space on religion. Unlike the previous studies which barely mentioned religion, Duchal prepared separate tables to show the relationship (by sex) between age and religion. She found that religion had been losing its hold since the first time budget studies of 1923 and, as a result, it was primarily the old women who were the believers.[69] Comparing time spent on reading, study, and social work with time spent on religious worship for the years 1923, 1934 and 1964, Duchal remarked that 'agricultural workers' religion at present has significantly decreased, while their time on reading, study, and social work has significantly increased'.

One further category in the Duchal study must be considered. That is the time spent on the private plot. Both the Lenkova and the Bibik studies stated that time would be best utilized when farmers spent less time on the private plots. In these two studies, but especially in Lenkova, the private plot assumed the role of *bête noire*.[70] This is not the case with the Duchal study. Perhaps this can be related to the government's changing attitude toward the private plot. The 1960 Lenkova and Bibik studies were heavily influenced by Khrushchev's pronouncements against the private plot. The 1964 study, although completed just prior to Khrushchev's downfall, seemed to discuss the private plot as a more positive phenomenon.

Duchal also explored the problem of how to classify time spent on the private plot. The result of one's labours on the private plot is classified, according to Duchal, as time for satisfying personal needs; hence the time is non-working time. But the labour helps to increase commodity production and is also of a socially useful nature; hence, it is working time. Duchal advocated a special study to resolve the dilemma.

Thus we have seen how the researchers of kolkhozniks' time budgets gathered samples, used similar methods, and approached the task of discovering how kolkhozniks spent their time. Each successive study was an improvement upon the preceding study. The Lenkova study gave but few variables in relation to time expenditures. The Bibik study increased the number of these variables and, at the same time, compared a backward and a progressive kolkhoz. The novelty of this study lay in the researchers' statements informing the reader of the limits of the research and the representativeness of the study.

> The data received from the investigation cannot be applied to all kolkhozniks in the country. Our investigation covered a relatively small number of persons (not

over 500). In addition, the data examined, pertaining only to one weekday and one free day taken at a certain season of the year, cannot fully reflect the true relationship in time expenditures for a longer period.[71]

The authors then offered suggestions for future time budget research: 1) carry out time budget studies in each period of the year, and do not restrict the investigation to kolkhozes in one zone; 2) compare time budgets of kolkhoz and sovkhoz workers; 3) use time budgets when planning the development of social and cultural measures in the village; 4) work out measures to improve the structure of time for all of the kolkhozniks and for individual groups – by sex, occupation, etc. The Duchal study went into considerable detail about the composition of the sample and stressed the significance of education for the kolkhoznik. The study also reflected the changing outlook of the authorities on certain topics, such as the private plot. Finally, the last study, which concentrated on the change in the use of free time, documented the authors' contention that there is an essential qualitative difference between free-time use in central districts and remote villages.

Conclusion

The significance of time budget research lies in its descriptive, quantitative and critical functions. The problem of ascertaining how an individual utilizes his/her non-working time had become one of great practical concern in the Soviet Union. With the reduction of the working day, more and more of an individual's time was less and less directly supervised. If the state was to mould society, then the working people – and particularly the youth – must be shown the correct and most rational way of utilizing this time. This could not be accomplished if no one knew how time was spent.

The results from the research were to be used for planning a more rational use of non-working time by establishing a system of communal facilities and cultural amenities. Each of the researchers offered suggestions for improving living conditions and increasing the material and cultural level of the workers. While doing this, they tended to emphasize what the regime stressed (for example, an increase in the number of children's establishments or more communal eating facilities) or they may have offered their own ideas. Zemtsov, for example, was interested in staggering the working hours so as to relieve the transportation network. In all cases, the communal interest was stressed at the expense of the private.

The tables described above by no means represent the bulk of the time budget presentations. On the contrary, they are but a small part of the reports. Descriptions of (existing) facilities, such as the book supplies in the local library or the conditions of the local cinema, abound in the time budget presentations. As such, they form a body of information about selected areas of the former Soviet Union.

Time budget research had another function which became increasingly evident. Criticism of existing conditions, in addition to the discussion of the actual amounts of time spent on various activities, formed a good part of the reports. Sometimes the criticism was merely voiced, but at other times the author presented the data with the aim of persuading the reader to accept specific proposals. Most of the criticism fell within accepted limits. It also paralleled many of the regime's complaints, but often the researcher could back up his/her observations with more specific facts than the regime spokespersons. The complaints were mostly concerned with the absence or inadequacy of facilities and services – with objective, rather than subjective, factors.

---

1 G. A. Prudenskii, 'Svobodnoe Vremia Trudiashchikhsia v Sotsialistichiskoi Obshchestve,' *Kommunist,* Vol. 15 (1960), p.10.

2 The (1965) Pskov study, which was linked to and regulated by the European Coordination Centre for Research and Documentation in Social Sciences' multi-nation time budget research, did cordinate more factors.

3 The Pskov study was based on the adult population of urban and industrial areas. The basic unit of this study, then, was the urban, industrial centre.

4 R. E. F. Smith, *A Russian-English Dictionary of Social Science Terms* (London, 1962), p.136.

5 V. G. Baikova, A. C. Duchal and A. A. Zemstov, *Svobodnoe Vremia i Vsestoronnee Razvitie Lichnosti,* Moscow, 1965, p.271. (Emphasis mine.) This may perhaps be explained by Baikova's insistence on developing the ITRs as leaders and organizers of production, as a technical vanguard.

6 S. V. Beliaev *et al.,* 'Izuchenie Biudzheta Vremeni Trudiashchikhsia Kak Odin iz Metodov Konkretno-Sotsiologicheskogo Issledovaniia,' *Vestnik LGU,* No. 23 (1961), pp.96-110.

7 It was possible that the problems of the sample would be resolved by the European Coordination Centre for Research and Documentation in Social Sciences' multi-nation research on time use. Alexander Szalai, the Hungarian chairman of the committee, suggested that the household be the basic unit of the survey. Having established criteria for the survey site (in this case, not the factory or the place of work), Szalai suggested that not all of the people found in the household should be part of the survey population; certain groups, such as school children and the aged, would be excluded. Out of all of the households in the survey, a certain number would be picked *at random.* Then, from every household picked, a list of eligible persons would be drawn up and from this list the interviewees would be chosen *at random.* Thus this method involves a double random sample. It is quite plausible that such methods would have been adopted by the Soviets, especially since the Soviet representative to the multi-nation study was G. V. Prudenskii, the man whose original Siberian research methods form the basis of the UNESCO work. See the preliminary report by Alexander Szalai, 'The Mutlinational Comparative Time Budget Research12:57 Project: A Venture in International Research Cooperation,' *The American Behavioral Scientist,* X, No. 4 (December, 1966), pp.1-31.

8 This differentiation had been recognized by some Soviet psychologists. In a discussion on the transfer to the five-day work week, they noted that the worker's sluggish attitude the day after a day off and his anticipatory feelings (and their effect) preceding the day off made it more (economically) profitable to combine, rather than split up, the two days off. They concluded that it would be disastrous if this occurred twice, instead of once, a week. M.

Babadzhanian, G. Goriachev and E. Markova, 'Piatidnevka s Tochki Zreniia Psikhologa,' *Ekonomicheskaia Gazeta*, 11 July 1967, p.31.
9 See S. G. Strumilin, *Problemy Ekonomiki Truda*, Moscow, 1957, p.733, and *Rabochii Den' i Kommunizm*, Moscow, 1959, p.64.
10 G. A. Prudenskii (ed.), *Vnerabochee Vremia Trudiashchikhsia*, Novisibirsk, 1961, p.254. The actual questionnaires were included in the Appendix.
11 *Ibid.* p.233.
12 *Sovkhoz* – state farm.
13 See Appendix III and IV for these charts. An exception to this is the questionnaire form for the *Komsomol'skaia Pravda* poll on yearly holidays. [See Appendix I.]
14 B. Kolpakov and G. Prudenskii, 'Opyt Izmereniia Vnerabochego Vremeni Trudiashchikhsiia,' *Vop Fil*, No. 9 (1964), pp.27-34.
15 *Ibid.* p.29. (Emphasis mine.)
16 It is quite possible that this suggestion would not be carried out on account of the link-up of Prudenskii and the Siberian department with the European Coordination Centre for Research and Documentation in Social Sciences' time budget research group. This group, for the purpose of collecting comparable data, established its own forms and questions for the time budget study.
17 *Ibid.*
18 G. A. Prudenskii, *Vremia i Trud*, Moscow, 1965, p.343.
19 Prudenskii, *Kommunist*, 15 (1960), pp.40-48.
20 G. S. Petrosian, *Vnerabochee Vremia Trudiashchikhsia v SSSR*, Moscow, 1965, p.194.
21 *Ibid.* pp.8-9.
22 The problem of simultaneous action was raised by Petrosian, Patrushev and Volkov, the last in a critical review of Prudenskii's *Vremia i Trud*. G. N. Volkov, 'Trud i Vremia Kak Predmet Kompleksnogo Issledovaniia,' *Vop Fil*, No.1 (1966), p.162. For a solution to this problem, see the UNESCO time budget research.
23 This type of research is the same as Prudenskii's 'target research'.
24 Petrosian, *Vnerabochee Vremia...*, p.8.
25 *Ibid.* pp.21-22.
26 Once again, time classifications could have become standardized by and related to the European Coordination Centre for Research and Documentation in Social Sciences' research.
27 See Chapter 6 for a discussion of the *Komsomol'skaia Pravda* poll on the use of free time.
28 G. V. Osipov and S. F. Frolov, 'Vnerabochee Vremia i Ego Ispol'zovanie,' *Sotsiologiia v SSSR*, II, G. V. Osipov (ed.), Moscow, 1966, pp.227-244.
29 *Ibid.* pp.228-229. (Emphasis mine.)
30 *Ibid.* p.243.
31 V. A. Artemov, 'O Nekotorykh Metodakh Analiza Biudzhetov Vremeni Trudiashchikhsia,' *Sotsiologicheskie Issledovaniia: Voprosy Metodologii i Metodika*, R. B. Ryvkina (ed.), Novosibirsk, 1966, pp.398-420.
32 Leningrad figures from Beliaev *et al., Vestnik LGU*, No.4 (1961), p.48; Kiev figures from Goncharenko *et al., Fil Nauki*, No.1 (1963), p.36.
33 Beliaev *et al., Vestnik LGU*, 4 (1961), pp.96-110.
34 M. P. Goncharenko *et al.*, 'Metodika i Nekotorye Rezultaty Konkretnogo Sotsial'nogo Issledovaniia Biudzheta Vrememi Trudiashchikhsia,' *Fil Nauki*, No.1 (1963), pp.29-39.

35 Some of Petrosian's other generalizations were also not upheld in the Kiev and Leningrad studies. For example, Petrosian found that the ITRs spent the most time for work connected with production, whereas in both of the other studies the workers headed the list.
36 Petrosian, *Vnerabochee Vremia...*, p.102.
37 See F. Gayle Durham's *The Use of Free Time by Young People in Soviet Society*, (Cambridge, Massachusetts, 1966) for a detailed discussion of the age factor.
38 *Ibid.* p.101. This table is a shortened version of the one which appears in the Petrosian study.
39 Petrosian, *Vnerabochee Vremia...*, p.105.
40 Goncharenko *et al.*, *Fil Nauki*, No.1 (1963), p.36.
41 V. I. Bolgov, *Vnerabochee Vremia i Uroven' Zhizni Trudiashchikhsia*, Novosibirsk, 1964, p.34.
42 Petrosian, *Vnerabochee Vremia...*, p.111.
43 This did not hold for those with a higher education: they spent less time than those with an incomplete higher education, but more time than those with a secondary education.
44 See V. G. Baikova, 'Svobodnoe Vremia i Povyshenie Nauchno-Tekhnicheskogo Urovnia Inzhenernogo-Tekhnicheski Rabotnikov,' *Vop Fil*, No.4 (1965), pp.69-74.
45 R. Lamkov, 'Opyt Izucheniia Vnerabochego Vremeni,' *Voprosy Organizatsii i Metodiki Konkretnogo-Sotsiologicheskikh Issledovanii*, (eds.) G. K. Ashin *et al.*, Moscow, 1963, pp.146-157.
46 *Ibid.* p.153.
47 *Ibid.* p.154.
48 *Ibid.* p.155.
49 Petrosian, *Vnerabochee Vremia...*, p.93.
50 *Ibid.* p.123.
51 Beliaev *et al.*, *Vestnik LGU*, 23 (1961), pp.55 and 52.
52 Goncharenko *et al.*, *Fil Nauki*, No.1 (1963), p.38.
53 V. D. Patrushv, *Intensivnost'Truda pri Sotsializme*, Moscow, 1963, p.288.
54 *Krai* – territory; an administrative subdivision of the RSFSR usually including autonomous *oblasti*.
55 *Ibid.* p.211.
56 *Ibid.* p.228.
57 Petrosian, *Vnerabochee Vremia...*, p.131.
58 *Ibid.* p.132.
59 *Ibid.* pp.136-140.
60 Grushin, in *Svobodnoe Vremia: Aktual'nye Problemy* (Moscow, 1967), specifically complained that such 'quotas' were worked out for Akademgorod, but were ignored in the end.
61 Petrosian, *Vnerabochee Vremia...*, p.179.
62 *Ibid.* p.188.
63 L. Lenkova, 'Ob Ispol' zovanii Vremeni Kolkhoznikami,' *Ekonomika Sel'skogo Khoziaistva*, 1 (1962), pp.43-48; L. Bibik, 'Opyt Obsledovaniia Biudzheta Vremeni Kolkhoznikov, '*Biulletin' Nauchnoi Informatsii: Trud i Zarabotnaia*, Vol.6 (1961), pp.45-52. This statement holds up to the end of the 1960s.
64 The following discussion is taken mainly from Baikova, Duchal, and Zemtsov, *Svobodnoe Vremia...* (previously cited). Unless specified, this is where the Duchal notes come from. Also see A. S. Duchal, 'Izmenenie Strukury Rabochego i Svobodnogo Vremeni Krest'ian za Gody Sovetskoi Vlasti,' *Vop Fil*, No.4 (1964), pp.74-80.

65 M. M. Berezhnoi and S. I. Ovchinnikov, 'Opyt Issledovaniia Izmenenii v Strukture Svobodnogo Vremeni Kolkhoznikov,'*Fil Nauki*, Vol.5 (1966), pp.21-27.

66 This is not quite an accurate description of the last study which had a minimum discussion of these topics.

67 Duchal in Baikova, Duchal and Zemtsov, *Svobodnoe Vremia*..., p.264.

68 Duchal, *Vop Fil*, No.4 (1964), p.79.

69 Duchal in Baikova, Duchal, and Zemtsov, *Svobodnoe Vremia*... , p.259. An interesting footnote to this discussion comes from B. A. Grushin. In his 1967 free-time poll write-up he specifically disagrees with Prudenskii's (and hence, Duchal's and others') assertion that time on religious activities has 'disappeared'. 'The facts speak otherwise.' See B. A. Grushin, *Svobodnoe Vremia: Aktual'nye Problemy* (Moscow, 1967), p.85.

70 The last 1964 study does not discuss the private plot.

71 Bibik, 'Biulletin Nauchnoi Informatsii: Trud i Zarabotnaia Plata', No. 6 (1961), p.51.

8

Perestroika and Soviet Sociology*

The reflexive interrelations between the development of sociology and changes in social structure have been a continuing focus of interest within the sociological community.[1] The discussion of such interrelations falls into two main groups. Those in the 'sociology of sociology' vein seek to argue that particular theories or bodies of work are derivative from, at least implicit, social or political agenda.[2] While such work can be illuminating, it can also easily slide towards the position of denying any internal autonomy to sociology as a discipline. In the case of the second group, sociological research is seen as playing a significant, even on occasion major, role in shaping national – or international – priorities.[3] In this case, the problems of a simple reductionism are usually avoided; the difficulties here are rather those of a genuinely 'critical evaluation', the carrying out of which is really dependent on clearly establishing the purposes and frames of reference belonging to the sociologists whose work is under examination.[4]

The case of Soviet sociology is of particular interest in this regard. Having been an outstanding example of the problems encountered in the course of the attempted institutionalization of the discipline,[5] Soviet sociology played the role of midwife to major changes which were profoundly restructuring Soviet society. The present chapter locates the relationship between sociology and *perestroika* in the context of the struggle to establish the integrity of sociology as a discipline in the Soviet Union.

Expansion and Retrenchment: The 1960s and 1970s

Sociology in the Soviet Union endeavoured to reinstate itself as a legitimate discipline after the nadir of the Stalin era. Beginning with Khrushchev's Twentieth Party Congress speech in 1956 and the ensuing thaw, sociology began to re-emerge as the Communist Party at last unlocked the door for its subsequent development in the late 1950s; unlocked, but did not open the door since the main feature of these years was the struggle by sociology for the right to exist as an independent academic discipline. Although the Soviet Sociological Association was formed in 1958, it was not until the Twenty-Third Party Congress in March-April 1966 that sociology was recognized officially as a discrete discipline with distinct functions. That Congress did discuss the future development of sociology and an increased

* A version of this chapter originally appeared in the *British Journal of Sociology*, Vol. 43 (1), March 1992, pp.1-10.

role for sociological research in the solution of economic, political and ideological problems. However, only in 1968 was sociology finally given its own Institute in the USSR Academy of Sciences (the Institute of Concrete Social Research). Until then, it remained basically the illegitimate offspring of philosophy.

Nevertheless, in the 1960s and 1970s, sociology blossomed. Successive Congresses of the CPSU emphasized the need for thorough investigations of social structure, systematic opinion polling, and the study of changes in labour patterns and life styles and of the connection between economic and social development.[6] Further significant promotion of the institutionalization of sociology was represented by the Resolution of the CPSU Central Committee 'On measures for further development of the social sciences and the enhancement of their role in communist construction' (1968). This set out for the first time at party level the goals of sociology as a science. While these were still cast within the formalism of an orthodox historical materialism, the Resolution did represent a significant further move in the legitimation of the discipline, and this was manifested in a wide range of activity. Conferences and seminars were held and the first graduate programme of training was established at the Institute. Areas of sociological research continued to grow, in spite of the chronic discussion of the definition of and legitimacy of sociology as a discipline. Empirical work focused on an increasingly wide subject matter while more and more advanced methods were employed to study those topics always considered acceptable. This period was characterized also by persistent criticism of the utilization of statistics, that is, the careless construction of or use of 'home-made' statistics, the assumption that correlation means causation, or the drawing of 'statistical' conclusions from unrelated facts, as well as the condemnation by sociologists of the practice of withholding (central) statistical material or not even collecting basic socio-demographic data about the structure of Soviet society. A large majority of empirical research at this time produced an awareness of the lack of adequate social and sociological information, which lack acted as a stimulus for the collection of basic data.

This period of expansion, which was both quantitative and qualitative, came to an end at the beginning of the 1970s. The change was clearly identifiable in developments at the Institute of Concrete Social Research. Its first director, Alexei Rumiantsev, was a leader in the field of sociology, but with his dismissal in 1971 and eventual replacement in 1972 by Mikhail Rutkevich, the Institute (the real centre and co-ordinator of Soviet sociology) removed and dispersed many prominent and qualified sociologists.[7] There was a definite turnover in personnel at other research institutes, laboratories and journals, both at the centre and at the periphery of Soviet sociology. A good example of this was the director of the Institute, Vladimir Yadov, who was asked to leave the Institute of Socio-Economic Problems (attached to the Academy of Sciences in Moscow), being labelled a 'slanderer of Soviet reality'.[8] Many sociologists were either silenced or joined other non-sociological departments, such as economics or ethnography. As the more liberal elements in Soviet sociology were temporarily silenced, the party played an increasing role both in conducting sociological research and in educating new members in the profession. At the same time, research results, sent to various party bodies, often landed on the archive shelves.[9] Not only was the research itself more party oriented and less independent, but also there was even more stress than usual placed on solving practical problems.

Since the early 1970s, direct party interference in sociological research increased, more areas of study were prohibited, and more studies were secret.[10] The one positive outcome of this period was the establishment in 1974 of the first journal of sociology, *Sotsiologischeskie Issledovaniia* (*Sociological Research*), which until 1990 was published bi-monthly and since then appears every month. In addition, the first joint symposium with a capitalist country, Finland, took place in 1978.[11]

These characteristics of retrenchment, dispersal and problem-solving continued into the early 1980s. In general, this period – from the late 1970s to the early 1980s – was one of contradictory developments. On the one hand, following the dismissal of Rutkevich as Director of the Institute in 1976, more sociology was published, especially in the field of methodology. New projects were also initiated. On the other hand, the Ministry of Education continued its policy of impeding the establishment of departments of sociology at the universities. In fact, only in 1984 were undergraduate programmes in sociology begun at some universities, including Moscow and Leningrad.

Sociology and Perestroika

In hindsight, a possible resolution of these developments began to emerge slowly in a disjuncture between the Brezhnev period and the brief, but telling, Andropov period. As Alec Nove suggests, social scientists, including the many sociologists who were dispersed from Moscow, were already working as 'constructive dissidents, i.e. those who prematurely advocated *perestroika*'.[12] The best known of these 'constructive dissidents' was Tatiana Zaslavskaya whose seminal paper analyzing and criticizing the conditions of the Soviet economy and society was presented to the economics departments of the Party Central Committee and the USSR Academy of Sciences in 1983, soon after Brezhnev's death. Only a few copies of her memorandum were produced for those conference participants who were originally on the list before printing. However, many samizdat copies were made during the night before the conference. Leaked to the West via the *Washington Post*, her seminal memorandum was then read by the Politburo, including Gorbachev and Andropov. Consequently she fell foul of the authorities: the Novosibirsk District Party Committee discussed her 'crime' as her ideas were censured.[13]

Zaslavskaya's very courageous and undoubtedly path-breaking memorandum stated flatly that the Soviet economic system was obsolete and Soviet bureaucracy was a very real impediment to much needed change. Relying on her sociological research at the Novosibirsk Institute of Industrial Economics, she also maintained that, contrary to official belief, many contradictions existed within Soviet society; that is, the monolithic picture of society was definitely a myth: the Soviet Union was not socially homogeneous. As Zaslavskaya has written subsequently,[14] reinforcing Nove's proposition regarding 'constructive dissidents', the ideas of *perestroika* were around even during the stagnation period of Brezhnev. However, real change came when the reforming element in the party leadership, especially Mikhail Gorbachev himself, endorsed her analysis of the problems facing Soviet society. As a result, social scientists of the 'intellectual/critical school' were able to take advantage of *glasnost'*.

At the beginning of 1987, Zaslavskaya herself published in *Pravda* a critical evaluation of the role and state of Soviet sociology.[15] Clearly reflecting the new-found openness in which issues could be discussed, she called upon sociology to: 1) gather 'full, accurate and truthful information about the real state of affairs', 2) specify the party's course of acceleration of economic development, and 3) provide the management of *perestroika* with reliable 'feedback'. However, she argued, sociology was not as yet able to perform these tasks because of past problems. What were they?

In the first instance, the rate of growth of sociology had been slow. In fact, said Zaslavskaya, Soviet sociology was certainly less developed than sociology in Poland or Hungary, not to mention in capitalist systems. Sociologists had only one professional outlet for their writing (unlike the US, for example) and, above all, there were many problems associated with the education and training of sociologists: 'there is no system that is at all well developed for passing on sociological knowledge'. She then stated that as a general rule, the professional standard of research was not high nor was the status of sociology as yet recognized by all. (The debate about legitimacy obviously continued.) Zaslavskaya called for sociologists to unite and tackle these problems. She also singled out the low level of gathered and/or published social statistics, the 'concealed' information which hindered the research work of the serious sociologists. Echoing sociologists in the 1960s, she asked why data on such topics as crime, suicide, alcohol and drug (ab)use and migration were not available.[16] In other words, Zaslavskaya pointed out the political, as well as the bureaucratic, obstacles to sociological research.

Zaslavskaya later published an article in *Sotsiologischeskie Issledovaniia* (Sociological Research), similar to the *Pravda* one just discussed but now directly aimed at sociologists *per se*.[17] Here, she used slightly different figures: for example, membership in the Soviet Sociological Association was listed as 6,000 (not 8,000) individual members and 1,200 (not 1,500) collective members; figures for doctorate and candidate degrees in applied sociology were, respectively, 15-20 (not 5-8) doctorates and 50 (not 25) candidate degrees. She also said here that, at the highest party and state levels, it was still necessary to change attitudes towards sociology as a science. She offered the following concrete recommendations for an improved sociology:

- create sociological faculties and departments in universities in those cities where there are already professional sociological collectives (such as Gorky, Minsk, Odessa, etc.);
- open up departments of 'applied sociology' or 'economic sociology' in leading *vuzy* (higher educational establishments) throughout the country;

- create a system of additional training to raise the level of those sociologists who do not already have a sociological education;
- expand the system of sociological instruction for party workers, for Soviet and economic organizations, etc.; and
- enlarge the output of scholarly and methodological sociological literature, as well as popular sociological literature.

In sum, therefore, Zaslavskaya was advocating both the expansion *and* the improvement of sociology in the Soviet Union.

Zaslavskaya was by no means alone either in her criticism of the state of sociology or in offering suggestions for its future development in the age of *perestroika*. But she certainly carried more weight than others as she was the President of the Soviet Sociological Association. Since the publication of her critique in 1987, she also became the first director of the new All-Union Centre for the Study of Public Opinion.

It is important to understand the policy as well as the personal implications of this appointment. Public opinion research played a central and vital role in the development of Soviet sociology. Since its inception in the early 1960s, public opinion research expanded and improved, reflecting the pragmatic trend in sociology, the growing belief among decision-makers in the functional value of such research, and the greater acceptance of sociological research by the country at large.[18] The function of such research has been to act as a feedback mechanism for a system notoriously lacking in institutional means by identifying, let alone responding to, popular concerns and aspirations. In the last few years of the Soviet Union, the mass media, especially the press, utilized and popularized public opinion research extensively, using surveys and polls to uncover the 'real needs' of the population as well as acting as a mouthpiece of social criticism. This was accompanied by the often expressed complaint about 'questionnaire mania'.[19]

'Questionnaire mania' was first diagnosed as a disease in the 1960s as questionnaire research was flimsily conducted by a fair proportion of sociologists (or so-called sociologists). Even with the very significant improvements which took place in the broad area of methodology, however, two established Soviet sociologists commented in 1989:

> The overall methodological and methodical level of sociological studies as yet fails to meet modern requirements even at academic institutions [let alone at the other research centres not attached to academic institutions - EAW]. In this light, building up methodology and techniques featuring quantitative methods and computers in empirical sociological studies acquires special importance.[20]

The director of the (once again renamed) Institute of Sociology, Vladimir Yadov, like his predecessor, Ivanov,[21] was also concerned about the process of conducting sociological research. The Institute, which hoped again to become the centre and co-ordinator of fundamental research (both by its links throughout the Soviet Union and through international projects, of which about fifty were taking place) ran a methodological seminal to try and combat some of the problems mentioned above.[22]

However, of equal if not greater importance is the fact that Yadov and his colleagues were concerned about the *theoretical* state of Soviet sociological research. Under the cloak of *glasnost'*, Grushin, renowned for his work on public opinion research, wrote: we 'need to create a new language which would adequately describe reality', at the same time, indicating that journalists and film makers have already begun this process.[23] Or we have Zaslavskaya saying that too little effort has gone into creating a fundamental sociological theory. Gavrilets, known for his work on models and methods of research, suggested that sociologists withdraw the term 'Marxist-Leninist sociology' and substitute 'Soviet sociology'.[24] Here is the crux of the matter. With all of the changes within Soviet society, leading Soviet sociologists were openly questioning the continual use of Marxist-Leninist theory as the *sole* sociological theory capable of understanding and analyzing Soviet society and, by implication, questioning the status of such 'theory' itself.

Take the area of stratification, for example. Sociologists in the 1960s stated that, while the path towards social unity and classless society was originally paved by the liquidation of an exploiting class, classes still do exist, namely, the two non-antagonistic classes of workers and peasants; there was, in addition, it was proposed, one stratum, the intelligentsia. More and more research showed increasing stress placed on examining intra-class, rather than inter-class, differences; like their Western counterparts, workers were found to be alienated and intellectuals to be reproducing themselves. Sociologists began to ask for new definitions of 'class' as they discovered that Soviet society was a differentiated and stratified society in which different classes and different groups within the classes had varied attributes, interests, life styles. I recall that those of us who attended the Seventh World Congress of Sociology in Varna (Bulgaria) in 1970 expected to learn about these new definitions. At the meeting about social stratification in socialist societies, one Soviet sociologist in his forties went to the blackboard and began to draw a diagram of the future structure of a socialist society, using class and non-class terms. As he was about to explain his complex drawing, Rutkevich (mentioned earlier as the hatchet man of the 1972 Institute of Social Research purges) leapt to his feet, reprimanded this young man, and hastily erased the diagram, saying that it was just 'conjecture'. In the climate of the 1970s, new definitions of class were not easily able to surface.

But it is not 1970 any longer. In the *perestroika* period some Soviets began to certainly publicly question the Marxist paradigm. In the field of stratification, for example, this was inevitably the case as changes in property and ownership began to take place; hence, property relations were beginning to change. Moreover, as the role of the Communist Party changed within the Soviet Union, it no longer was necessary for all Soviet sociologists to proclaim historical materialism as *the* theory of sociology. There was room for utilizing a variety of theoretical approaches to analyze Soviet social forces. Yadov said we need 'other approaches'. 'World sociology [and here he spoke clearly to his own colleagues – EAW] is waiting for a leader who will venture to suggest in principle a new paradigm, integrating macro-theoretical and micro-theoretical approaches to the study of the totality of the social organism and social process'.[25] Charismatic overtones and totalizing tendencies aside, parallels with the general thrust of much sociological theorizing in the West over the last decades are obvious. Soviet sociology was actively seeking new theoretical paradigms to comprehend the changing nature of Soviet reality.

Postscript

I ended the original *British Journal of Sociology* article on a practical note, asking: What is to be done? Our Soviet colleagues, having sustained sociology in circumstances of great difficulty, attempted to maintain and advance the discipline under changed circumstances which offered both challenges and dangers. We in Britain began to help them in this task. In the summer of 1989, Teodor Shanin of Manchester University, aided by the ESRC, the British Council, the British Academy, and the Maxwell and Soros foundations, initiated a crash summer school for twenty-one aspiring Soviet sociologists. A similar programme was held in the summer of 1990 in Kent direct by Ray Pahl and the following summer a third was scheduled to take place.[26] But surely this was only the tip of the iceberg: could we not offer a Marshall Plan in sociology, especially in the areas of methodology and theory (including 'applied theory')? This could have become a two-way exchange for undergraduates, graduates, and academics who would visit – learn, research, teach – us, as well as the reverse. I argued in the article that, with the advent of *perestroika*, no matter what its outcome or even in spite of its outcome, we could not afford not to participate more actively. After all, our American colleagues helped out extensively at a number of universities with a wide variety of programmes, as well as initiating co-operative ventures in publishing sociological materials.

1 See R. Nisbet, *The Sociological Tradition*, New York, Basic Books, 1967; G. Hawthorn, *Enlightenment and Despair: A History of Sociology*, Cambridge, Cambridge University Press, 1976; R. Friedrichs, *Sociology of Sociology*, New York, Free Press, 1970; A. Gouldner, *The Coming Crisis of Western Sociology*, New York, Basic Books, 1970; L. Bramson, *The Political Context of Sociology*, Princeton, NJ, Princeton University Press, 1961; M. Bulmer (ed.), *Essays on the History of British Sociological Research*, Cambridge, Cambridge University Press, 1985.

2 Gouldner, *op. cit.*; N. Genov (ed.), *National Trends in Sociology*, London, Sage, 1989; V. Shlapentokh, *The Politics of Sociology in the Soviet Union*, Boulder, Colorado, Westview Press, 1987.

3 P. Abrams, *The Origins and Growth of British Sociology, 1834-1914*, Chicago, University of Chicago Press, 1968.

4 See, for example, the work of Carol Weiss (*Evaluating Action Programs: Readings in Social Action and Education*, London, Allyn and Bacon, Inc., 1972) on evaluation research

and, on a more general level, the work of Anthony Giddens (*New Rules of Sociological Method*, London, Hutchinson and Co., 1976) on the *double* hermeneutic.

5 E. A. Weinberg, *The Development of Sociology in the Soviet Union*, London, Routledge and Kegan Paul, 1974. Also see articles by E. Beliaev and P. Butorin, 'Institutionalization of Soviet Sociology: Its Social and Political Context', *Social Forces*, Vol. 61, No. 2, 1982, pp.418-35, and V. Zaslavsky, 'Sociology in the Contemporary Soviet Union', *Social Research*, Vol. 44, No. 2, 1977, pp.330-53.

6 V. Ivanov and G. Osipov, 'Traditions and Specific Features of Sociology in the Soviet Union' in N. Genov (ed.), *National Trends in Sociology*, London, Sage, 1989, p.175.

7 T. I. Zaslavskaya, '*Perestroika* and Sociology', *Social Research*, Vol. 55, Nos. 1-2, 1987a, pp.267-76. The case of Yuri Levada should be raised here. As a member of the Institute of Concrete Social Research, Doctor of Philosophical Science Levada wrote a two-volume course entitled 'Lectures in Sociology' in 1969 which created quite a storm. He was severely criticized for what was conceived of as his attempt to separate sociology from historical materialism as well as his perceived leaning toward 'bourgeois sociology'. Because of his 'lack of ideological rigidity', not only were his lectures banned but the sociological community was castigated as well as thoroughly scrutinized. Levada himself was dismissed from his work at Moscow State University and lost the chance for promotion, being refused the title of professor. See the documents in *Sotsiologiia i Vlast': Dokumenti 1969-1972,* (Vol. 2), edited by G. Osipov *et al.*, Russian Academy of Sciences and Russian State Archive, Moscow, 2001, p.22.

8 T. I. Zaslavskaya, 'Friends or Foes? Social Forces Working For and Against P*erestroika*' in A. Aganbegyan (ed.), *Perestroika Annual,* London, Futura, 1988, p.255.

9 *Ibid.*

10 Schlapentokh, *op. cit.*

11 Communication, 'The First Soviet-Finnish Symposium of Sociology, Helsinki, January 24-25 1978, *Acta Sociologica*, Vol. 21, No. 2, 1978, pp.179-80. See also L. Jonson's article in the same issue of *Acta Sociologica*.

12 A. Nove, *Glasnost' in Action: Cultural Renaissance in Russia*, London, Unwin Hyman, 1989, p.159. Also see M. Lewin, *The Gorbachev Phenomenon*, London, Radius, 1988.

13 What followed was a very difficult period of her life. See her own discussion of this in a BBC TV interview of the series *Women in Politics*, 23 July 1989. Also see A. Brown, 'Tat'yana Zaslavskaya and Soviet Sociology: An Introduction', *Social Research*, Vol. 55, Nos. 1-2, 1988, pp.261-6.

14 Zaslalvskaya, *op. cit.*, 1988.

15 Zaslavskaya, *op.cit.*, 1987a.

16 If they are available for suicide, for example, we could all see the parallel figures which show that in the first few years after Khrushchev and Gorbachev became First Secretaries of the Party, the suicide rate dropped dramatically: a few years later, it began to rise again.

17 T. I. Zaslavskaya, 'Rol' Sotsiologii v Uskorenii Razvitiia Sovetskovo Obshchestva' (The Role of Sociology in the Acceleration of the Development of Soviet Society), *Sotsiologischeskie Issledovaniia*, No. 2, 1987b, pp.3-15.

18 See Chapter 6.

19 One prominent Soviet sociologist estimated that 60 per cent of all sociology in the world deals with public opinion questionnaires (V. C. Korobeinikov quoted in V. D. Voinova, 'Mezhdu Proshlym i Budushchim ili Kakim Byt' Institutu Sotsiologii?' (Between the Past and the Present or What Must be the Institute of Sociology?), *Sotsiologicheskie*

Issledovaniia, No. 2, 1989, p.151). In the light of this, he suggested the creation of a Soviet-American commercial information centre to study public opinion.

20 Ivanov and Osipov, *op. cit.*, p.189.

21 See an interview with V. N. Ivanov, 'Nevozmozhnoe Stanovitsia Vozmozhnym' (The Impossible Becomes the Possible), *Sotsiologicheskie Issledovaniia*, No. 1, 1989, pp.115-21.

22 Ye. N. Fetisov, 'Vperedi Bol'shaya Rabota' (We Have Much Work to Do!), *Sotsiologischeskie Issledovaniia*, No. 3, 1989, pp.123-4.

23 Voinova, *op. cit.*, p.151.

24 *Ibid.*

25 V. A. Yadov, 'Razmyshleniia o Predmete Sotsiologii' (Reflections on the Subject of Sociology), *Sotsiologicheskie Issledovaniia*, No. 2, 1990, p.15. The referee for the article in the *BJS* raised a question as to the nature and degree of the Soviet response to the expanding literature in the West on the subject of micro-macro relations. I found little evidence of any such response in print. My strong impression was that even at the level of discussion, the question was premature in the Soviet context which was largely, to adapt Weiss's phrase, at a formative stage of theoretical reorientation. Soviet sociology had yet to engage with the work of Bourdieu, Touraine, Giddens, Elias and others, and it is for that reason, among others, that I issued the plea with which this chapter concludes.

26 Looking back at their summer experience, two Soviet participants at the 1989 school stressed the importance of building 'footbridges' between the two sociological traditions and strengthening scientific contacts between the two countries; they also indicated that the school helped them to 'look at old things in a new way' (S. Yampol'skaya and I. Salovskaya, 'Manchester School for Young Sociologists', *Sotsiologischeskie Issledovaniia*, No. 5, 1990, p.149. Shanin's assessment of the 1989 school was that the Soviet participants found 'their exposure to multiplicity of styles of teaching, methods of approach, alternative perspectives and human contacts was particularly useful ...' (T. Shanin, *First Summer School of Soviet Sociologists: Director's Report*, Manchester, Manchester University, 1989, p.7), while Pahl emphasised the 1990 change which ensured that each student worked on producing a scholarly article with the help of an individual advisor, thus leading to the development of contacts within the UK for the Soviet students (R. E. Pahl, *Summer School for Soviet Sociologists: Final Report*, Canterbury, University of Kent, 1990, p.3).

9
Concluding Thoughts – Past, Present and Future

This book has not been an exhaustive study of the development and flourishing of Soviet sociology, but was rather designed to show the beginnings and some changes in the growth of the discipline, especially accentuating the period up to the 1970s. This revised edition of the original book was sparked by two independent requests, one from my graduate students who were using the original book as a textbook on the development of sociology in order to teach a younger generation of post-Soviet sociologists about the history of their own discipline, and more importantly, by meeting younger Russian sociologists at conferences in the West who seemed curious to read a Westerner's – hopefully, a more or less non-biased one at that – approach to the history of their newly evolving discipline. The latter group were keen that such a book would be neither a white-wash nor a total condemnation of the past: in other words, they stressed that they did not wish to read a re-written history of the discipline in the light of the downfall of the Soviet Union.[1] This project was revitalised with these requests in mind.

Fighting for Legitimacy

Sociology fought for legitimacy within the Soviet system from the Twentieth Party Congress in 1956, seeking recognition and support within three distinct spheres – the academic community, the population at large and the official world.

The struggle for the right to exist as an independent academic discipline took place on several levels. On one of these, sociology had to demonstrate the necessity for a social science – let alone a discipline – in addition to historical materialism. After all, was not historical materialism already Marxist sociology? On another level, sociology had to emphasize that it was not an outgrowth of bourgeois sociology. Thus, its roots in the Soviet past had to be stressed. Here the advocates of sociology could rely not only upon quotations about the subject from Marx and Lenin, but also upon the revived interest and work of sociologists from other socialist countries, in particular Czechoslovakia, Poland and Rumania. The discussions which had begun in the 1950s on sociology's right to exist diminished in intensity, but did not entirely cease before 1991. Although the problem of the relationship between historical materialism and sociology was not permanently 'solved', for all practical purposes sociology won recognition as an independent science. The next step was to secure the right to teach the discipline and carry out research.

With regard to the question of popular acceptance, the public was first urged to participate in sociological research in the 1960 when the youth newspaper, *Komsomol'skaia Pravda*, opened its Public Opinion Institute. The Institute began its investigations by ascertaining the opinions on very general subjects, such as war, but later concentrated on less abstract and more practical problems, such as the service industries. These polls helped to accustomed the public to 'sociological' methods, specifically to questionnaires and it is probably correct to assume that sociology was equated with questionnaire research in the minds of the general public. Academic acceptance for public opinion research was evident in October 1970, when Rumiantsev, then the director of the Institute of Concrete Social Research, asked the Central Committee of the CPSU to establish an independent institute for public opinion research.[2]

As far as the official world is concerned, it is apparent that work in the ill-defined subject of sociology was again permitted in the late 1950s. The following indicate the slow-growing acceptance of sociology. The Twentieth Party Congress of the CPSU in 1956 and the subsequent thaw did allow sociology to take its first steps. The 1960 Party Programme in heralding the building of communism requested the help of social scientists in its construction. The Twenty-Third Party Congress in 1966 specifically recognized sociology as an independent discipline, as sociology was seen as an instrument which, by providing both information and analysis, helped to prevent the regime from losing contact with reality and might help in planning and controlling society, as well as understanding it. In 1968, the Politburo accepted suggestions from the USSR Academy of Sciences about the organization of the first major academic institution, the Institute of Concrete Research, which began to function actively in the period of 1969-72. In 1972 the Institute was renamed the Institute of Sociological Research and in 1988 the Central Committee of the CPSU adopted a resolution on 'Enhancing the role of Marxist-Leninist sociology in the solution of major problems of Soviet society', which recognized sociology as an independent and legitimate discipline, renaming the Institute of Concrete Social Research, the Institute of Sociology.

Although the legitimation of sociology was achieved in broad terms, Soviet sociologists continued to encounter certain structural obstacles. Until 1968, when sociology was finally given its own Institute in the Academy of Sciences, it remained the illegitimate offspring of philosophy. There can be no doubt that some of the continuous demands for the establishment of the Institute were related to the would-be benefits of direct monetary backing; complaints about inadequate, if at times non-existent, financing were frequent. The establishment of the Institute also affected co-operation and/or co-ordination between sociologists themselves and between them and other social scientists. Soviet sociologists seemed to call repeatedly for this, implying that co-operation might have achieved better research facilities and the sharing of data and techniques. Another problem was reduced when at least one journal, *Sotsiologicheskie Issledovaniia*, was published specifically intended for sociologists, thus alleviating the necessity for articles on sociology to appear in a wide variety of journals as well as in the daily press. There was the further problem of obtaining statistical materials: either statistics in certain 'unsafe' areas were gathered and kept secret, or they were not collected at all. Either way, the sociologists' work was hindered.

Limits of the Soviet System

One might of course argue that all of these constraints are minor in comparison with the limits that the overall Soviet system imposed. Could, in fact, sociology develop within such a system? Undoubtedly, considerable, if uneven, development had taken place since the 1917 Revolution. In the very broadest sense, the discipline was very much tied up with the atmosphere inside the Soviet Union; as a barometer, the practice of sociology indicated the degree to which the Soviet Union would permit a concrete examination of existing social conditions. This study has traced this progression. But what are the factors, peculiar to the system, which limited sociologists?

The general ethos within which Soviet sociology operated can best be described as one of 'problem-solving'. The question as to why some areas were studied and others were not can certainly be explained in this way. This is particularly so to the extent that one recognizes the dual significance of this problem-solving orientation. On one level, research into non-concrete, non-utilitarian fields was rarely undertaken; research attempted to answer actual problems in concrete terms. Equally significant, however, is the fact that by encouraging a broad empiricist concern with isolated problems of whatever significance, the orientation prevented the development of theory and research into the dynamics of the whole society. Most importantly, the problem-solving approach effectively prevented the development of studies concerned with the distribution of power in the Soviet Union and with such factors as power and ideology as determinants or functions of patterns of industrialization and social change. The problem-solving prospective would appear to be closely related to the circumstances surrounding the revival of sociology from the mid-1950s onwards. A discipline emphasising the need for fact gathering and interpretation could advance its claims within a climate of political re-orientation in which the regime sought to emphasize a break with the dogmas of the past and to establish and maintain contact with social reality. 'Concrete sociological research' is an apt title for sociology in the Soviet Union.

To a greater or lesser extent, the system did dictate what was to be researched, what was to be investigated. Soviet sociologists studied some areas of society in great depth while studiously avoiding others. For example, the period of the cult of personality – that is, twenty or more years of Soviet history – was pointedly ignored. Other topics – in 'non problem' areas – had to be approached by circuitous routes. Thus the role of sex was only gradually being considered in research on the family. But, on the whole, research which had critical implications for the existing social system or which tended to imply change in directions either beyond the control of or alien to the broad goals of the regime was not undertaken. While it is quite possible that some sociological research was conducted which had not been published and which examined more sensitive areas, the amount was probably quite small. The same, however, may not be true for those findings which in one way or another differed from those anticipated.[3]

At the same time, it is virtually impossible to correlate what sociologists actually did or did not study with what they were or were not permitted to investigate. Soviet researchers chose an area of research on a variety of grounds, either because: 1) he/she was directed or encouraged to study that topic; or 2) he/she knew that the area was previously studied and hence was acceptable; or 3) he/she would be financed for the research; or 4) he/she would be able to improve his/her academic position; or 5) he/she found it intrinsically interesting, etc. The researcher then faced the question of how to investigate the problem. If certain methods or approaches were considered non-acceptable either on empirical grounds or for ideological reasons, then the researcher followed a more or less prescribed course of action. But this type of restraint increasingly became less operative. It was at the editorial level of both journals and publishing houses that the work of the sociologist may have been constrained. Once again, however, it is difficult to know what had been edited out of or added to his/her work and on what grounds the omissions and additions occurred.

Professional disagreements or perhaps different professional approaches could account for some of the above 'editorialising'. In fact, Schlapentokh, a Soviet sociologist who emigrated to the West in Soviet times, saw his fellow sociologists not as a monolithic group but as falling into one of three groups: the professionals (or liberals) whose mission was to debunk the ideology and objectively explain social behaviour; the ideologists (or conservatives) who sought to defend the official ideology by utilizing the prestige of empirical sociology; or the managerial sociologists who attempted little or no confrontation as they got on with reputable purposeful research, with 'every member of the discipline know[ing] the camp to which he or she, and everyone else, belongs.' Each group, of course, had vested interests.[4]   Another Soviet (non-émigré) writer has categorised his fellow sociologists as the: 1) '*dogmatists*, to whom everything is clear; 2) *revisionists*, who attempt to improve social science on the basis of classical Marxism, and sometimes with an admixture of classical sociology; 3) specialists, who know something about sociology, economics and law etc. in foreign countries, but nothing about life in their own country ...' Within all of these three categories, continues Kordonskii, were both theorists and empiricists.[5] Vested interests and empirical versus theoretical divisions accounted for many divisions, as we know to be the case in many academic disciplines outside of the Soviet Union. Most recently, documents in the second volume of *Sotsiologiia i Vlast* reveal controversy both between established parts of the sociological community and leading representatives of the power structure, and within the sociological environment itself.[6]

However, we do not know specifically what type of material was not published nor on what grounds. Another constraint faced by Soviet sociologists was access or lack of access to 'bourgeois' work in the libraries. I had a personal and enlightening experience relevant to this issue. As a graduate student at the LSE, I met Tatiana Zaslavskaya in the late 1960s. I agreed to send a variety of Western sociological books to her in Novosibirsk. The trouble arose, however, when she thanked me for sending a tome by Max Weber, when I had actually sent her a book by Robert Merton. This 'confusion' happened twice, at which point I decided not to send any more books to my Soviet colleague! Finally, while the researcher may have been limited over the choice of research, methodological approach and the outlets for publication, the ultimate influence of his/her research may have been inconsequential; certain research findings would not have been implemented because, among other reasons, they would affect vested interests.

Other 'intangible' constraints on the Soviet sociologist include ghosts of the past. The cult of personality certainly left its mark. 'The fear of responsibility, a fear surviving from the times when unthinking "quotationitis" often substituted for serious research, still lingers...'[7] This can certainly explain a large, but decreasing, number of relatively innocuous and useless pieces of work which were supposedly sociological in nature but were, in fact, a mere 'stringing together' of quotations from classical Marxist-Leninist-Stalinist sources. The role of Soviet history in shaping sociology cannot be ignored.

What role did Marxism-Leninism play in shaping sociological research? Soviet social theorists would have been the first to stress that social science – and hence sociology – is not value free. The researcher is a member of a society and consequently reflects the norms and values of that society. The result was that 'Marxist sociology and Marxist ideology are internally and indissolubly bound together'[8] and that 'sociology is a party science. The world outlook of the scientist, his social and political sympathies, his social position affect the methodology and even the method of research and, consequently, the results.'[9] But do they? This argument appears to amount to little more than that the system determined the areas from within which questions of sociological research may be approached. Any alternative view is dependent on the position that there is a specifically identifiable and distinctive Soviet sociology. Little evidence can be adduced to support such a position. This is to recognize that Soviet sociology is distinctive in a national rather than in an intellectual, that is, specifically Marxist, way.

Some Soviet sociologists began to reach the point at which they actively questioned or directly criticized Marxism. Nonetheless, the position stated by N. Preobrazhenskii in 1922 was generally still operative when the Soviet Union ceased to exist.

> Marxists may argue in part about the theory of method(s), still more about the means of its application; their concrete works may be completely different in content..., but they do not argue and do not compete with each other in the sphere of the basic position of Marxism.[10]

And yet, leading Soviet sociologists during *perestroika* were in fact questioning 'the basic position of Marxism' as the only or sole acceptable theory to be used in analyzing Soviet society. The possibility that Marxism in the form of a critical approach to social analysis would become institutionalized in the Soviet Union was extremely remote. With more and more empirical research, certain aspects of Marxism-Leninism were being questioned – accepted, discarded or modified – and new theories advanced as the theoretical foundation began to alter.[11] The beginnings of this were evident, for example, in the discussion of social stratification.

From Glasnost to Perestroika

With *glasnost* and *perestroika* came a changing role for sociology. As *perestroika* progressed, sociologists played a more confident and active part in the general transformation and liberalization of Soviet society. Armed with knowledge about the realities of Soviet social problems, sociologists were able to criticize the regime and expose actual social situations as well as participate in the reformation. Sociology became a tool of reform, a tool of liberalization, an instrument for changing political realities. Dissent and criticism became virtues. Sociology as social engineering became more plausible.

Sociology was actively involved in politics and the political agenda of the communist party.[12] In her inaugural address as President of the Soviet Sociological Association, Zaslavaskaya indicated that sociology was to supply the government with 'full, precise and truthful information about the needs, interests, values and behaviour of social groups under the given conditions as well as about the possible effects of this behaviour on social processes.'[13] And at a conference organized by two committees of the International Sociological Association in Moscow in 1989, Borodkin from Novosibirsk appealed to Soviet sociologists to participate in political life and political commitment, reduce social tension and social conflict, and articulate interests of deprived social groups.[14]

In sum, since 1956 Soviet sociology was a discipline attempting to develop within the context of a particular society. The ideological orientation of the Soviet regime clearly produced a particular set of problems for the development of 'an independent sociology'. Broadly speaking, these problems were manifested in two ways: in the form of questions as to the possible relationship between this ideological basis and any conceivable sociology, and in the form of a perceived threat to the regime from the development of the discipline. From the discussion of the structural and ideological factors above, it is clear that the latter may have had greater specific significance for sociology's continued development. Nevertheless, this should not obscure the fact that Soviet sociology also shared problems common to other sociologies throughout the world.

Public Opinion and Time Budget Research

In the 1960s and 1970s, public opinion research did not seek to enquire about attitudes representative of the population in general nor was research about non-controversial themes nor unwanted public opinion explored (see Chapter 6). Some time elapsed after the opening of the All-Union Centre for Public Opinion Research in 1988 before the Centre (VTsIOM) began to examine some non-controversial issues and to engage in a really systematic survey of popular attitudes. By the end of 1989, formerly 'controversial' topics such as the popularity of individual politicians and the role of the communist party were feasible areas to research. By 1991, as Wyman notes, 'no issue was in principle off-limits for study'.[15] It was even acceptable to obtain previously untapped public opinion as public opinion had a legitimate right to exist and be analyzed.

The early 1990s saw a vast increase in those academics, researchers, institutions and other organizations, including the more liberal press, involved in conducting mass opinion studies. But with the spread of public opinion research came a repetition of most of the very same criticism expressed in the 1960s: that is, criticism about how representative the samples were of a very large population, how the questionnaires were constructed (e.g. what was the exact wording of any particular question and was it too vague or ambiguous); why the percentages of responses did not necessarily add up to 100 per cent; what margins of error were permissible; and what did the figures actually mean (see White's discussion). The use of the results from the polls were often speculative, if at times mainly quite casual.[16] Calls were expressed for better training and more professional responsibility by those organizations carrying out public opinion research – both academic and commercial.

Some organizations were praised for their research, most notably the State Statistics Committee, followed by VTsIOM. Although too numerous to name, other important organizations include: International Foundation for Political-Legal research = Interlegal (1989); 'Indem' Foundation = Information Science for Democracy (1990); Foundation 'Public Opinion' (1990); and 'Vox Populi', an outgrowth of VTsIOM (by Grushin).[17] Also commended were those individual Russian sociologists who helped to establish the basic infrastructure for the study of public opinion in Russia, people such as Yuri Levada and Boris Grushin. These are the people now concerned with utilizing and questioning different research methodologies and also debating professional questions (including professional ethics) in relation to this type of research. There is no doubt that research techniques have improved and public opinion pollsters have certainly become more professional. By the mid-1990s methods used in public opinion research were certainly moving toward international standards.[18]

Unlike in Soviet times, a wide range of attitudes are currently being investigated, including ascertaining opinions about political, social, economic, religious, national/ethnic, etc., topics. It is also possible to compare surveys carried out in the late Gorbachev period with those taking place since the fall of the Soviet Union and also to compare attitudes between different surveys conducted at different time periods since 1991 (e.g. 1994 and 1999). For example, the Moscow School of Political Studies (established 1992) jointly with the Centre for Post-Collectivist Studies (established 1995) publishes the journal *Russia on Russia* which carries discussions of many of the surveys conducted by VTsIOM. [See also the website www.wciom.ru for the latest surveys.]

The other area examined in detail in this book is that of time budget research. The only update I wish to mention here is the most recent work of Vasilii Patrushev, namely, *The Time Budget and Changes in the Living Activities of City Dwellers Between 1965 and 1998*.[19] Patrushev's research group at the Institute of

Sociology at the Russian Academy of Sciences conducted time budget research in 1965 and 1986, and most recently in 1997-98 in the city of Pskov, taken to be a 'typical Russian city' (see Chapter 7). Overall the research substantiated the fact that women in the age group 18-25 have had and have less free time then men: in 1965 they had 21 hours of free time compared to 33 hours of free time per week for men; by 1987 women had gained five hours of free time; and by 1997-98 they had 29 hours of free time compared to 31 hours for men.

Two other striking conclusions may be drawn from the three studies. The first is that between 1965 and 1986 the reduction in domestic work (that is, housework) for women was due to the increased availability of labour- and time-saving appliances and not at all to an increase in men sharing or even taking over the responsibilities for the housework. The second conclusion concerns the change between 1986 and 1997-98 in actual paid working hours for women, that is, in 1997/98 women worked seven hours less than they did in 1986, a drop from 40 hours to 33 hours per week. Patrushev suggests that this shift reflects compulsory short-term working; in other words, this reflects the effects of unemployment on women, which of course would vary from city to city. And a final note about these time budgets: as mentioned above in regard to public opinion research, the latest sample covered just 231 people (88 men and 143 women), compared with 2,671 people in 1965 and 1,853 people in 1986, so common errors of sampling should most probably be assumed.

The Future of Russian Sociology

The discussion of the role and development of sociology in Russia since 1991 has for some Russians been a continuation of a general consensus regarding the analysis of sociology in the *perestroika* period. By this I mean that, according to this view, sociology was and will be seen as being essentially a tool for social reform. Zaslavskaya, for example, states this explicitly in her seminal pieces on *perestroika* (see Chapter 8). Or put succinctly by Gray (1993): Russian sociology is a 'reliable handmaiden to desired social reform', as well as a handmaiden to 'enlightened' social reform.[20] From *perestroika* to post-1991 Russia and thereafter, this implies using whatever data are actually collected to aid the reform agenda, to transform [Soviet/Russian] society, and to make sociology socially relevant. It also highlights the increasing openness – glasnost, if you will – of examining new topics of research, often in areas which used to be off-limits, either for political and/or ideological reasons, as well as being able both to expose and analyze actual social situations.[21]

Alongside this view is another approach which implies adopting as well as adapting sociological and social methodologies, often of Western origin. With the downfall of the USSR has come the availability and acceptability of utilizing these – non-Marxist – approaches, methods and methodologies, let alone 'theories', in the pursuit of analyzing Russian society. These 'approaches' have stimulated the new generation of Russian sociologists, some of whom are being educated in the West, and who are contributing to foreign journals and symposia; new journals are appearing in Russia itself; and a new community of sociologists is evolving who have little history or sympathy with the Soviet past, some of whom nowadays are collaborating with foreign scholars.

But what are the problems presently faced by Russian sociology? Russian critics of Russian sociology in recent years complain that sociology is currently distinguished by 'theoretical confusion' and 'lack of discrimination' (*vseyadnost'*, literally omnivorousness) and by urgently needing appropriate tools of research.[22] The discipline is also criticized for the fact that with the demise of the Soviet Union came the increasing commercialization of sociology.[23] This often took the form of an increase in the number of public opinion surveys proliferating throughout the country, mainly because public opinion surveys were an easy and cheap form of research. The consequences of this proliferation, say Russian sociologists, are that the public significantly equates sociological research with public opinion research. A further note of criticism concerns the general reduction in state financing to all educational institutions and research institutes. This reduction has consequently and adversely affected both the growth and the carrying out of contemporary sociological work and has hindered the education and training of the new and future generation(s) of sociologists.

In trying to re-establish a specifically Russian sociology as distinct from Soviet sociology, Russian authors indicate that sociologists need to know the past in order to educate the new generation.[24] Sometimes this involves establishing the subject and method(s) of sociology as a growing and developing discipline distinct from, for example, history or philosophy in tsarist times. This might involve examining: the evolution of the philosophy of Russian sociology; the growth of the subject and methods of sociology as a separate discipline among other social sciences; and the interaction of sociology and the political process.[25] By examining Russian social thought current at the end of the nineteenth/beginning of the twentieth century, proponents of this position contend that this would facilitate a better understanding of contemporary social theory. There are some problems I see here: some books chronicling the history of Russian sociology have a very wide understanding of the definition of sociologist. For example, they include Georgi Plekhanov, intellectual leader of the Russian Social-Democrat movement, or Piotr Lavrov, philosopher and ideologist of populism, as sociologists. Others argue that sociologists started in the juridical schools of Russia (including B. N. Chicherin and M. M. Kovalevsky), moved to historical work (N. I. Kareev, N. P. Pavlov-Silvansky and V. O. Kliuchevsky), and then onwards to the study of the political or revolutionary process (P. N. Miliukov and M. Ostrogorski).[26]

There is no doubt that it is valuable to unearth and circulate thinking about the Russian past, but do we equate social thinkers with sociologists? If the answer is yes – and it seems to be the case for current Russian writers – then two related outcomes are credible. The first allows the Russians to establish 'their' own distinctive lineage of social thought in comparison with Soviet sociology: this implies that Russian sociology could and should be much freer than Soviet sociology since Soviet sociology was so actively connected with the party-state or, even more forcibly argued, that Soviet sociology was an 'imperial sociology'.[27]

The other outcome extends the argument even further: Russian sociologists may also establish 'their' social thought in comparison with sociological theories advanced in the West and this allows Russian sociology potentially to become independent from the West. As indicated above, there are a number of Russian authors today who, with these aims in mind, are investigating Russian sociologists who worked in tsarist times with the express intention of showing the existence, as well as the worth, of these non-Bolshevik academics, advancing the argument that these men contributed to Russian as well as to world sociology before 1917. On a somewhat different tack, others, such as Kachanov, have argued that the aim of Russian sociology is to create an original national sociology.[28] The flag of Russian nationalism is certainly evident in some of these accounts.

Questions about the future of sociology in Russia remain. There are indications that the old nineteenth century Slavophile vs Westernizer debates are surfacing again. In a similar way, there is an emerging question as to whether Russian sociology will become a largely national academic discipline or aspire to becoming an internationally recognized discipline and internationally collaborating discipline. As with Soviet sociology, Russian sociology performs functions, faces obstacles and shares problems in common with other sociologies at the beginning of the twenty-first century.

---

1 In 1997, an editorial committee made up of academics from the Institute of Social-Political Research of the Russian Academy of Science and the Centre for the Conservation of Contemporary Documentation of the Russian Federal Archive Service began to publish what is hoped to be a series of collected documents entitled *Sociology and Power* (*Sotsiologiia i Vlast'*, Vol. 1 (1953-1968) and Vol. 2 (1969-1972), Moscow, Russian Academy of Sciences and Russian State Archive, 1997 and 2001 (Vol. 1 is edited by L. Moskvichev and Vol. 2 by G. Osipov *et al.*). The primary goal of the two volumes published to date is to demonstrate the actual status of Soviet sociology and Soviet sociologists and their respective relation to the power structure, specifically the Central Committee of the CPSU. The publication of official documents and memoirs from party, state and scientific organizations' archives from the 1950s to the 1990s (although Volume 2 only goes up to 1972) demonstrates, say the authors, the 'dramatic and even tragic' (Vol. 1, p.5) history of Soviet sociology and its 'persecution' as a discipline. [Some of the sources are still not declassified.] The documents publicize 'full details of the entire political spiritual atmospheres of the historical period under review.' (*Ibid.* p.7.)
2 *Ibid.* Vol. 2, p.16.
3 For a discussion about relations between party and the natural sciences and similar as well as different problems faced in the natural sciences, see L. Graham, *Science and Philosophy in the Soviet Union*, New York, 1972; L. Graham, *Science in Russia and the Soviet Union*, Cambridge, 1993; D. Joravsky, *Soviet Marxism and Natural Science*, New York, 1961; S. Solomon, 'Reflections on Western Studies of Soviet Science', in L. L. Lubrano and S. G. Solomon (eds.), *The Social Context of Soviet Science*, Boulder, Colorado, 1980; J. L. Roberg, *Soviet Science Under Control: The Struggle for Influence*, London, 1998; M. Adams, 'Science, Ideology and Structure: The Kol'tsov Institute, 1900-1970' in Lubrano and Solomon, *op. cit.*

4 V. Shlapentokh, *The Politics of Sociology in the Soviet Union*, Boulder, Colorado, Westview Press, 1987, p.85.

5 S. Kordonskii quoted in A. Filippov, 'A Final Look Back at Soviet Sociology', *International Sociology*, 1993, 8(3), p.366.

6 *Sotsiologiia i Vlast'*, *op. cit.*, (Vol. 2), p.19.

7 S. Kovalev, 'Voprosy Teorii: Trebovaniia Zhizni i Obshchestvennye Nauki', *Pravda*, 6 May 1966, p.3.

8 F. V. Konstantinov, 'Vorposy Teorii:Filosofiia Revoliutsionnoi Epokhi', *Pravda*, 24 July 1967, p.3.

9 V. Shlapentokh, *Sotsiologiia Dlia Vsekh*, Moscow,

10 N. Preobrazhenskii, 'Blizhaiskie Zadachi Sotsialisticheskoi Akademii', Vestnik Sotsialisticheskoi Akademii', *Vestnik Sotsialisticheskoi Akademii*, No. 1, 1922, p.6.

11 D. Shalin, 'Sociology for the *Glastnost* Era: Institutional and Substantive Changes in Recent Soviet Sociology', *Social Forces*, 1990, 68(4), p.1028.

12 See an interesting article about the growth of political sociology in the Soviet Union/Russia by V. Voronkov and E. Zdravomyslova, 'Emerging Political Sociology in Russia and Russian Transformation', *Current Sociology*, 1996, 44(3), pp.40-52.

13 T. I. Zaslavskaya, quoted in Filippov, *op. cit.*, p.361.

14 J. Musil, 'Moscow Conference Report II: A View from Eastern Europe', *International Journal of Urban and Regional Research*', 1990, 14(2), p.317.

15 M. Wyman, *Public Opinion in Postcommunist Russia*, London, Macmillan, 1997, p.6.

16 S. White, 'Public Opinion and Political Science in Post-Communist Russia', *European Journal of Political Research*, 1995, pp.507-26; *Russia's New Politics*, 2000, pp.182-94.

17 See footnote 28 in Filippov, *op. cit.*, p.370, for more organizations.

18 White, *op. cit.*, p.523.

19 V. Patrushev, *Zhizn' Gorozhanina* (1965-1998), Moscow, Academic, 2000 and V. Patrushev, *Biudzhet Vremeni i Peremeny v Zhizhnedeitatel'nosti Gorodskish Zhitelei v 1965-1998 Godakh*, Moscow, Institute of Sociology RAN, 2001.

20 D. Gray, 'Russian Sociology: The Second Coming of August Comte', *American Journal of Economics and Sociology*, 1993, 53(2), p.173 and p.170.

21 E. Z. Myrskaya, 'Soviet Sociology: Fateful History and Present-Day Paradoxes of Fate', *Canadian Journal of Sociology*, 1991, 16(7), pp.75-78. See also A. Jones, 'Soviet Sociology, Past and Present', *Contemporary Sociology*, 1989, 18, pp.316-19.

22 A. O. Boronoev and V. V. Koslovskii (eds.), *Rossiiskaia Sotsiologiia: Istoriko-Sotsiologicheskie Ocherki*, Moscow, Russian State Humanitarian University, 1997, p.5.

23 The commercialization of sociology is discussed in both volumes of *Sotsiologiia i Vlast'* (1997 and 2001). See also T. I. Zaslavskaya, 'Rol' Sotsiologii v Preobrazovanii Rossii', *Sotsiologicheskie Issledovaniia*, 1996, No. 3, p.6.

24 See, for example, E. Kukushkina, *Russkaia Sotsiologiia XIX-nachala XX Veka*, Moscow, Moscow University, 1993.

25 For example, see A. Medushevskii, *Istoriia Russkoi Sotsiologii*, Moscow, Moscow Higher School, 1993.

26 See Boris Kargalitsky's chapter on the Russian intelligentsia (in B. Kargalitsky, *Russia Under Yeltsin and Putin*, London, Pluto Press, 2002) where he discusses how the restoration of capitalism has been accompanied by idealization of the past.

27 Filippov, *op. cit.*

28 I. L. Kachanov, 'Rossiiskaia Sotsiologia kak Sobytie', *Sotsiologicheskie Issledovaniia*, 2001, 3, pp.3-8.

Glossary

Apparat: system/machinery of administration; staff, personnel of the system/machinery of administration; the organization

Byt: daily life; (mode of) life; customs; habit

Gorkom: urban committee, usually of the party

Gosplan: State Planning Commission

ITR (inzhenerno-tekhnicheskie rabotniki): engineering and technical personnel, with a higher or secondary technical education, engaged in technical management of industry or transport

Kollektiv: collective; group; team; the (whole) body of employees, etc.

Krai: territory; an administrative subdivision of the RSFSR usually including autonomous *oblasti*

Narod: the people of a state; nation(ality); national group; (common) people; folk

Narodnost': nation(ality); ethnic national group(ing); nationalism; national characteristics

Oblast': region; an administrative sub-division of a Union Republic

Partiinost': 'Party-mindedness'; partisanship; seeing things and acting as one committed to realizing the future as envisioned by the party; group feeling; commitment

Raikom: district committee of the party

Raion: district; administrative area within *oblast'*, *krai* or republic

Sovkhoz: state farm

Sovnarkhoz: Regional Economic Council

Tekhnikum: specialized secondary school/institute, with two-to-four year courses, including general education, normally from age fourteen

Vuz: Higher educational establishment, a university or institute with degree courses

Zakonomernost': order; regularity; sequence; pattern; conformity to systematic/established law of nature or society

Appendix I
Komsomol'skaia Pravda
Public Opinion Polls

I. What do the Soviet people think? How do they appraise the present correlation of the forces of peace and war?

(*Komsomol'skaia pravda*: 19 May 1960)

1. Will mankind succeed in averting a war?
2. On what do you base your belief?
3. What must be done above all to strengthen peace?

II. How has your standard of living changed?

(*Komsomol'skaia pravda*: 7 October 1960)

1. How has your living standard changed in recent years?
   (Risen, Remained the same, Declined)
2. In what way is this manifested? To what do you first and foremost attribute this?
3. Which problem do you consider to be most urgent (underline):
   Shortening of the working day
   Increase in the output of consumer goods
   Housing construction
   Improvement in *byt* services (continued)
   Increase in food output
   Higher wages
   Expansion of the number of children's institutions
4. What do you suggest for the quickest solution to the problem you have indicated above?

III. What do you think about your generation?

(*Komsomol'skaia pravda*: 6 January 1961)

1. What do you think of your generation? Does it please you, and are you satisfied with its pursuits? (Yes or No)
2. On what do you base your statement?
3. In your opinion, what traits are the strongest in Soviet young people? Where

are they most clearly in evidence?

4. In your opinion, are there any negative characteristics common among young people? If your answer is yes, what are they?
5. What justification do you have for your opinion?
6. Which of the following, in your opinion, is more typical of your peers (underline one):
    Purposefulness – lack of goals?
7. Do you personally have a goal in life?
    (Yes, No, Have not thought about it)
8. What is it?
9. What must you do to achieve it?
10. What have you already done?
11. Do you think you will achieve this goal?
    (Yes, No, Don't know)
12. On what do you base your conviction?

IV. What do you think about the scouts of the future?

Part One (*Komsomol'skaia pravda*: 16 August 1961)

1. What do you see as the very strongest aspects of the life of the collectives of communist labour (in production, relations between people, culture, daily life, etc.)?
2. Which aspects of the development of the movement do you consider to be the most long-term?
3. The most important task of each komsomol is to join actively in the fight for communist labour. With which of the following problems do you connect (in the first place) the further mass spread of the movement?
    interest in new techniques
    raising education and culture
    improvement of professional mastery
    growth of consciousness
    possibly, what other problem?
4. From your point of view, what are the shortcomings which occur in the competition for communist labour?
5. What is your opinion about the existing procedure of acquiring honorary titles by the collectives? Are any changes needed in this procedure?
6. In what way should the wide mass of workers take part in awarding honorary titles? In your opinion, who ought to have the right of the deciding vote?
7. In your opinion, may a person be deprived of an honorary title? If yes, in which cases?

Part Two (*Komsomol'skaia pravda*: 23 September 1961)

1. What causes you the greatest difficulty in the struggle for the rank of collective of communist labour? What do you consider your most important achievement?

2. What new features distinguish your collective's labour (in regard to productive relations, creativity, consciousness, working without reward, etc.)?
3. What changes occurred in your life (culture, *byt*, relations between people, etc.) since the time you chose by precept 'to live in a communist way'?
4. To what degree and in what way does your collective influence the life of other people (patronage, educational work, help in work, etc.)? What, in your opinion, deserves wide dissemination from this experience?
5. From your point of view, which shortcomings occur in the competition for communist labour?
6. Same as 3 of Part One.
7. In what forms, in your opinion, will the movement for communist labour be developed in the future?
8. What is your opinion about the existing system of awarding honorary titles to collectives? Does this system need any changes?
9. Same as 6 of Part One.
10. Same as 7 of Part One.

V. What is your opinion of the young family?

(*Komsomol'skaia pravda*: 10 December 1961)

1. In your opinion, what are the strongest traits characterizing the Soviet family?
2. What do you value most in your own family?
3. From what still-existing survivals of the past, in your opinion, is it necessary for young families to free themselves?
4. What features in the upbringing of children in the Soviet family do you consider the best and most advanced?
5. In your opinion, what difficulties in the upbringing of children do families encounter at the present time?
6. What ways would you suggest for overcoming these difficulties?
7. Which of the following would be the most important in eliminating the vestiges of woman's inferior position in everyday life? (Underline)
    Expansion of the public forms of satisfying the needs of the family (personal service shops, enterprises of public eating, etc.)
    Lessening the woman's labour at production (emancipation from heavy work, night shifts, etc.)
    Expansion of the network of children's institutions (crèches, kindergartens, boarding schools, schools keeping open late, etc.)
    Participation of husband, of children in carrying out housework
    Lightening housework by means of mechanization
    Possibly, any other problem
8. In your opinion, how well prepared are young married people to create a family? How does a lack of preparation manifest itself?
9. In your opinion, is the existing marriage procedure in need of changes? If so, what changes?
10. Are changes needed in the existing procedure for the dissolution of a marriage?

11. How do you explain the break-up of young families?
12. What measures can you suggest for strengthening the young family?

Moscow University students: In the name of what are you studying?

(*Komsomol'skaia pravda*: 1 September 1962)

1. Which of the motives prompted you to devote yourself to your chosen speciality:
    tradition of the family
    romanticism of the profession
    the relative case of the job
    the desire to acquire popularity and glory
    sense of mission
    high pay for the given profession
    striving to move in cultured society
    impossibility to study your calling
    not thought of it
    possibly, what other kind of motive
2. What aim do you place before yourself in your work?
3. Will you succeed in attaining it?
    yes
    no
    don't know
4. What are you keen on besides your speciality (literature, art, technology, social work, sports, etc.)?
5. On completion of university, where and how do you intend to use the knowledge you have received?
6. Could something hinder your intentions? If yes, precisely what?

VI. How do you spend your free time?

(*Komsomol'skaia pravda*: 4 January 1963)

1. How much time, on the average, do you spend each day on the following:
    a. your main work (in the case of students, your studies)
    b. supplementary work to earn money
    c. everyday needs (housework, shopping for food and other items, making use of communal and service institutions, etc.)
    d. in transit from home to place of work (each way)
    e. evening or correspondence study at educational institutions
    f. care of children
    g. sleep
2. What do you do with the remaining free time? (How much time do you give to volunteer work, reading, sports, etc.? How often do you go to the cinema, the theatre, sports events, etc.?)

3. What do you do on your day off?
4. What would you like most of all to do with your free time?
5. What keeps you from spending your free time as you would like to:
   lack of time
   lack of the necessary conditions – amateur arts circles, sports groups, organized evening entertainment, etc.
   lack of cultural institutions
   lack of personal means
   fatigue after work
   inability to organize your time
   other reasons
6. What are the most important ways you see for making better use of leisure time?

VII. To Mars, with what?

(*Komsomol'skaia pravda*: 1 March 1963)

What should be carried in a rocket that is sent to Mars?
1. Photographs of what news event of the century should be placed in the capsule?
2. What document of importance for the history of mankind should we place in the capsule?
3. An account of what great person of our epoch?
4. A portrait of which person whose exploit has glorified the twentieth century?
5. A description of what outstanding scientific discovery of modern times?
6. A model of what technological invention?
7. What modern implement of labour?
8. What object of everyday life most typical of our times?
9. What sports equipment should we place in the capsule?
10. What work of literature?
11. What score of what musical work?
12. What feature film?
13. A reproduction of what painting or sculpture?
14. A model of what work of architecture?
15. There is still one empty space in the capsule. Suggest your own exhibit. What should it tell the Martians about life on earth?

VIII. Let's project – televisions, radios, etc.

(*Komsomol'skaia pravda*: 26 June 1964)

1. What type of television would you prefer?
   a. table
   b. on legs
   c. portable
   d. hinged (hung) in the corner

  e. mounted in sectional furniture
  f. furnished with earphones
  g. with a revolving screen
  h. with a screen (by the diagonals)
     35 centimetres 47 centimetres 59 centimetres and more
  If you wish, propose its construction

2. Do you need remote control?
  Television   Yes No
  Radio receiver   Yes No

3. Do you need an automatic record changer on the record-player?
               Yes No

4. What exterior decoration do you prefer?
  a. polished, dull
  b. natural colours of light, red warm wood
  c. plastics, coloured plastics (bright or muted tone)

5. Which brands do you have:
  Television
  Radio-receiver
  Record-player
  Tape recorder

6. What do you like about them?
  Exterior
  Loudness
  Position of controls
  Other technical data

7. What do you not like that we need to change?

IX. An innovation demands a name

(*Komsomol'skaia pravda*: 28 October 1964)

Please supply names for the following:
  Television
  Wireless set – radio receiver
  Radio-gramophone, radiogram
  Tape recorder – radio
  Magnetic tape recorder
  Record-player
  Dynamics of a relaying system

Children and words

(*Komsomol'skaia pravda*: 2 August 1964)

Twenty-five out of the fifty words which were listed:
  Altar' – altar

Baryshnik – profiteer
Bespridannitsa – dowerless girl
Biurokrat – *bureaucrat*
Goven'e – preparation for receiving the sacrament
Gol' perekatnaia – utter destitution
Domovoi – house spirit
Edinolochnik – private peasant
Katsap – (Polish) a Great Russian
Kustar' – homeworker (producer for the market); handicraft worker
Lapotnik – dealer in, maker of, bast shoes; primitive person (obsolete)
Mireod – peasant employer of labour; land grabber, usurer
Nakhlebnik – parasite
Polkulachnik – kulak follower or adherer
Podkhalim – yes-man, lickspittle
Seredniak – a middle peasant with own modest resources, but not
    employing labour
Sklochnitsa – squabbler, troublemaker
Skopidom – miser
Spetsy – specialist (especially of those remaining in the USSR after 1917
    but distrusted by the authorities)
Sutiaga – litigious person
Tolkuchka – second-hand merchant
Troitsa – Trinity (holiday – Whitsun)
Khanzha – sanctimonious hypocrite
Khokhol – nickname of the Little Russians

X. How do you rate the service industries?

(*Komsomol'skaia pravda*: 20 November 1964)

1. What, in your opinion, are the basic deficiencies in different spheres of
    service?
    Rate the following services:
        Trade
        Communal eating
        Transport
        Medical network (hospitals, pharmacies, sanatoria and others)
        Combines (integrated works) of everyday services (workshops,
            laundries, hairdressers, hotels and others)
        Cultural establishments (theatres, cinemas, clubs, libraries and
            others)
        Sports centres (stadia, sports halls, swimming pools and others)
        Communications enterprises (post, telegraph, telephone)
    Rate the services listed above *according to*:
        Unnecessary expenditures of time (because of a shortage of
            service points, duration of fulfilment of orders, etc.)

Inconvenient hours of service
Unsatisfactory organization of supplies
Work of poor quality, poor fulfilment of orders
Low calibre of service personnel

2. What services which you do not have the opportunity of using would you like to use?
3. In your opinion, the basic reasons for the deficiencies which you have noted include?
4. What do you value most of all in the existing work of the services?
5. What would you suggest to improve the system of services?

XI. Komsomol members about the komsomol

(*Komsomol'skaia pravda*: 26 April 1966)

1. Which trends in the komsomol's work ought to be developed first and foremost?
    a. participation in the management of the affairs of society
    b. participation in solving economic questions
    c. championing the interests and defending the rights of youth
    d. education of youth
2. With what questions is your komsomol organization primarily concerned?
3. What do you consider to be the greatest success and the greatest failure in the action of your organization?
4. How has the komsomol helped and what role did it play in attaining your life plans?
5. Have you ever raised any questions before your organization?
    If not, why not?
    If yes, were you satisfied by their conclusions?

    a. Are changes needed in the present practice of admission into the komsomol?
        If yes, precisely what?
    b. Are changes needed in the present system of reports and elections in the komsomol? If yes, precisely what?
6. What are the main qualities that a present-day komsomol leader should possess?

XII. Holidays – How can you best spend them?

Part One (*Komsomol'skaia pravda*: 23 June 1966)

1. In your opinion, what are the basic positive aspects of the organization of the annual holiday of our country's population?
2. In your opinion, what are the basic inadequacies in the organization of the holiday?

3. On the whole, how do you evaluate the organization of the annual holiday?
   Good   Satisfactory   Poor
4. Which categories of people have the best organized leisure and which the worst (age, occupation, social position, etc.)?
   In what ways is this manifested?
5. Which types of holiday do you consider the most valuable?
   - those promoting the strengthening of health and morals, raising culture and developing relations between people (underline any one)
   - staying in houses of rest, sanitoria, pensions, etc
   - staying in places of rest under your own steam (without passes)
   - tourism (walking, by water, etc.) journeys
   - excursions, trips to cities
   - staying at home, at a dacha, in a village with relatives
   - staying at a sports camp, in homes for fishermen and hunters, etc
   - journeys with youth groups (detachments) to construction, to *sovkhoz*, kolkhoz, etc

   Explain why you think this.
6. What, in your opinion, can play a decisive role in improving the holiday of workers today? (mark any one)
   - extending the construction of rest houses, tourist camps and centres, hotels, etc., bettering the organization of leisure
   - increasing income (as a means of carrying out leisure)
   - raising the culture of leisure, the ability to organize it wisely
   - increasing the duration of holidays
7. In your opinion, which areas of leisure should be developed today in the first place? (underline any one)
   - traditional zones of leisure (Crimea, Caucasus, Pre-Baltic, suburban regions of large centres)
   - new, still unopened zones of leisure

   If the latter, then which regions do you have in mind?
8. What do you consider to be most expedient:
   to preserve the existing tradition of having a holiday once a year, or
   to change it, dividing (according to desire) a holiday in two sections?
9. According to established tradition, the majority of the people of our country take a holiday exclusively in the summer or at the beginning of the autumn. Do you think this is right, and why does this occur? Should we change the present tradition? If yes, then what, in your opinion, must be done for the development of leisure at other times of the year?
10. In your opinion, what today limits most of all the possibility of parents and children having a holiday together?
    What ways do you propose for the solution of the problem?
11. What do you consider to be the basic problems in the organization of the leisure of youth aged fifteen to eighteen?
    What do you propose to do in this direction?
12. Which conditions must we create in the first place in order to guarantee the subsequent development of mass tourism in our country?

XII. How would you like to spend your holiday?

Part Two (*Komsomol'skaia pravda*: 29 July 1966)

1. What do you think a good rest should give to a healthy person? (indicate by
    order of importance)
    -   remove tiredness, give strength for further work
    -   strengthen health, toughen physically
    -   expand the horizon (views), get new knowledge
    -   distract from usual cares
    -   increase number of acquaintances, connections with interesting
        people
2. What, in your opinion, has the most significance for the realization of good
    and valuable leisure (underline):
    material possibilities or the ability of a person to rest
3. In your opinion, when we plan the future leisure of the population, which
    group(s) of holiday makers must we have in mind, first and foremost?
    -   leisure with the family
    -   leisure in the company of friends, colleagues, professional colleagues
    -   leisure with unknown company
    -   leisure alone
4. In view of the working out of measures on the subsequent improvement of the
    organization of leisure in the country, which types of leisure - in your opinion
    - should be shown preference?
    -   leisure by travelling with a free travel warrant or without a free
        travel warrant
    -   leisure in one place or by transferring from one place to another
5. In view of the development of the material base of leisure, to what should we
    today turn our main attention? (underline any one)
    -   construction of many-storeyed buildings of a city type
    -   construction of small homes (cottages) for several people
    -   construction of light, prefabricated little homes
    -   construction of tents, camps
6. What do you think? Is it necessary to attract the (monetary) means of the
    population for the extension of the material base of leisure? (underline)
    Yes   No   Don't know
    If yes, how do you introduce this?
7. Why do you suppose that tourism received such wide development especially
    in the last years, and how?
8. In your opinion, the further spread of mass tourism in our country depends on
    the development of what kind of transportation? (underline)

    Depends on:

    Public transportation (rail,   Individual transportation
    sea, bus and other   OR   (increase number of
    communications)   personal cars, scooters,
                                                launches and others)

9. What kind of role in the choice of place and means of leisure do the existing sources of information play today? (indicate by order of importance)
    -   advertising prospectus
    -   radio and television
    -   advice of friends and acquaintances
    -   special information, books, pictures, atlases
    -   newspaper and magazine articles
    -   artistic literature, films
10. What can you suggest for improving information about difference types of leisure?

XIII. The reader about himself and about the newspaper

(*Komsomol'skaia pravda*: 12 October 1966)

1. How did you become acquainted with our newspaper?
    -   subscribed at home
    -   read the newspaper subscribed to by your institution
    -   bought it at a kiosk
    -   read it at a street display stand
    -   read it at your neighbour's, acquaintance's
    -   read it at a library, club, recreation and reading room
2. For how many years have you subscribed to the newspaper?
3. Do you intend to subscribe to *Komsomol'skaia pravda* in 1967?
    Yes   No
    On what is your decision based?
4. How regularly do you read the paper?
    Daily
    Several times a week
    Only on Saturdays and Sundays
    Irregularly
5. Which sections of our paper interest you most of all? (mark by degree of importance – not more than three)
    -   problems of youth, of komsomol life
    -   economics, questions of industry and agriculture
    -   propaganda of Leninism, problems of theory, analysis of practical activity
    -   sports
    -   international life
    -   science and technology
    -   materials on historical-revolutionary, military-patriotic themes
    -   questions of morals and *byt*
    -   culture, literature, art
    -   problems of secondary and higher education
6. Which other newspapers do you subscribe to and read regularly?

7. Are other newspapers on the same plane as *Komsomol'skaia pravda*, or do
    they answer your needs better?
8. What do you see as the strong aspects of *Komsomol'skaia pravda*?
9. Which materials under the regular headings of the newspaper do you more or
    less read regularly? Which practically never? 49 choices were listed here
    (e.g. letters to the editor, etc.). The Public Opinion Institute was listed in
    sixteenth place.
10. How much time, on the average, do you usually spend reading our newspaper
    during the day?

	Work days	Sundays
10-15 minutes		
15-30 minutes		
30 minutes to one hour		
More than one hour		

11. Is this time adequate for you to read everything that you would like to read in
    the paper?

	Work days	Sundays
Yes		
No		

Appendix II
Time Budget Research

A. Time budget blank for workers and office workers

I.   General information about the respondent and his family
    Data from the enquiry ---------- Number of time budget -----------
    Shift – day, evening, night

1.   Republic, *krai, oblast'*
        City, workmen's settlement
    Branch of industry
2.   Where one works (name of enterprise, institution, organization)
3.   Sex
4.   Age (completed years)
5.   Education:
        Up to third grade
        Elementary
        Seventh year
        General secondary school
        Special secondary school
        Higher, incomplete
        Higher
6.   Where one studies:
        At day educational institutions or schools
        At night educational institutions
        By correspondence (educational institutions)
        Course for raising qualifications and schools of progressive methods
        Other forms of study (network of party education, of universities of culture, and others)
7.   In what capacity does one work (position or specific duties)
8.   For non-workers, indicate the source of one's means of subsistence:
        Pension
        Stipend
        Dependent on others
        Other sources of means of subsistence
9.   Wage category (for a worker), number of grades in the wage category
10. Average per cent of fulfilling production norms (for piecework) during the past month:
        up to 100 per cent
        100-105 per cent

      105-110 per cent
      110-125 per cent
      125 per cent and more

11. Overall length of service, ...
      According to speciality
12. Extra wages for the past month
13. General daily income, on the average, for one member of the family for -------
    month, 196—
14. Of all the members of the family (present)
    Of those:
        Workers
        Housewives
        Pensioners (non-workers)
    Children:
        up to one year old
        from one to six
        from seven to eleven
        adolescents from twelve to fifteen
        other members of the family
15. Number of children found in children's institutions
    Of these:
        In kindergartens and nurseries
        In school (including schools which stay open late)
        In boarding school
16. Size of the living space, on the average, for one member of the family
17. Family occupies (figure encompasses the family circle):
        Separate flat
        One room in a common flat
        Two or more rooms in a common flat
        A part of a room
        Dormitory
        Private house
        Private flat
18. Presence in the flat of communal comforts (figures encompass the family
    circle):
        Central heating
        Stove heating
        Sanitation
        Water supply
        Hot water
        Bath and shower
        Refuse disposal
        Gas
19. Presence in the family of cultural-*byt* inventory (figures encompass the family
    circle):
        Sewing machine

      Washing machine
      Refrigerator
      Vacuum cleaner
      Radio receiver
      Television
      Bicycle
      Motorcycle, scooter
      Private passenger car

20. Use of the enterprise's public eating facilities by member of the family:
      Regularly, two or three times a day
      Regular, once a day
      Every now and then

21. Number of books in personal library:
      Belles lettres
      Special
      Political

B. Distribution of time – sample time budget

Different Time Expenditures   *Working Days*   *Rest Day*

I. Working Time
    1. Time of actual work (fixed – contracted time)
    2. Time for actual work (overtime)
    3. Wasted time and non-productive working time
    4. Regulated breaks in work (industrial gymnastics,
        time for nursing mothers, etc.)
    5. Start and finish of shift

II. Non-working time, connected with work in production
    6. Eating
    7. Waiting in queues in the dining room or buffet
    8. Going to the dining room or buffet and returning
    9. Leisure and other time expenditures
    10. Time to take care of oneself before and after the shift (undressing,
        dressing, washing)
  Moving to the place of work and returning
    11. Walking to and from the transportation stop
    12. Waiting for transportation
    13. Riding to work and back
    14. Walking to work and back

III. Housework
  Shopping for non-food products
    15. Time on the way to and from the store
    16. Staying in the store (without waiting in queues)

    17. Waiting in queues

Shopping for food products

    18. Time on the way to and from the store

    19. Staying in the store (without waiting in queues)

    20. Waiting in queues

    21. Time shopping in the market place (excluding travel to and from)

Food preparation

    22. Lighting the stove, carrying the ashes, bringing firewood and coal

    23. Carrying water (such water that was not for food preparation, if there is no water supply)

    24. Preparing or warming up the dinner, lunch or breakfast

    25. Washing dishes (after having all the food for the day)

Care of the premises, the furniture and *byt* apparatus

    26. Tidying up the premises (washing and polishing the floors, making the bed)

    27. Tidying up the yard (rubbish, snow)

    28. Repairing the flat, the furniture, *byt* apparatus and other work of taking care of the premises

Care of clothing, footwear, linen (washing)

    29. Washing and ironing (besides nappies)

    30. Repairing shoes and clothing

    31. Cleaning clothes and footwear

Use of everyday (*byt*) service enterprises

    32. Visiting the laundry

    33. Visiting workshops for repairing and cleaning clothes and shoes

    34. Visiting workshops repairing furniture and *byt* apparatus

    35. Visiting clothing and shoe workshops

    36. Visiting hiring places

Looking after the children

    37. Taking care of the unweaned babies, day and night (feeding, bathing, changing nappies, rocking to sleep and washing)

    38. Washing, dressing, feeding and putting the other (weaned) children to bed

    39. Taking children to the kindergarten, to the school or the day-crèche

    40. Visiting children's hospitals and consultations

    41. Working in subsidiary economy (taking care of cattle, birds, gardens and vegetable gardens)

Other types of housework

    42. Knitting, sewing, making domestic articles

    43. Storing up fuel (supply, sawing up)

    44. Other types of housework

IV. Looking after oneself

    45. Dressing, washing, combing one's hair and shaving at home

    46. Washing at home

    47. Time for (medical) treatment at home

    48. Time to and from the medical establishment

49. Time waiting at the medical establishment
50. Consultation time at the doctor's
51. Time to and from the bath and the shower
52. Waiting in queues at the bath and the shower
53. Using the bath and the shower
54. Time to and from the hairdresser
55. Waiting in queues at the hairdresser
56. Time for immediate service at the hairdresser

V.   Physiological needs
Time for food (besides lunch break)
57. Time expended on eating at home
58. Time on the way to the dining room, the café, the tea room and back again
59. Waiting in queues at a dining room, a café and a tea room
60. Time for eating in a dining room, a café and a tea room
Sleep
61. Sleeping during the day
62. Sleeping at night

VI. Free time
Upbringing of the children
63. Checking school tasks, participation in preparing the children's lessons, reading, conversations and training in labour skills
64. Strolling and playing with the children
65. Visiting gatherings of relatives and meeting with teachers
Study and raising qualifications
66. Preparation for studies and reading special literature at home and in libraries
67. Studies in educational institutions (schools, academies, *tekhnikumy* [specialized secondary schools], institutes, etc.) without time for the journey
68. Studies at industrial-technical courses, at schools of progressive methods and at dress-making courses (without time for the journey)
69. Time for the journey to educational institutions, courses, reading rooms and libraries
70. Studies in the network of party education
Social work
71. Preparation and reading of reports, of lectures in the network of party education, of industrial and technical courses, of schools of progressive methods
72. Participation in meetings, sessions, conferences, etc.
73. Participation in mass Sunday work
74. Fulfilment of other public mission
Creative activity and amateur work
75. Invention and rationalization
76. Literary creativity, painting, sculpting

77. Participation in amateur talent activities
78. Photography, radio amateurism
79. Other types of amateur work

Physical culture and sport

80. Physical exercises, other than at production
81. Amateur occupation with sports and sporting games (volleyball, football, hunting, fishing, skating, etc.)
82. Pursuits at athletic schools and sections, participation in competitions

Leisure and entertainment

83. Reading newspapers
84. Reading magazines and *belles lettres*
85. Attending lectures and discussions
86. Listening to the radio
87. Looking at programmes on television
88. Going to the cinema
89. Going to theatres
90. Going to concert halls, clubs, House of Culture
91. Going to museums and exhibitions
92. Going to parks, gardens, stadiums, mass outdoor fetes, walking without children
93. Singing, playing on musical instruments at home
94. House table games (dominoes, chess, checkers, lotto, cards, etc.)
95. Receiving guests and visiting relatives and friends
96. Inactive leisure
97. Other types of leisure

VII. Other time expenditures

98. Visiting institutions for personal business (savings banks, district and executive committees, post offices, militia, etc.)
99. Unallocated time

TOTAL

Besides this, time expenditures

    (under the conditions of a simultaneous outlay of time, taken into account by other items)
    Reading newspapers
    Reading books and magazines
    Listening to radio and television broadcasts

Date of completion
Signature of registrar

Bibliography

Abrams, P. (1968), *The Origins and Growth of British Sociology, 1834-1914*, University of Chicago Press, Chicago.

Adams, M. (1980), 'Science, Ideology and Structure: The Kol'tsov Institute, 1900-1970', in Lubrano, L. L. and Solomon, S. G. (eds.), *The Social Context of Soviet Science*, Westview Press, Boulder, Colorado.

Andrusz, G. (1990), 'Moscow Conference Report I: The Re-emergence of Soviet Sociology', *International Journal of Urban and Regional Research*, Vol. 14, No. 2, p.302.

Afanas'ev, V. G., Golubev, A. N. and Petrov, I. G. (eds.) (1968), *Problemy Nauchnogo Kommunizma: Konkretnye Sotsiologicheskie Issledovaniia i Ideologicheskaia Deiatel'nost'* (*Problems of Scientific Communism: Concrete Sociological Research and Ideological Activity*), No. 2, Moscow.

Afanas'ev, V. G. and Petrov, Iu. A. (1969), 'O Dissertatsionnykh Rabotakh po Filosofii v 1967/68 Uchebnom Godu' ('On Dissertations in Philosophy for the 1967-8 Academic Year'), *Vop Fil*, No. 1.

----- (1969), 'O Dissertatsionnykh Robotakh po Filosofii i Sotsiologii v 1968/69 Uchebnom Godu' ('On Dissertations in Philosophy and Sociology for the 1968-9 Academic Year'), *Vop Fil*, No. 12.

Aganbegian, A. G., Osipov, G. V. and Shubkin, V. N. (eds.) (1966), *Kolichestvennye Metody Sotsiologii* (*Quantitative Methods in Sociology*), Moscow.

Aitov, N. (1972), 'Na Perekrestke Mnenii: Gorod – Proportsii Razvitiia' ('At the Crossroads of Opinions: The City – Proportions of Development'), *Izvestiia*, 17 February. Translated (1972) by the *CDSP*, Vol. 24, No. 7.

Aleksandrov, A. (1966), 'Slovo o Sotsiologii' ('A Word about Sociology'), *Literaturnaia Gazeta*, 21 April. Translated (1966) by the *CDSP*, Vol. 23, No. 17.

Aleksandrov, G. *(1945)*, 'O Nekotorykh Zadachakh Obshchestvennykh Nauk v Sovremennykh Usloviiakh' ('On Several Tasks of the Social Sciences in Contemporary Conditions'), *Bol'shevik*, No. 14.

Anan'ev, B. G., El'meev, V. Ia. and Kerimov, D. A. (eds.) (1967), *Chelovek i Obshchestvo* (*Man and Society*), Vol. 2, Leningrad.

Anan'ev, B. G. and Kerimov, D. A. (eds.), (1966), *Chelovek i Obshchestvo* (*Man and Society*), Vol. 1, Leningrad; (1968), Vol. 3, Leningrad; (1969), Vol. 4, Leningrad; (1969), Vol. 5 Leningrad; (1969), Vol. 6: *Chelovek i Obshchestvo: Sotsial'nye Problemy Molodezhi* (*Man and Society: Social Problems of Youth*), Leningrad.

Anan'ev, B. G., Kerimov, D. A. and Pashkov, A. S. (eds.) (1970), *Chelovek i Obshchestvo: Problemy Sotsial'nogo Planirovaniia* (*Man and Society: Problems of Social Planning*), Vol. 7, Leningrad.

Anan'ev, B. G. and Pashkov, A. S. (1971), 'Kompleksnoe Issledovanie Sotsial'nykh Problem' ('Complex Research of Social Problems'), *Chelovek i Obshchestvo*, Vol. 8, Leningrad.

Annan'ev, B. G. and Spiridonov, L. I. (eds.) (1971), *Chelovk i Obshchestvo: Problemy Sotsializatsii Individa* (*Man and Society: Problems of Socialization of the Individual*), Vol. 9, Leningrad.

Andreev, G. L. *et al.* (1967*)*, 'Nauchnyi Ateizm za 50 Let' ('Scientific Atheism for Fifty Years'), *Vop Fil*, No. 12.

Andreeva, G. M. (1963), 'Priemy i Metody Eempiricheskikh Issledovanii v SovremennoiBurzhuaznoi Sotsiologii', ('Modes and Methods of Empirical Research in Contemporary Bourgeois Sociology'), *Voprosy Organizatsii i Metodiki Konkretno-sotsiologicheskikh Issledovanii*, Ashin, G. K. *et al.* (eds.), Moscow.

---- (1964), 'Metodologicheskaia Rol' Teorii na Raznykh Etapakh Sotsial'Nogo Issledovaniia' ('Methodological Role of Theory at Different Stages of Social Research'), *Vop Fil*, No. 7.

---- (1965), *Sovremennaia Burzhuaznaia Empiricheskaia Sotsiologiia: Kriticheskii Ochrek (Contemporary Bourgeois Empirical Sociology: Critical Essay)*, Moscow.

---- (1966), 'Metodologicheskie Osnovy Burzhuaznoi Empiricheskoi Sotsiologii' ('Methodological Bases of Bourgeois Empirical Sotsiology'), *Metodologicheskie Voprosy Obshchestvennykh Nauk*, Chesnokov, D. I. et al. (eds.), Moscow.

---- (1967), 'O VI Mezhdunarodnom Kongresse Sotsiologov' ('On the Sixth World Congress of Sociologists'), *Vestnik MGU*, No. 1.

---- (1970), 'O Sootnoshenii Mikro- i Makrosotsiologii' ('About the Correlation of Micro- and Macro-sociology'), *Vop Fil*, No. 7.

Andreeva, G. M. and Nikitin, E. P. (1966), 'Metod ob Iasneniia v Sotsiologii' ('Method of Explanation in Sociology'), *Sotsiologiia v SSSR*, Vol. 1, Osipov, G. V. (ed.) Moscow. Translated (1966) by *Soviet Sociology*, Vol. 5, No. 1.

Andrianov, N. (1970), 'Puti k Istine: Zametki ob Ateisticheskoi Propagande' ('Paths to Truth: Notes on Atheist Propaganda'), *Pravda*, 7 September. Translated (1970) by the *CDSP*, Vol. 22, No. 37.

---- (1966), 'Antiobshchestvennye Iavleniia, Ikh Prichiny i Sredstva Bor'bu s Nimi' ('Anti-social Phenomena, Their Causes and Means of Struggle with Them'), *Kommunist*, No. 12. Translated (1966) by the *CDSP*, Vol. 18, No. 36.

Antosenkov, E. (1970), *Labour Turnover in USSR National Economy: Socio-economic Nature and Principles of Control*, Novosibirsk.

Antosenkov, E. (ed.) (1969), *Opyt Issledovaniia Peremeny Truda v Promyshlennosti: po Rezul'tatam Ekonomicheskogo i Sotsiologicheskogo Obsledovaniia Tekuchesti Rabochikh Kadrov (The Experience of Research on Labour Turnover in Industry: According to Results of an Economic and Sociological Enquiry into the Turnover of Working Cadres)*, Novosibirsk.

Anufrieva, R. A. and Vasilenko, V. A. (1967), 'Sotsiologiia na Ukraine i ee Perspektivy' ('Sociology in the Ukraine and its Prospects'), *Vop Fil*, No. 9.

Aptekman, D. M. (1965), 'Prichiny Zhivuchesti Rligioznogo Obriada Kreshcheniia v Sovremennykh Usloviiakh' ('Causes of the Vitality of the Ceremony of Baptism Under Modern Conditions'), *Vop Fil*, No. 3. Translated (1965) by *Soviet Sociology*, Vol. 4, No. 2.

Artemov, V. A. (1966), 'O Nekotorykh Metodakh Analiza Biudzhetov Vremeni Trudiashchikhsia' ('On Several Methods of Analysis of Working People's Time Budgets'), *Sotsiologicheskie Issledovaniia: Voprosy Metodologii i Metodiki*, Ryvkina, R. V. (ed.), Novosibirsk.

Artemov, V. A. *et al.* (1967), *Statistika Biudzhetov Vremeni Trudiashchikhsia (Statistics of Time Budgets of Working People)*, Moscow.

Artemov, V. A. and Kutyrev, B. P. (1969),'Biudzhet Vremeni i Sotsial'no-ekonomicheskoe Planirovanie' ('Time Budget and Socio-economic Planning'), *Fil Nauki*, No. 6.

Arutunian, Iu. V. (1966), 'Sotsial'naia Struktura Sel'skogo Naseleniia' (Social Structure of the Rural Population'), *Vop Fil*, No. 5. Translated (1966) by the *CDSP*, Vol. 18, No. 25.

---- (1966), 'Konkretno-sotsial'noe Issledovanie Sela' ('Concrete Social Research of the Village'), *Vop Fil*, No. 10.

---- (1968), *Opyt Sotsiologicheskogo Izucheniia Sela* (*The Experience of a Sociological Study of the Village*), Moscow.

---- (1968), 'Sotsial'nye Aspekty Kul'turnogo Rosta Sel'skogo Naseleniia' ('Social Aspects of the Cultural Growth of the Rural Population'), *Vop Fil*, No. 9.

---- (1969), 'Rural Sociology' and 'Rural Social Structure', *Town, Country and People*, Osipov, G. V. (ed.), London.

---- (1971), *Sotsial'naia Struktura Sel'skogo Naseleniia* (*Social Structure of the Rural Population*), Moscow.

Ashin, G. K. *et al.* (eds.) (1963), *Voprosy Organizatsii i Metodiki Konkretno-sotsiologicheskikh Issledovanii* (*Questions of the Organization and Method of Concrete Sociological Research*), Moscow.

Baikova, V. G., Duchal, A. S. and Zemtsov, A. A. (1965), *Svobodnoe Vremia i Vsestoronnee Ravzitie Lichnosti* (*Free Time and the All-round Development of the Individual*), Moscow.

Baskin, M. P. (1964), 'Krizis Burzhuaznoi Sotsiologii – Otrazhenie Degradatsii Burzhuaznoi Ideologii' ('Crisis of Bourgeois Sociology – A Reflection of the Degradation of Bourgeois Ideology'), *Sovremennaia Burzhuaznaia Sotsiologiia*, Osipov, G. V. (ed.), Moscow.

Beliaev, E. V. *et al.* (1961), 'Izuchenie Iudzheta Vremeni Trudiashchikhsia Kak Odin iz Metodov Konkretno-sotsiologicheskogo Issledovaniia' ('The Study of the Time Budget of Working People as One of the Methods of Concrete Sociological Research'), *Vestnik LGU*, No. 23. Translated (1962) by *Soviet Sociology*, Vol. 1, No. 1.

---- (1966), 'Vsesoiuznyi Simpozium Sotsiologov' ('All-Union Symposium of Sociologists'), *Vop Fil*, No. 10.

Beliaev, E. and Butorin, P. (1982), 'Institutionalisation of Soviet Sociology: Its Social and Political Context', *Social Forces*, Vol. 61, No. 2.

Belov, M. V. (1965), '*Voprosy Filosofii* na Cherepovetskom Metallurgicheskom Zavode' ('*Voprosy Filosofii* at Cherepovetsk Metallurgical Factory'), *Vop Fil*, No. 11.

Belykh, O. V. *et al.* (1966), 'Ob Opyte Konkretnykh Sotsial'nykh Issledovanii' ('On the Experience of Concrete Social Research'), *Fil Nauki*, No. 3.

Besedina, V. and Mamonova, T. (1966), 'Sprosim Nashikh Muzhchin' ('We Ask Our Men'), *Komsomol'skaia Pravda*, 27 May. Translated (1966) by the *CDSP*, Vol. 18, No. 29.

Blauberg, I. V. and Naumova, N. F. (eds.) (1970), *Sotsial'nye Issledovaniia: Teoriia i Metody* (*Social Research: Theory and Methods*), Vol. 5, Moscow.

Bogomolov, A. S. and Petrov, Iu. A. (1971), 'O Dissertatsionnykh Rabotakh po Filosofii v 1969-70 Uchebnom Godu' ('On Dissertations in Philosophy for the 1969-70 Academic Year'), *Vop Fil*, No. 1.

Bolgov, V. I. (1970), 'Kategoriia Vremeni v Sotsial'nom Izmerenii i Planirovanii I Problema Ekonomii Vremeni' ('The Category of Time in Social Measuring and Planning and the Problem of the Economics of Time'), *Sotsial'nye Issledovaniia: Problemy Biudzheta Vremeni Trudiashchikhsia*, Vol. 6, Moscow.

Bolgov, V. I. (ed.) (1970), *Sotsial'nye Issledovaniia: Problemy Biuzheta Vremeni Trudiashchikhsia*, Vol. 6, Moscow.

Boronoev, A. O. and Koslovskii, V. V. (1997), 'Introduction', in Boronoev, A. O. and Koslovskii, V. V. (eds.), *Rossiiskaia Sotsiologiia: Istoriko-Sotsiologicheskie Ocherki* (*Russian Sociology: Historical-Sociological Aspects*), Russian State Humanitarian University, Moscow.

Bramson, L. (1961), *The Political Context of Sociology*, Princeton University Press, Princeton, New Jersey.

Brown, A. (1988), 'Tat'yana Zaslavskaya and Soviet Sociology: An Introduction', *Social Research*, Vol. 55, Nos. 1-2.

Brym, R. J. (1990), 'Notes on the Discipline: Sociology, Perestroika and Soviet Society', *Canadian Journal of Sociology*, Vol. 15, No. 2, pp.207-15.

Bukharin, N. (1925), *Historical Materialism: A System of Sociology*, New York.

Bulmer, M. (ed.) (1985), *Essays on the History of British Sociological Research*, Cambridge University Press, Cambridge.

Chagin, B. A. (1967), 'Razvitie Sotsiologicheskoi Mysli v SSSR v 20-e Gody' ('Development of Sociological Thought in the USSR in the 1920s'), *Fil Nauki*, No. 5.

---- (1971), *Ocherk Istorii Sotsiologicheskoi Mysli v SSSR (Sketch of the History of Sociological Thought in the USSR*, Leningrad.

Chesnokov, D. I. (1967), *Istoricheskii Materialism i Sotsial'nye Issledovaniia (Historical Materialism and Social Research)*, Moscow.

Chesnokov, D. I. *et al.* (eds.) (1966), *Metodologicheskie Voprosy Obshchestvennykh Nauk (Methodological Questions of the Social Sciences)*, Moscow.

Communication, (1978), 'The First Soviet-Finnish Symposium of Sociology, Jan. 24-25 1978', *Acta Sociologica*, Vol. 21, No. 2, Helsinki.

Dagel', P. S. (1967), 'Klassifikatsiia Motivov Prestupleniia i ee Kriminologicheskoe Znachenie' ('Classification of Motives of Crime and its Criminological Significance'), *Nekotorye Voprosy Sotsiologii i Prava*, Petrov, L. A. (ed.), Irkutsk.

---- (1929), 'Diskussiia o Marksistskom Ponimanii Sotsiologii' ('Discussion about the Marxist Concept of Sociology'), *Istorik Marksist*, No. 12.

Dmitriev, A. V. and Toshchenko, Z. T. (1994), 'Sotsiologicheskii Opros i Politika (Sociological Poll and Politics)', *Sotsiologicheskie Issledovaniia*, No.5, pp.42-51.

Dobrynina, V. I. (ed.) (1970), *Molodezh' i Trud (Youth and Labour)*, Moscow.

Dynnik, M. A. *et al* .(eds.) (1965), *Istoriia Filosofii (History of Philosophy)*, Vol. 6, books one and two, Moscow.

Erunov, B. A. (1964), *Sila Obshchestvennogo Mneniia (The Force of Public Opinion)*, Leningrad.

Fedoseev, P. N. (1966), 'Marksistskaia Sotsiologiia, ee Zadachi i Perspektivy' ('Marxist Sociology, Its Tasks and Prospects'), *Vestnik AN SSSR*, No. 7.

---- (1967), 'Marksistskaia Sotsiologiia i Konkretnye Sotsiologicheskie Issledovaniia' ('Marxist Sociology and Concrete Sociological Research'), *Partiinaia Zhizn'*, No. 20. Translated (1967) by the *CDSP*, Vol. 19, No. 48.

---- (1968), 'Sotsiologicheskie Issledovaniia v SSSR' ('Sociological Research in the USSR'), *Sotsial'nye Issledovaniia*, Vol. 2, Moscow.

Fetisov, Ye. N. (1989), 'Vperedi Bol'shaya Rabota' (We Have Much Work to Do!), *Sotsiologischeskie Issledovaniia*, No. 3.

Filimonov, E. G. (1967), 'Problemy Konkretno-Sotsiologicheskikh Issledovanii Religioznosti v Sovetskoi Literature (1961-66)' ('Problems of Concrete Sociological Research of Religiosity in Soviet Literature: 1961-66'), *Konkretnye Issledovaniia Sovremennykh Religioznykh Verovanii*, Klibanov A. I. *et al.* (eds.), Moscow.

Filippov, A. (1993), 'A Final Look Back at Soviet Sociology', *International Sociology*, Vol. 8, No. 3, pp.355-73.

Fischer, George (1967), 'Sociology', *Science and Ideology in Soviet Society*, Fischer, G. (ed.), New York.

Friedrichs, R. (1970), *Sociology of Sociology*, Free Press, New York.

Frolic, B. Michael (1970), 'The Soviet Study of Soviet Cities', *Journal of Politics*, Vol. 32, No. 3.

Furman, D. E. (1968), 'Diskussiia o Structure Marksistskoi Sotsiologicheskoi Teorii' ('A Discussion about the Structure of Marxist Sociological Theory'), *Vestnik MGU*, No. 5.

Genov, N. (ed.) (1989), *National Trends in Sociology*, Sage, London.

Giddens, A. (1976), *New Rules of Sociological Method*, Hutchinson and Co., London.

Glezerman, G. E. and Afanas'ev, V. G. (eds.) (1965), *Opyt i Metodika Konkretnykh Sotsiologicheskikh Issledovanii* (*The Experience and System of Rules of Concrete Sociological Research*), Moscow.

Golosenko, I. A. (ed.) (1996), *N I Kareev: Osnovy Russkoi Sotsiologii* (*N I Kareev: Foundations of Russian Sociology*), Ivan Limbakh, St Petersburg.

Gordon, L. and Levin, B. (1968), 'Nekotorye Sotsial'no-Bytovye Posledstviia Piatidnevki v Bol'shikh i Malykh Gorodakh' ('Several Socio-*byt* Consequences of the Five-day Week in Large and Small Cities'), *Voprosy Ekonomiki*, No. 4. Translated (1969) by *Soviet Sociology*, Vol. 7, No. 4.

Gouldner, A. (1970), *The Coming Crisis of Western Sociology*, Basic Books, New York.

Graham, L. (1972), *Science and Philosophy in the Soviet Union*, Alfred A Knopf, New York.

Graham, L. (1993), *Science in Russia and the Soviet Union*, CUP, Cambridge.

Gray, D. (1994), 'Russian Sociology: The Second Coming of August Comte', *American Journal of Economics and Sociology*, Vol. 53, No. 2, pp.163-74.

Greenfield, L. (1988), 'Soviet Sociology and Sociology in the Soviet Union', *Annual Review of Sociology*, Vol. 14, pp.99-123.

Greenfield, L. (1991), 'The "Purposeful Science" of Soviet Sociology', in Jones, A. (ed.), *Professions and the State: Expertise and Autonomy in the Soviet Union and Eastern Europe*, Temple University Press, Philadelphia.

Gremiako, L. L., El'meev, V. Ia. and Kerimov, D. A. (1966), 'Institut Sotsial'nykh Issledovanii' ('Institute of Social Research'), *Vop Fil*, No. 8.

Grushin, B. A. (1963), 'Institut Obshchestvennogo Mneniia *Komsomol'skoi Pravdy*' ('*Komsomol'skaia Pravda*'s Public Opinion Institute'), *Voprosy Organizatsii i Metodika Konkretno-Sotsiologicheskikh Issledovanii*, Ashin G. K. *et al.* (eds.), Moscow.

---- (1965), 'K Probleme Kachestvennoi Reprezentatsii v Vyborochnom Oprose' ('To the Problem of Qualitative Representation in Questionnaires'), *Opyt i Metodika Konkretnykh Sotsiologicheskikh Issledovanii*, Glezerman, G. E. and Afanas'ev, V.G. (eds.), Moscow.

---- (1965), 'Sotsiologiia i Sotsiologi' ('Sociology and Sociologists'), *Literaturnaia Gazeta*, 25 September. Translated (1965) in the *CDSP*, Vol. 17, No. 40.

---- (1967), *Svobodnoe Vremia: Aktual'nye Problemy* (*Free Time: Actual Problems*), Moscow.

---- (1967), *Mneniia o Mire i Mir Mnenii* (*Opinion about the World and the World of Opinion*), Moscow.

Grushin, B. and Chikin, V. (1962), *Ispoved'Pokoleniia* (*Confession of a Generation*), Moscow.

Hawthorn, G. (1976), *Enlightenment and Despair: A History of Sociology*, Cambridge University Press, Cambridge.

Hecker, Julius F. (1934), *Russian Sociology: A Contribution to the History of Sociological Thought and Theory*, London.

Iablokov, I. N. (1967), 'Ob Opyte Konkretnogo Issledovaniia Religioznosti', ('On the Experience of Concrete Research of Religiosity'), *Vestnik MGU*, No. 4.

Iadov, V. A. (1965), 'O Chem Govorit Opyt Organizatsii i Provedeniia Konkretnykh Sotsial'nykh Issledovanii v Leningrade' ('What the Experience of the Organization and Execution of Concrete Social Research in Leningrad Indicates'), *Fil Nauki*, No. 2. Translated (1965) by the *CDSP*, Vol. 17, No. 31.

---- (1966), 'Sotsiologiia: Problemy i Fkty: Otvetstvennost'' ('Sociology: Problems and Facts: Responsibility'), *Literaturnaia Gazeta*, 12 November. Translated (1966) by the *CDSP*, Vol. 18, No. 48.

---- (1966), 'Ob Ustanovlenii Faktov v Konkretnom Sotsiologicheskom Issledovanii' ('On Ascertaining Facts in Concrete Sociological Research'), *Fil Nauki*, No. 5.

---- (1966), 'Rol' Metodologii v Opredelenii Metodov i Tekhniki Konkretnogo Sotsiologicheskogo Issledovaniia' ('The Role of Methodology in Determining Methods and Techniques of Concrete Sociological Research'), *Vop Fil*, No. 10.

---- (1968), *Metodologiia i Protsedury Sotsiologicheskikh Issledovanii* (*Methodology and Procedures of Sociological Research*), Tartu.

Iankova, Z. (1970), 'O Bytovykh Roliakh Rabotaiushchei Zhenshchiny (K Probleme Osushchestvleniia Fakticheskogo Ravenstva Zhenshchiny s Muzhchinoi)' ('About Domestic Roles of Working Women: To the Problem of the Realization of Factual Equality of Women with Men'), *Problemy Byta, Braka i Sem'i*, Solov'ev, N., Lazauskas, Iu. and Iankova, Z. (eds.), Vil'nius.

Ianov, A. (1967), 'Vremia Vzroslet'' ('Time to Mature'), *Komsomol'skaia Pravda*, 2 June. Translated (1967) by the *CDSP*, Vol. 19, No. 25.

Igitkhanian, M. Kh. (1963), 'Dukhovnyi Oblik Sovetskoi Molodezhi' ('The Spiritual Image of Soviet Youth'), *Vop Fil*, No. 6. Translated (1963) by the *CDSP*, Vol. 15, No. 39.

Ikonnikova, S. N. and Lisovskii, V. T. (1969), *Molodezh' o Sebe, o Svoikh Sverstnikakh* (*Youth About Itself, About Its Coevals*), Leningrad.

Iochuk, M. T. (1967), 'Mezhdunarodnyi Forum Sotsiologov' (International Forum of Sociologists'), *Vestnik AN SSSR*, No. 2.

Iovchuk, M. T. *et al.*(eds.) (1965), *Marksistsko-Leninskaia Filosofiia i Sotsiologiia v SSSR i Evropeiskikh Sotsialisticheskikh Stranakh* (*Marxist-Leninist Philosophy and Sociology in the USSR and European Socialist Countries*), Moscow.

Iurkevich, N. G. (1970), *Sovetskaia Sem'ia: Funktsii i Usloviia Stabil'nosti* (*The Soviet Family: Functions and Conditions of Stability*), Minsk.

Iu, K. (1961), 'V Statisticheskoi Sektsili Moskovskogo Doma Uchenykh' ('In the Statistical Section of the Moscow House of Scholars'), *Vestnik Statistiki*, No. 6.

Ivanov, V. N. (1989), 'Nevozmozhnoe Stanovitsia Vozmozhnym' ('The Impossible Becomes the Possible'), *Sotsiologicheskie Issledovaniia*, No. 1.

Ivanov, V. and Osipov, G. 'Traditions and Specific Features of Sociology in the Soviet Union' in Genov, N (ed.), *National Trends in Sociology*, Sage, London.

Jones, A. (1989), 'Soviet Sociology, Past and Present', *Contemporary Sociology*, Vol. 18 (May), pp.316-19.

Joravsky, D. (1961), *Soviet Marxism and Natural Science*, Columbia University, New York.

Kachalevskii, E. (1971), 'Esli Videt' Perspektivu: Partiinaia Zhizn'' ('If One Sees the Long-range Perspective: Party Life'), *Pravda*, 6 December. Translated (1971) by the *CDSP*, Vol. 23, No. 49.

Kachanov, I. L. (2001), 'Rossiiskaia Sotsiologia kak Sobytie ('Russian Sociology' as an Event)' *Sotsiologicheskie Issledovaniia*, No. 3, pp.3-8.

Kantorovich, V. (1966), 'Rodstvennaia Nam Nauka' ('A Science Kindred to Us'), *Literaturnaia Gazeta*, 5 May and 14 May. Translated (1966) by the *CDSP*, Vol. 18, No. 26.

---- (1967), 'Sotsiologiia i Literatura' ('Sociology and Literature'), *Novyi Mir*, No. 12.

Kapeliush, Ia. S. and Prigozhin, A. I. (1966), 'Sobranie Sovetskoi Sotsiologicheskoi Assotsiatsii' ('Meeting of the Soviet Sociological Association'), *Vop Fil*, No. 6.

Kargarlitsky, B. (2002), *Russia Under Yeltsin and Putin*, Pluto Press, London.

Kasiukov, I. and Mendeleev, A. (1967), 'Nuzhen li Talant Sem'ianinu?' ('Must a Family Man have Talent?'), *Nedelia*, No. 12. Translated (1967) by the *CDSP*, Vol. 19, No. 13.

Kelle, V. Zh. (1967), 'O Nekotorykh Napravleniiakh Razvitiia Istoricheskogo Materializma' ('On Several Directions of the Development of Historical Materialism'), *Vop Fil*, No. 10.

Kharchev, A. G. (1963), 'O Nekotorykh Razultatakh Issledovaniia Motivov Braka v SSSR' ('On Several Results of Research on Motives for Marriage in the USSR'), *Fil Nauki*, No. 4. Translated (1964) by *Soviet Review*, Vol. 5, No. 2.

---- (1963), 'Sotsiologicheskie Issledovaniia v Pol'she' ('Sociological research in Poland'), *Vop Fil*, No. 6.

---- (1964), *Brak i Sem'ia v SSSR* (*Marriage and the Family in the USSR*), Moscow.

---- Osipov, G. V. (ed.) (1969), 'Marriage Motivation Studies', *Town, Country and People*, London.

Khorev, B. (1969), 'Kakoi Gorod Nuzhen?' ('What Kind of City is Needed?'), *Literaturnaia Gazeta*, 2 April. Translated (1969) by the *CDSP*, Vol. 21, No. 14.

Khvostov, V. M. (1920), *Osnovy Sotsiologii. Uchenie o Zakonomernosti Obshchestvennykh Protsessov* (*The Bases of Sociology. A Study of the 'Zakonomernosti' of Social Processes*), Moscow.

Kim, V. V. and Liubtin, K. N. (1967), 'Razvitie Filosofskikh Issledovanii v Sverdlovske' ('Development of Philosophical Research in Sverdlovsk'), *Fil Nauki*, No. 6.

Kirillova, M. A. and Pankratova, M. G. (1967), 'Simpozium Sotsiologov po Issledovaniiu Problem Sem'i i Byta' ('Symposium of Sociologists on the Study of the Problems of the Family and *Byt*'), *Fil Nauki*, No. 4.

Klibanov, A. I. (1967), 'Piat'Desiat let Nauchnogo Issledevaniia Religioznogo Sektantstva' ('Fifty Years of Scientific Study of Religious Sectarianism'), *Voprosy Nauchnogo Ateizma*, No. 4, Moscow. Translated (1970) by *Soviet Sociology*, Vol. 8, Nos. 3-4.

Klopov, E. V. (1969), 'Biudzhet Vremeni i Sotsial'noe Planirovanie' ('Time Budget and Social Planning'), *Vop Fil*, No. 9.

Klushin, V. I. (1964), 'Sotsiologiia v Petrogradskom Universitete (1920-24)' ('Sociology in Petrograd University – 1920-4'), *Vestnik LGU*, No. 5.

---- (1970), *Bor'ba za Istoricheskii Materialism v Leningradskom Gosudarstvennom Universitete (1918-25 Gody)* (*The Fight for Historical Materialism in Leningrad State University – 1918-25*), Leningrad.

Kogan, L. N. (ed.) (1969), *Molodezh', ee Interesy, Stremleniia, Idealy* (*Youth, its Interests, Aspirations, Ideals*), Moscow.

Kogan, L. N. and Loktev, V. I. (1969), 'Sociological Aspects of the Modelling of Towns', *Town, Country And People*, Osipov, G.V. (ed.), London.

Kolbanovskii, V. V. and Slesarev, G. A. (1961), 'Obshchee Sobranie Sovetskoi Sotsiologicheskoi Assotsiatsii' ('General Meeting of the Soviet Sociological Association'), *Vop Fil*, No. 5.

Kolpakov, B. T. and Patrushev, V. D. (1971), *Biudzhet Vremeni Gorodskogo Naseleniia* (*Time Budget of the Urban Population*), Moscow.

Kolpakov, B. and Prudenskii, G. (1964), 'Opyt Izmereniia Vnerabochego Vremeni Trudiashchikhsia' ('The Experience of the Measurement of Working People's Non-Working Time'), *Voprosy Ekonomiki*, No. 9.

Komsomol'skaia Pravda: Polls listed in chronological order, by topic:

Peace and War
(1960), 'Institut Obshchestvennogo Mneniia *Komsomol'skoi Pravdy'* (*'Komsomol'skaia Pravda*'s Public Opinion Institute'), 19 May.

(1960), 'Udastsia Li Chelovechestvu Predotvratit' Voinu? Da! Otvechaet Tridtsatyi Meridian' ('Will Mankind Succeed in Preventing War? Yes! Answered the Thirtieth Meridian'), 19 May.

How has your Standard of Living Changed?
(1960), 'Kak Izmenilsia Uroven' Vashei Zhizni?' ('How has your Standard of Living Changed?'), 7 October.

Grushin, B. and Chikin, V. (1960), 'O Chem Rasskazali Ankety' ('What the Questionnaires Tell'), 7 October.

What do you Think about your Generation?
(1961), 'Chto vy Dumaete o Svoem Pokolenii ('What do you Think about your Generation?'), 6 January; 11 January.

(1961), 'Molodoe Pokolenie o Samom Sebe' ('The Young Generation about Itself'), 26 January.

Grushin, B. and Chikin, V. (1961), 'Isopoved' Pokoleniia' ('Confessions of a Generation'), 21 July; 22 July.

Scouts of the Future
(1961), 'Chto vy Dumaete o Razvedchikakh Budushchego?' ('What do you Think About the Scouts of the Future?'), 16 August; 23 August; 30 August; 23 September.

Grushin, B. and Chikin, V. (1962), 'Razvedka i Nastuplenie' ('Reconnaissance and Attack'), 14 September.

What is your Opinion about the Young Family?
(1961 and 1962), 'Vashe Mnenie o Molodoi Sem'e?' (What is your Opinion about the Young Family?'), 10 December; 17 December; 24 December; 6 January.

Verza, Olga (1964), 'Twelve Problems of a Young Family', *Moscow News*, 1 February.

Grushin, B. (1964), '"Poeziia" i "Proza" Semeinoi Zhizni' ('The Poetry and Prose of Family Life'), 9 July.

Moscow University Students
(1962), 'My Razdvinem Granitsy Poznaniia' ('We are Extending the Boundaries of Understanding'), 1 September.

How do you Spend your Free Time?
(1963), 'Kak Vy Provodite Svobodnoe Vremia?' ('How Do You Spend Your Free Time?'), 4 January; 11 January; 20 January.

(1963), 'Zhit' Nel'zia "Prosto – Naprosto"' ('It is Simply Impossible to Live!'), 25 January.

Shalaev, A. (1963), 'Prizvanie – Grazhdanin' ('A Vocation – Citizen'), 17 February.

Gromova, T. (1963), 'A Poka Zhdu ...' ('I'm Still Waiting'), 27 March.

Dolinina, N. (1963), 'Kogda Uchitel' Smotrit na Chasy' ('When a Teacher Looks at his Watch'), 26 May.

Peremyslov, A. (1963), 'Kommuny Doma Prorastaiut' ('Communal House Projects get Bigger and Bigger'), 7 June.

Polianichko, V. (1963), 'Prikhodite v Dom Schastlivykh' ('Come to the House of the Lucky Ones'), 21 August.

Egorov, A. (1963), 'Podnimite Perchatku, Il'ia Il'ich!' ('Pick up the Gauntlet, Il'ia Il'ich!'), 24 November.

Gromova, T. and Ronina, G. (1963), 'Kogda Vremia Zaniato Nami' ('When we are Busy'), 27 December.

(1964), 'Iskusstvo Zhit' – v Imenii Tsenit'vremia' ('The Art of Living – Is the Ability to Value Time'), 8 January.

(1964). 'Tol'ko Vpered, za Begushchim Dnem!' ('Ever Onwards, Day by Day!'), 30 January.

Gromova, T. and Ronina, G. (1965), 'Starsheklassnik Posle Urokov' ('Senior Pupils After Class'), 18 June.

Grushin, B. (1966), 'Kak vy Provodite Svobodnoe Vremia?' ('How do you Spend Your Free Time?'), 24 February; 25 February; 26 February.

To Mars, With What?
(1963), 'Na Mars – S Chem.?' ('To Mars, With What?'), 1 March; 17 March; 12 April.
(1963), 'Oktiabr' Kosmos Mir' ('The October Revolution, the Cosmos and Peace'), 18 June.
Oganov, B. and Chikin, V. (1963), 'O Vremeni i o Sebe' ('About Time and About Oneself'), 20 October; 22 October; 23 October; 24 October.

Let's Project – Televisions, Radios, etc.
(1964), 'Proektiruem Sami' ('Let's Project'), 26 June; 10 July; 28 October.

An Innovation Demands a Name
(1964), 'Novinka Prosit Im'ia ('An Innovation Demands a Name'), 28 October; 13 November.
(1965), 'Novinka – Luchshee Im'ia' ('Innovation – The Best Name'), 12 November.

Children and Words
(1964), '1000 Detei o Piatidesiati Slovakh' ('1000 Children on Fifty Words'), 2 August.
(1964), Kassil', Lev 'Ikh Glazami' ('Through Their Eyes'), 2 August.
Gromova, T. and Ronina, G. (1964), 'Ot Feviati do Desiati ...' ('From Nine to Ten'), 2 August.
(1964), 'Otnesemsia Ser'ezno!' ('Let's Treat it Seriously!'), 2 August.

Service Industries
(1964), 'Khorosho Li Vas Obsluzhivaiut?' ('How do you Rate the Service Industries?'), 20 November.
Kliamkin, I. (1965), 'Motor Torgovli' ('Motive Force of Trade'), 7 January.
Il'ina, N. (1965), 'Ushla Na Bazu, Tseluiu, Obnimaiu ...' ('I Went to the Store, I Kiss and Embrace ...'), 19 February.
Tsipis, Ia. and Tishchenkov, E. (1965), 'Mashina Izuchaet Spros' ('The Machine Studies the Demand'), 27 February.
(1965), 'Kakoi Nam Nuzhen Servis' ('What Kind of Service Do We Need?'), 27 February.
(1965), Iun', O 'I Liubo, o ... Dorogo' ('It's a Real Pleasure, But So Dear!'), 30 March.
(1965), '346 Interv'iu v Prilavke' ('346 Interviews at the Counter'), 21 April.
Struev, A. I. (1965), '10 Voprosov o Prilavke' ('10 Questions About the Counter'), 14 December.
Tarasov, N. N. (1966), 'Na Vkus, Na Tsvet i Po Neobkhodimosti' ('To Taste, To Colour, and According to Necessity'), 5 January.
Artem'ev, S. P. (1966), 'I Mechty Na Dorogakh' ('With All We Do, Let's Not Forget Our Dreams'), 27 January.

Komsomol Members about the Komsomol

Grushin, B. (1966), 'Komsomol'tsy o Komsomole' ('Komsomol Members about the Komsomol'), 26 April.

(1966), 'Komsomol'tsy o Komsomole' ('Komsomol Members about the Komsomol'), 17 May.

Ronina, G. (1966), 'Slishkom Malo Znaiu ...' ('I Know too Little'), 13 September.

Holidays – How Can You Best Spend Them and How Would You Like to Spend Them?

(1966), 'Vremia Otpuskov - Kak Luchshe Provesti Ego?' ('Holiday Time - How Can You Best Spend It?'), 23 June; 30 June; 8 July; 20 July.

(1966), 'Kak Vy Khotite Provesti Svoi Otpusk?' ('How Would You Like to Spend Your Holiday?'), 29 July.

(1966), 'V Zime Svoe Ocharovanie' ('Winter Too Has Its Charm'), 22 September.

Shelomov, N. (1966), 'Industriia Otdykha' ('The Industry of Leisure'), 27 September.

(1966), 'Otdykh – Zdorov'e – Trud' ('Leisure, Health, Labour'), 23 November.

Komsomol'skaia Pravda Reader about Himself and the Newspaper

(1966), 'Chitatel' o Sebe i o Gazete' ('The Reader about Himself and about the Newspaper'), 12 October.

Naming Children

(1967), 'Piat' Voprosov Papam i Mamam' ('Five Questions for Fathers and Mothers'), 10 September; 17 September; 29 September.

(1967), 'Kak Vybiraiut Imena' ('How Names are Chosen'), 31 December.

Kon, I. S. (1960), 'O Rabote Sotsiologicheskogo Seminara' ('On the Work of the Sociology Seminar'), Vestnik *LGU*, No. 1. Translated (1960) by the *Soviet Review*, Vol. 1, No. 1.

(1965), 'Tsennoe Issledovanie' ('Valuable Research'), *Fil Nauki*, No. 1. Translated (1965) by the *CDSP*, Vol. 17, No. 19.

Kon, I. S. and Iadov, V. A. (1967), 'Na VI Vsemirnom Sotsiologicheskom Kongresse' ('At the Sixth World Congress of Sociology'), *Fil Nauki*, No. 1.

Konstantinov, F. (1967), 'Voprosy Teorii: Filosofiia Revoliutsionnoi Epokhi' ('Questions of Theory: Philosophy of the Revolutionary Epoch'), *Pravda*, 24 July. Translated (1967) by the *CDSP*, Vol. 19, No. 30.

---- (1965), 'Istoricheskii Materialism – Marksistskaia Sotsiologiia' ('Historical Materialism Marxist Sociology'), Kommunist, No. 1. Translated (1965) by the *CDSP*, Vol. 17, No. 8.

Konstantinov, F. and Kelle, V. (1965), *Istoricheskii Materialism – Marksistskaia Sotsiologiia (Historical Materialism – Marxist Sociology)*, Moscow.

Konstantinov, F. V., Osipov, G. V. and Semenov, V. S. (eds.) (1964), *Marksistskaiai Burzhuaznaia Sotsiologiia Segodnia (Marxist and Bourgeois Sociology Today)*, Moscow.

Kosolapov, R. I. and Simush, P. I. (1969), 'Partiinaia Rabota i Konkretnye Sotsiologicheskie Issledovaniia' ('Party Work and Concrete Sociological Research') *Ideologicheskaia Rabota Partiinykh Organizatsii*, Korolev, A. M. and Mosiagin, S. I. (eds.), Moscow.

Kovalev, A. M. (1967), 'Eshche Raz o Sotsiologii Marksizma i Nauchnom Kommunizme' ('Once More about the Sociology of Marxism and Scientific Communism'), *Fil Nauki*, No. 1.

---- (1969), 'O Sootnoshenii Istoricheskogo Materializma, Nauchnogo Kommunizma i Konkretnykh Issledovanii' ('About the Correlation of Historical Materialism, Scientific Communism and Concrete Research'), *Vestnik MGU*, No. 2.

Kovalev, S. (1966), 'Voprosy Teorii: Trebovaniia Zhizni i Obshchestvennye Nauki' ('Questions of Theory: Life's Demands and the Social Sciences'), *Pravda*, 6 May. Translated (1966) by the *CDSP*, Vol. 18, No. 18.

Kovalevskii, M. M. (1913), 'Sotsiologiia na Zapade i v Rossii' ('Sociology in the West and in Russia'), *Novye Idei v Sotsiologii*, Vol. 1, Kovalevskii, M. M. and deRoberty, E. V. (eds.), St Petersburg.

Kovalevskii, M. M. and deRoberty, E. V. (1913-4), *Novye Edei v Sotsiologii* (*New Ideas in Sociology*), Vols. 1-4, St Petersburg.

Kozlovskii, V. E. And Sychev, Iu. A. (1970), 'Obsuzhdenie Kursa Lektsii Iu. A. Levady po Sotsiologii' ('Discussion of the Lecture Course by Iu. A. Levada on Sociology'), *Fil Nauki*, No. 3.

Kravchenko, I. I. and Faddeev, E. T. (1966), 'O Sotsial'noi Strukture Sovetskogo Obshchestva' ('On the Social Structure of Soviet Society'), *Vop Fil*, No. 5.

Kravchenko, I. I. and Trubitsyn, O. N. (1972), 'Problemy Izmeniia Sotsial'noi Struktury Sovetskogo Obshchestva' ('Problems of the Change of the Social Structure of Soviet Society'), *Vop Fil*, No. 6.

Kudriavtsev, V. (1966), 'Analiz Plius Tekhnika' ('Analysis Plus Technique'), *Izvestiia*, 30 September. Translated (1966) by the *CDSP*, Vol. 18, No. 39.

---- (1967), 'Prestupnost': Sootnoshenie Sotsial'nogo i Biologicheskogo: Da No Li Pri Rozhdenii?' (Crime: Correlation of the Social and the Biological: Are You Born with It?'), *Literaturnaia Gazeta*, 29 November. Translated (1967) by the *CDSP*, Vol. 19, No. 49.

---- (1968), *Prichinnost' v Kriminologii* (*Crime in Criminology*), Moscow.

---- (1971), 'Problemy Prichinnosti v Kriminologii' ('Problems of Crime in Criminology'), *Vop Fil*, No. 10.

Kugel', S. A. (1969), 'Izmenenie Sotsial'noi Struktury Sotsialisticheskogo Obshchestva Pod Vozdeistviem Nauchno-Tekhnicheskoi Revoliutsii' ('Change of the Social Structure of Socialist Society Under the Influence of the Scientific-Technical Revolution'), *Vop Fil*, No. 3.

Kukushkina, E. (1993), *Russkaia Sotsiologiia XIX-Nachala XX Veka* (*Russian Sociology - 19th-Beginning 20th Century*, Moscow University, Moscow.

Kurylov, A. K., Smol'kov, V. G. and Shtraks, G. M. (eds.) (1969), *Iz Opyta Konkretnykh Sotsiologicheskikh Issledovanii* (*From the Experience of Concrete Sociological Research*), Moscow.

Lazutkin, E. S. (1966), 'Ekonomiko-Sotsiologicheskie Issledovaniia' ('Economic and Sociological Research'), *Vop Fil*, No. 3.

Leont'ev, L. (1966), 'Sotsiologiia i Ekonomicheskaia Nauka' ('Sociology and Economics'), *Literaturnaia Gazeta*, 26 May. Translated (1966) by the *CDSP*, Vol. 18, No. 26.

Levada, Iu. A. (1969), 'Lektsii po Sotsiologii' ('Lectures on Sociology'), *Informatsionnyi Biulleten' Nauchnogo Soveta AN SSSR Po Problemam Konkretnykh Sotsial'nykh Issledovanii*, Nos. 20-1, Moscow.

Levada, Y. (ed.) (1990), *Est' Mnenie! Itogi Sotsiologicheskovo Oprosa* (*There are Opinions! Sums of Sociological Polls*), Progress, Moscow.

Levada, Y. (1995), 'Democratic Disorder and Russian Public Opinion Trends in VCIOM Surveys, 1991-95', *Studies in Public Policy*, 255, 3-17.

Levina, E. and Syrina, E. (1966), 'Razmyshleniia o Mikroraione' ('Reflections on the Microdistrict'), *Zvezda*, No. 10. Translated (1967) by the *CDSP*, Vol. 19, No. 3.

Lewin, M. (1988), *The Gorbachev Phenomenon*, Radius, London.

Lewin, M. (1988), *The Gorbachev Phenomenon: An Historical Interpretation*, Century Hutchinson Ltd., London.

188   *Sociology in the Soviet Union and Beyond*

Naumova, N. F. (1968), 'Sotsiologiia Truda, ee Uspekha i Problemy' ('Sociology of Labour, Its Successes and Problems'), *Vop Fil*, No. 7.

---- (1970), 'Nravstvennye Antinomii Sovremennoi Burzhuaznoi Sotsiologii' ('Moral Antimony of Contemporary Bourgeois Sociology'), *Vop Fil*, No. 2.

Nikitin, D. (2001), 'Russian Social Science in Transition: Applied Political Research and Social Criticism', *Sociological Practice*, Vol. 3, No. 2, pp.157-73.

Nisbet, R. (1967), *The Sociological Tradition*, Basic Books, New York.

Nove, A. (1989), *Glasnost' in Action: Cultural Renaissance in Russia*, Unwin Hyman, London.

Novikov, N. V. (1966), *Kritika Sovremennoi Burzhuaznoi 'Nauki o Sotsial'nom Povedenii' (Critique of Contemporary Bourgeois 'Science of Social Behaviour')*, Moscow.

Novikov, N. V., Osipov, G. V. and Iankova, Z. A., (eds.) (1968), *Sotsial'nye Issledovaniia (Social Research)*, Vol. 2, Moscow.

Novikov, N. V., Osipov, G. V. and Slesarev, G. A. (eds.) (1965), *Sotsial'nye Issledovaniia (Social Research)*, Vol. 1, Moscow.

---- (1970), *'O Lektsiakh Po Sotsiologii* Iu. A. Levady' ('On *Lectures on Sociology* by Iu. A. Levada'), *Vestnik MGU: Seriia Filosofiia*, No. 3.

---- (1958), 'O Sozdanii Sovetskoi Sotsiologicheskoi Assotsiatsii' ('On the Creation of the Soviet Sociological Association'), *Vop Fil*, No. 8.

Okulov, A. F. *et al.* (eds.) (1967), *Voprosy Nauchnogo Ateizma: Pobedy Nauchno-Ateisticheskogo Mirovozzreniia v SSSR za 50 Yet (Questions of Scientific Atheism: Victories of a Scientific Atheist World-view in the USSR for Fifty Years)*, No. 4, Moscow.

Osipov, G. *et al.* (ed.) (2001), *Sotsiologia i Vlast':Dokumenti 1969-1972: Vol. 2 (Sociology and Power: Documents 1969-1972)*, Russian Academy of Sciences and Russian State Archive, Moscow.

Osipov, G. V. (1962), 'Nekotorye Cherty i Osobennosti Burzhuaznoi Sotsiologii' ('Several Characteristics and Features of Bourgeois Sociology'), *Vop Fil*, No. 8. Translated (1962) by the *CDSP*, Vol. 14, No. 42.

---- (1964), *Sovremennaia Burzhuaznaia Sotsiologiia (Contemporary Bourgeois Sociology)*, Moscow.

---- (1970), 'Teoriia i Praktika Sovetskoi Sotsiologii' ('Theory and Practice of Soviet Sociology'), *Sotsial'nye Issledevaniia: Teoriia i Metody*, Vol. 5, Moscow.

---- (ed.) (1966), *Sotsiologiia v SSSR (Sociology in the USSR)*, Vols. 1 and 2, Moscow.

---- (ed.) (1966), *Industry and Labour in the USSR*, London.

---- (1968), 'Sotsiologiia kak Nauka' ('Sociology as a Science'), *Sotsial'nye Issledovaniia*, Vol. 2, Moscow.

---- (ed.) (1969), *Town, Country and People*, London.

Osipov, G. V. *et al.* (eds.) (1965), *Rabochii Klass i Tekhnicheskii Progress: Issledovanie Izmenenii v Sotsial'noi Structure Rabochego Klassa (The Working Class and Technical Progress: Research on the Change in the Social Structure of the Working Class)*, Moscow.

Osipov, G. V., Kharchev, A. G. and Iankova, Z. A. (eds.) (1970), *Sotsial'nye Issledovaniia: Problemy Braka, Sem'i i Demografii (Social Research: Problems of Marriage, the Family and Demography)*, Vol. 4, Moscow.

Osipov, G. V. and Szczepanski, Ia. (eds.) (1969), *Sotsial'nye Problemy Truda i Proizvodstva (Social Problems of Labour and Production)*, Moscow.

Osipov, G. V., Zimanov, S. Z. and Saliev, A. (1969), 'Plany Filosofskikh i Sotsiologicheskikh Issledovanii' ('Plans of Philosophical and Sociological Research'), *Vop Fil*), No. 2.

Ostroumov, S. S. and Chugunov, V. E. (1965), 'Izuchenie Lichnosti Prestupnika po Materialam Kriminologicheskikh Issledovanii' ('Study of the Criminal Personality from Materials of Criminological Research'), *Sovetskoe Gosudarstvo i Pravo*, No. 9. Translated (1966) by the *Soviet Review*, Vol. 7, No. 2.

Ovchinnikov, B. D. (1969), 'Sootnoshenie Sotsial'nogo i Biologicheskogo v Ssviazi s Problemoi Prestupnosti' ('The Correlation of the Social and the Biological in Connection with the Problem of Crime'), *Vestnik LGU*, No. 23.

Ovsiannikov, M. F. and Petrov, Iu. A. (1966), 'O Sostoinaii Dissertatsionnoi Raboty po Filosofii v 1964-65 Uchebnom Godu' ('On the State of Dissertations in Philosophy in the 1964-5 Academic Year'), *Vop Fil*, No. 2.

---- (1967), 'O Dissertatsionnoi Rabote po Filosofii v 1965-66 Uchebnom Godu' ('On Dissertations in Philosophy in the 1965-6 Academic Year'), *Vop Fil*, No. 1.

---- (1967), 'O Dissertatsionnoi Rabote po Filosofii v 1966-67 Uchebnom Godu' ('On Dissertations in Philosophy in the 1966-7 Academic Year'), *Vop Fil*, No. 11.

Pahl, R. E. (1990), *Summer School for Soviet Sociologists: Final Report*, University of Kent, Canterbury.

Pashkov, A. S. (ed.) (1971), *Chelovek i Obshchestvo (Man and Society)*, Vol. 8, Leningrad.

Patrushev, V. (2000), *Zhizn' Gorozhanina (1965-1998) (Life of the City Dweller, 1965-98)*, Academia, Moscow.

Patrushev, V. (2001), *Biudzhet Vremeni i Peremeny v Zhiznedeiatel'nosti Gorodskish Zhitelei V 1965-1998 Godakh (The Time Budget and Changes in the Living Activities of City Dwellers Between 1965 and 1998)*, Institute of Sociology RAN, Moscow.

Patrushev, V. D. (1966), 'Ob Izuchenii Biudzheta Vremeni Trudiashchikhsia' ('On the Study of Working People's Time Budgets'), *Vestnik Statistiki*, No. 11. Translated (1966) by *Soviet Sociology*, Vol. 1, No. 1.

---- (1968), 'Biudzhet Vremeni Gorodskogo Naseleniia Sotsialisticheskikh i Capitalisticheskikh Stran' ('Time Budgets of the Urban Population of Socialist and Capitalist Countries'), *Fil Nauki*, No. 5.

---- (1970), 'O Prakticheskom Ispol'zovanii Dannykh Biudzhetov Vremeni' ('On the Practical Use of Time Budget Data'), *Sotsial'nye Issledovaniia: Problemy Biudzheta Vremeni Trudiashchikhsia*, Vol. 6, Moscow.

Paweczynska, Anna, (1966), 'Principles and Problems of Public Opinion Research in Poland', *Empirical Sociology in Poland*, Szczepanski, J. (ed.), Warsaw.

Pchelintsev, O. S. (1966), 'Problemy Razvitiia Bol'shikh Gorodov' ('Problems of the Development of Large Cities'), *Sotsiologiia v SSSR*, Vol. 2, Osipov, G.V. (ed.), Moscow. Translated (1966-7) by the *Soviet Review*, Vol. 7, No. 4.

Perevedentsev, V. I. (1966), *Migratsiia Naseleniia i Trudovye Problemy Sibiri (Migration of the Population and Labour Problems in Siberia)*, Novosibirsk. Translated (1968-9) by *Soviet Sociology*, beginning with Vol. 7, No. 3.

---- (1967), *Narodonaselenie i Ekonomika (Human Population and the Economic System)*, Moscow.

---- (1969), 'Spornoe Mnenie: Goroda i Gody' ('Controversial Opinion: Cities and Years'), *Literaturnaia Gazeta*, 26 February. Translated (1969) by the *CDSP*, Vol. 21, No. 9.

---- (1970), 'Migratsiia Naseleniia i Ispol'zovanie Trudovykh Resursov' ('Population Migration and the Use of Labour Resources'), *Voprosy Ekonomiki*, No. 9. Translated (1971) by *Problems of Economics*, Vol. 13, No. 11.

Petrosian, G. S. (1965), *Vnerabochee Vremia Trudiashchikhsia v SSSR (Non-working Time of Working People in the USSR)*, Moscow.

---- (1969), 'Natsionl'no-Etnograficheskie Razlichiia, Osobennosti Byta i Vnerabochee Vremia Trudiashchikhsia' ('National-Ethonographic Differences, Features of B*yt* and Non-Working Time of Working People'), *Fil Nauki*, No. 2.

Pickel, A. (2001), 'Between Social Science and Social Technology', *Philosophy of the Social Sciences*, Vol. 31, No. 4, pp.459-87.

Pimenova, A. L. (1966), 'Sem'ia i Perspektivy Razvitiia Obshchestvennogo Truda Zhenshchin Pri Sotsializme' ('The Family and the Prospects of the Development of Women's Social Labour Under Socialism'), *Fil Nauki*, No. 3.

Popova, I. M. (1960), 'Mesto i Rol' Sotsial'noi Psikhologii v Amerikanskoi Sotsiologii' ('The Place and Role of Social Psychology in American Sociology'), *Vestnik MGU*, No. 5. Translated (1961) by the *Soviet Review*, Vol. 2, No. 8.

Potaenko, K. L. and Tsegoeva, M. L. (1966), 'Izmeneniia Sotsial'noi Struktury Sovetskogo Obshchestva' ('Change in the Social Structure of Soviet Society'), *Fil Nauki*, No. 3.

Prigozhin, A. I (1969), 'Metodologicheskie Problemy Issledovaniia Obshchestvennogo Mneniia' ('Methodological Problems of Public Opinion Research'), *Vop Fil*, No. 2.

Provotorov, V. A. (1966), 'Obsuzhdenie Problem Sotsial'noi Struktury Obshchestva' ('Discussion of the Problems of Social Structure'), *Fil Nauki*, No. 1.

---- (1967), 'Sotsiologicheskie Issledovaniia v Partiinoi Rabote' ('Sociological Research in Party Work'), *Partiinaia Zhizn'*, No. 19.

Prudenskii, G. A. (ed.) (1961), *Vnerabochee Vremia Trudiashchikhsia (Non–working Time of Working People)*, Novosibirsk.

Rachkov, P. A., Ugrinovich, D. M. and Uledov, A. K. (eds.) (1970), *O Strukture Marksistskoi Sotsiologicheskoi Teorii (About the Structure of Marxist Sociological Theory)*, Moscow.

Razumovskii, I. (1926), 'Filosofiia i Iuridicheskaia Teoriia' ('Philosophy and Juridical Theory'), *Pod Znamenem Marksizma*, No. 12.

Roberg, J. L. (1998), *Soviet Science Under Control: The Struggle for Influence*, Macmillan, London.

Rozhin, V. P. (1962), 'O Predmete Marksistskoi Sotsiologii' ('On the Subject of Marxist Sociology'), *Voprosy Marksistskoi Sotsiologii*, Rozhin, V. P. (ed.), Leningrad.

---- (1966), 'Razvivat' Konkretnye Sotsiologicheskie Issledovaniia' ('To Develop Concrete Sociological Research'), *Vestnik MGU*, No. 5.

---- (1962), (ed.), *Voprosy Marksistsoi Sotsiologii (Questions of Marxist Sociology)*, Leningrad.

Rumiantsev, A. M. (1967), 'Vstupaiushchemu v Mir Nauki' ('To Those Entering the World of Science'), *Komsomol'skaia Pravda*, 8 June. Translated (1967) by the *CDSP*, Vol. 19, No. 30.

Rumiantsev, A., Burlatskii, F. and Osipov, G. (1968), 'Konkretnye Sotsial'nye Issledovaniia: Zadachi, Perspektivy' ('Concrete Social Research: Tasks and Prospects'), *Izvestiia*, 8 June. Translated (1968) by the *CDSP*, Vol. 20, No. 24.

Rumiantsev, A. M. and Osipov, G. V. (1968), 'Marksistskaia Sotsiologiia i KonkretnyeSotsial'nye Issledovaniia' ('Marxist Sociology and Concrete Social Research'), *Vop Fil*, No. 6.

Rumiantsev, A., Timofeev, T. and Sheinin, Iu. (1966), 'Dlia Progressa Nauki i Truda' ('For Progress of Science and Labour'), *Izvestiia*, 12 May. Translated (1966) by the *CDSP*, Vol. 18, No. 19.

Rusakov, R. S. and Karchemnik, V. D. (1970), 'O Rabote Instituta Istorii, Filologii i Filosofii SO AN SSSR v 1969 Godu' ('On the Work of the Institute of History, Philology and Philosophy of the SO AN USSR in 1969'), *Izvestiia Sibirskogo Otdeleniia Akademii Nauk SSSR*, No. 6.

Rutkevich, M. N. (1966), 'Izmenenie Sotsial'noi Struktury Sovetskogo Obshchestva i Intelligentsiia' ('Change in the Social Structure of Soviet Society and the Intelligentsia'), *Sotsiologiia v SSSR*, Vol. 1, Osipov, G. V. (ed.), Moscow.

---- (1966), 'O Poniatii Intelligentsii Kak Sotsial'nogo Sloia Sotsialisticheskogo Obshchestva' ('On the Notion of the Intelligentsia as a Social Layer of Socialist Society'), *Fil Nauki*, No. 4.

---- (1967), *Protsessy Izmeneniia Sotsial'noi Struktury v Sovetskom Obshchestve* (*Processes of Change of the Social Structure of Soviet Society*), Sverdlovsk.

---- (1967), 'Sotsial'nye Istochniki Popolneniia Sovetskoi Intelligentsii' (Social Sources of Replenishment of the Soviet Intelligentsia'), *Vop Fil*, No. 6. Translated (1967) by the *CDS*, Vol. 19, No. 35.

---- (1967), 'O Kriteriiakh Sotsial'nykh Razlichii Ikh Primenenii k Intelligentsii' ('About the Criteria of Social Differences and their Application to the Intelligentsia'), *Protessy Izmeniia Sotsial'noi Struktury v Sovetskom Obshchestve*, Rutkevich, M. N. (ed.), Sverdlovsk.

---- (1968), 'Problemy Izmeneniia Sotsial'noi Struktury Sovetskogo Obshchestva' ('Problems of Change of the Structure of Soviet Society'), *Fil Nauki*, No. 3.

---- (1970), 'Protsessy Sotsial'nykh Peremeshchenii i Poniatie "Sotsial'noi Mobil'nost"' ('Processes of Social Movement and the Concept of "Social Mobility"'), *Fil Nauki*, No. 5.

---- (1970), 'V. I. Lenin i Problemy Razvitiia Intelligentsii' ('V. I. Lenin and the Problems of the Development of the Intelligentsia'), *Doklady k VII Mezhdunarodnomy Sotsiologicheskomu Kongressu*, Zhemanov, O. N. (ed.), Sverdlovsk.

Rutkevich, M. N. and Filippov, F. P. (1970), *Sotsial'nye Peremeshcheniia* (*Social Movements*), Moscow.

Rutkevich, M. N. and Kogan, L. N. (1961), 'O Metodakh Konkretno-Sotsiologicheskogo Issledovaniia' ('On the Methods of Concrete Sociological Research'), *Vop Fil*, No. 3. Translated (1962) by the *Soviet Review*, Vol. 3, No. 11.

---- (1971),'Marksistskaia Sotsiologiia, Sotsial'noe Prognozirovanie i Planirovanie' ('Marxist Sociology, Social Forecasting and Planning'), *Fil Nauki*, No. 3.

Ryabushkin, T. *et al.* (ed.) (1982), *Sovetskaya Sotsiologia: Sotsiologicheskia Teoria i Sotsial'naia Praktika* (*Soviet Sociology: Sociological Theory and Social Practice*), Nauka, Moscow.

Ryvkina, R. V. (1964), 'Roi' i Znachenie Eksperimenta v Obshchestvennykh Naukakh' ('Role and Significance of the Experiment in the Social Sciences'), *Vop Fil*, No. 5.

---- (1966), (ed.) *Sotsiologicheskie Issledovaniia: Voprosy Metodologii i etodiki* (*Sociological Research: Questions of Methodology and Methods*), Novosibirsk.

Samsonov, Iu. B. (1967), 'Vsesoiuznoe Soveshchanie Sotsiologov' ('All-Union Conference of Sociologists'), *Vop Fil*, No. 10.

Schlapentokh, V. (1987), 'Evolution in the Soviet Sociology of Work - From Ideology to Pragmatism', *Work and Occupations*, Vol. 14, No.3, pp.410-33.

Seleskeridi, L. I. (1966), 'Chitatel'skaia Konferentsiia v Tbilsi' ('Readers' Conference in Tbilisi'), *Vop Fil*, No. 4.

Semenov, V. S. (1966), *Moscow Home Service*, 31 May.

---- (1967), 'VI Vsemirnyi Sotsiologicheskii Kongress' ('Sixth World Congress of Sociology'), *Vop Fil*, No. 8.

---- (1972), 'Novye Iavleniia v Sotsial'noi Structure Sovetskogo Obshchestva' ('New Phenomena in the Social Structure of Soviet Society'), *Fil Nauki*, No. 4.

Semenov, V. S. and Gretskii, M. N. (1971), 'Marksistsko-Leninskaia Nauka v Nastuplenii' ('Marxist-Leninist Science on the Offensive'), *Fil Nauki*, No. 2.

Sennikova, L. I. and Trubintsyn, O. N. (1972), 'Izmenenie Sotsial'noi Struktury Sovetskogo Obshchestva' ('Change of the Social Structure of Soviet Society'), *Fil Nauki*, No. 4.

(1967), 'Sessia Sotsiologov' ('Session of Sociologists'), *Pravda*, 23 November. Translated (1967) by the *CDSP*, Vol. 19, No. 47.

Shalin, D. (1976), 'On Current Trends in Soviet Sociology', *La Critica Sociologica*, 38, 173-84.

---- (1978), 'The Development of Soviet Sociology, 1956-1876', *Annual Review of Sociology*, Vol. 4, pp.171-91.

---- (1990), 'Sociology for the Glasnot Era: Institutional and Substantive Changes in Recent Soviet Sociology', *Social Forces*, Vol. 68, No. 4, pp.1019-39.

Shanin, T. (1989), *First Summer School of Soviet Sociologists: Director's Report*, Manchester University, Manchester.

Shargorodskii, M. D. (1962), 'Prichiny i Profilaktika Prestupnosti' ('Causes and Prevention of Crime'), *Voprosy Marksistskoi Sotsiologii*, Rozhin. V. P. (ed.), Leningrad. Translated (1964) by the *Soviet Review*, Vol. 5, No. 3.

Sherkovin, Iu. A. (1964), 'Obshchestvennoe Mnenie v Sovetskom Obshchestve' ('Public Opinion in Soviet Society'), *Vop Fil*, No. 11.

Shkaratan, O. I. (1967), 'Sotsial'naia Struktura Sovetskogo Rabochego Klassa' ('Social Structure of the Soviet Working Class'), *Vop Fil*, No. 1. Translated (1967) by the *CDSP*, Vol. 19, No. 12.

---- (1968), 'Rabochii Klass Sotsialisticheskogo Obshchestva v Epokhu Nauchno-Tekhnicheskoi Revoliutsii' ('The Working Class in Socialist Society in the Epoch of Scientific and Technical Revolution'), *Vop Fil*, No. 11.

---- (1970), 'Problemy Sotsial'noi Struktury Sovetskogo Goroda' ('Problems of the Social Structure of the Soviet City'), *Fil Nauki*, No. 5.

---- (1970), *Problemy Sotsial'noi Struktury Rabochego Klassa* (*Problems of the Social Structure of the Working Class*), Moscow.

Shliapentokh, V. (1970), *Sotsiologiia Dlia Vsekh* (*Sociology for Everyone*), Moscow.

Shlapentokh, V. (1987), *The Politics of Sociology in the Soviet Union*, Westview Press, Boulder, Colorado.

Shubkin, V. N. (1965), 'Molodezh Vstupaet v Zhizn'' ('Youth Enters Life'), *Vop Fil*, No. 5. Translated (1965) by the *CDSP*, Vol. 17, No. 30.

---- (1965), 'Nekotorye Voprosy Adaptatsii Molodezhi k Trudu' ('Several Questions of Adaptation of Youth to Labour'), *Sotsial'nye Issledovaniia*, Vol. 1, Moscow.

---- (1965), 'O Konkretnykh Issledovaniiakh Sotsial'nykh Protesessov' ('On Concrete Research of Social Processes'), *Kommunist*, No. 3. Translated (1965) by the *CDSP*, Vol. 17, No. 17.

---- (1966), 'Ob Ustoichivosti Otsenok Privlekatel'nosti Professii' ('On the Stability of an Assessment of the Attractiveness of Certain Professions'), *Sotsiologicheskie Issledovaniia: Voprosy Metodologii i Metodiki*, Ryvkina, R. V. (ed.), Novosibirsk.

---- (1966), 'Sotsiologiia: Problemy i Perspektivy' ('Sociology: Problems and Prospects'), *Pravda*, 13 March. Translated (1966) by the *CDSP*, Vol. 18, No. 11.

---- (1967), 'Kolichestvennye Metody v Sotsiologii' ('Quantitative Methods in Sociology'), *Vop Fil*, No. 3.

---- (1970), *Sotsiologicheskie Opyty: Metodologicheskie Voprosy Sotsial'nykh Issledovanii* (*Sociological Experiences: Methodological Questions of Social Research*), Moscow.

---- (1966), 'Sila i Slabosti Molodoi Nauki' ('Strength and Weaknesses of a Young Science'), *Literaturnaia Gazeta*, 6 August. Translated (1966) by the *CDSP*, Vol. 18, No. 32.

---- (1966), 'Sobranie Sovetskoi Sotsiologicheskoi Assotsiatsii' ('Meeting of the Soviet Sociological Association'), *Vop Fil*, No. 6. Translated (1966) by the *CDSP*, Vol. 18, No. 2.

Solomon, Peter H., Jnr., (1967), 'Soviet Criminology: the Effects of Post-Stalin Politics on a Social Science', unpublished Master's dissertation, Columbia University.

Solov'ev, N, Lazauskas, Iu. and Iankova, Z. (1970), *Problemy Byta, Braka i Sem'i* (*Problems of Byt, Marriage and the Family*), Vil'nius.

Sorokin, P. A. (1925), *Leaves from a Russian Diary (1917-22)*, London.

---- (1926), 'Russian Sociology in the Twentieth Century', *Publications of the American Sociological Society*, Vol. 21.

---- (1966), 'Sotsiologiia' ('Sociology'), *Kratkii Slovar' Po Filosofii*, Blauberg, I. V. (ed.), Moscow.

Stepanian, Ts. A. and Semenov, V. S. (eds.) (1968), *Klassy, Sotsial'nye Sloi i Gruppy v SSSR (Classes, Social Strata and Groups in the USSR)*, Moscow.

---- (eds.) (1968), *Problemy Izmeneniia Sotsial'noi Struktury Sovetskogo Obshchestva (Problems of the Change of the Social Structure of Soviet Society)*, Moscow,

Strumilin, S. G. (1957), *Problemy Ekonomiki Truda (Problems of the Economics of Labour)*, Moscow.

---- (1959), *Rabochii Den' i Kommunizm (Work Day and Communism)*, Moscow.

Suvorov, L. N. (1963), 'Marksistskaia Sotsiologiia i Konkretnye Sotsial'nye Issledovaniia' ('Marxist Sociology and Concrete Social Research'), *Fil Nauki*, No. 3.

Sviridov, G. (1970), 'Iz Praktiki Konkretnykh Sotsiologicheskikh Issledovanii' ('From the Work of Concrete Sociological Research'), *Partiinaia Zhizn'*, No. 16.

Szalai, A. (1966), 'The Multinational Comparative Time Budget Research08:57 Project: A Venture in International Research Cooperation', *American Behavioral Scientist*, Vol. 10, No. 4.

Takhtarev, K. M. (1924), Sravnitel'naia Istoriia Razvitiia Chelovecheskogo Obshchestva i Obshchestvennykh Form: Chast' Pervaia (Comparative History of the Development of Human Society and Social Forms: Part One), Leningrad.

Toschenko, Z. T. *et al.* (1999), *Sotsiologi Rossii i CNG:Bibliograficheski Spravochnik XIX-XX vv (Sociologists of Russia and SNG: Bibliographical Directory)*, Editorial URSS, Moscow.

Trapeznikov, S. P. (1967), 'Razvitie Obshchestvennykh Nauk i Povyshenie Ikh Roli v Kommunisticheskom Stroitel'stve' ('Development of the Social Sciences and Raising Their Role in Communist Construction'), *Vop Fil*, No. 11.

Ugrinovich, D. M. (1970), 'Religiia Kak Predmet Sotsiologicheskogo Issledovaniia' ('Religion as a Subject for Sociological Research'), *Ocherki Metodologii Poznaniia Sotsial'nykh Iavlenii*, Ugrinovich, D. M., Larmin, O. V. and Uledov, A. K. (eds.), Moscow.

---- (1970), 'O Predmete Marksistskoi Sotsiologii' ('On the Subject of Marxist Sociology'), *Ocherki Metodologii Poznaniia Sotsial'nykh Iavlenii*, Ugrinovich, D. M., Larmin, O. V. and Uledov, A. K. (eds.), Moscow.

Ugrinovich, D. M., Larmin, O. V. and Uledov, A. K. (eds.) (1970), *Ocherki Metodologii Poznaniia Sotsial'nykh Iavlenii (Essays on the Methodology of Knowledge of Social Phenomena)*, Moscow.

Uledov, A. K. (1966), 'O Filosofskoi Metodologii i Konkretnykh Metodakh Sotsial'no-Psikhologicheskogo Issledovaniia: Na Materialakh Izucheniia Obshchestvennogo Mneniia' ('On Philosophical Methodology and Concrete Methods of Socio-Psychological Research: On Materials of Studying Public Opinion'), *Metodologicheskie Voprosy Obshchestvennykh Nauki*, Chesnokov, D. I. *et al.* (eds.), Moscow.

Ustinovich, N. V. (1967), 'Sotsializm i Sem'ia' ('Socialism and the Family'), *Vop Fil*, No. 7.

Utevskii, B. S. (1964), 'Sotsiologicheskie Issledovaniia i Kriminologiia' ('Sociological Research and Criminology'), *Vop Fil*, No. 2.

Verbin, A. and Furman, A. (1965), *Mesto Istoricheskogo Materializma v Sisteme Nauk (The Place of Historical Materialism in the System of Sciences)*, Moscow.

Verbin, A. I., Kelle, V. Zh. and Koval'zon, M. Ia. (1958), 'Istoricheski Materializm i Sotsiologiia' ('Historical Materialism and Sociology'), *Vop Fil*, No. 5.

Vodzinskaia, V. V. and Iadov, V. A. (1963), 'U Pol'skikh Sotsiologov' ('Among Polish Sociologists'), *Fil Nauki*, No. 3.

Vol'fson, S. Ia. (1928), *Sotsiologiia Braka i Sem'i* (*Sociology of Marriage and the Family*), Moscow.

---- (1937), *Sem'ia Ibrak v Ikh Istoricheskom Ravzitii* (*Family and Marriage in their Historical Development*), Moscow.

Voinova, V. D. (1989), 'Mezhdu Proshlym i Budushchim Ili Kakim Byt' Institutu Sotsiologii?' ('Between the Past and the Present or What Must be the Institute of Sociology?'), *Sotsiologicheskie Issledovaniia*, No. 2.

Volovik, L. A. (ed.) (1969), *Sotsiologiia i Ideologiia* (*Sociology and Ideology*), Moscow.

Vol'skii, V. (1967), 'Partiinaia Zhizn': Krugozor Rukovoditelia' ('Party Life: The Leader's Outlook'), *Pravda*, 17 January. Translated (1967) by the *CDSP*, Vol. 19, No. 3.

Voronkov, V. and Zdravomyslova, E. (1996), 'Emerging Political Sociology in Russia and Russian Transformation', *Current Sociology*, Vol. 44, No. 3, pp.40-52.

Voronov, N. G. (1912), *Osnovaniia Sotsiologii* (*The Foundations Of Sociology*), Moscow.

Weinberg, E. A. (1974), *The Development of Sociology in the Soviet Union*, Routledge and Kegan Paul, London,.

Weiss, C. (1972), *Evaluating Action Programs: Readings in Social Action and Education*, Allyn and Bacon, Inc., London.

White, S. (1995), 'Public Opinion and Political Science in Postcommunist Russia', *European Journal of Political Research*, 27, 507-26.

White, S. (2000), *Russia's New Politics*, Cambridge University Press, Cambridge.

Wyman, M. (1997), *Public Opinion in Postcommunist Russia*, Macmillan, London.

Yadov, V. A. (1990), 'Razmyshleniia o Predmete Sotsiologii' ('Reflections on the Subject of Sociology'), *Sotsiologicheskie Issledovaniia*, No. 2.

Yampol'skaya, S. and Salovskaya, I. (1990), 'Manchester School for Young Sociologists', *Sotsiologischeskie Issledovaniia*, No. 5.

Zanin, V. I. (1970), 'Biudzhet Rabochego Vremeni' ('Budget of Working Time'), *Sotsial'nye Issledovaniia: Problemy Biudzheta Vremeni Trudiashchikhsia*, Vol. 6, Moscow.

Zaslavskaya, T. I. (ed.) (1970), *Migratsiia Sel'skogo Naseleniia* (*Migration of the Rural Population*), Moscow.

Zaslavskaya, T. I. (1987a), '*Perestroika* and Sociology', *Social Research*, Vol. 55, Nos. 1-2.

Zaslavskaya, T. I. (1987b), 'Rol' Sotsiologii v Uskorenii Razvitiia Sovetskovo Obshchestva' ('The Role of Sociology in the Acceleration of the Development of Soviet Society'), *Sotsiologischeskie Issledovaniia*, No. 2.

Zaslavskaya, T. I. (1988), 'Friends or Foes? Social Forces Working For and Against *Perestroika*' in Aganbegyan, A. (ed.) *Perestroika Annual*, Futura, London.

Zaslavskaya, T. I. (1990), 'International Sociological Association Conference on "Self-Management and Social Protection in the Urban Settlement and at the Enterprise", Moscow, 266-30, September 1989', *International Journal of Urban and Regional Research*, Vol. 14, No. 2, pp.297-301.

Zaslavskaya, T. I. (1996), 'Rol' Sotsiologii v Preobrazovanii Rossii ('The Role of Sociology in the Tansformation of Russia'), *Sotsiologicheskie Issledovaniia*, No. 3, pp.3-9.

Zaslavskaya, T. I., Shliapentokh, V. and Shubkin, V. (1967), 'Sotsiolog i Ego Rabota' ('The Sociologist and his Work'), *Izvestiia*, 10 October. Translated (1967) by the *CDSP*, Vol. 19, No. 41.

Zaslavsky, V. (1977), 'Sociology in the Contemporary Soviet Union', *Social Research*, Vol. 44, No. 2, pp.330-53.

Zdravomyslov, A. (1964), 'Sotsiologiia: Otkrytiia i Vozmozhnosti Kak Razvivat' Ovuiu Otrasl' Znaniia' ('Sociology: Discoveries and Possibilities to Develop a New Sphere of Knowledge'), *Sovetskaia Rossiia*, 21 May. Translated (1964) by the *CDSP*, Vol. 16, No. 2.

---- (1969), *Metodologiia i Protsedura Sotsiologicheskikh Issledovanii* (*Methodology and Procedures of Sociological Research*), Moscow.

Zdravomyslov, A. and Iadov, V. (1964), 'Opyt Konkretnogo Issledovanii Otnosheniia k Trudu' ('Experience of Concrete Research on Attitudes Toward Labour'), *Vop Fil*, No. 4. Translated (1964) by the *CDSP*, Vol. 16, No. 24.

---- (eds.) (1965), *Trud i Razvitie Lichnosti* (*Labour and the Development of the Individual*), Leningrad.

---- (1966), 'Effect of Vocational Distinctions on the Attitude to Work', *Industry and Labour in the USSR*, Osipov, G. V. (ed.), London.

Zdravomyslov, A. G., Rozhin, V. P. and Iadov, V. A (eds.) (1967), *Chelovek i Ego Rabota* (*Man and his Work*), Moscow.

Zhabskii, M. I. and Lenik, P. K. (1967), 'Sotsiologicheskoe Issledovanie Msasovogo Retsipienta Iskusstva' ('Sociological Research of the Influence of Art on the Masses'), *Vestnik MGU*, No. 4.

Zhemanov, O. N. (ed.) (1970), *Doklady k VII Mezhdunarodnomy Sotsiologicheskomu Kongressu* (*Reports to the Seventh World Congress of Sociology*), Sverdlovsk.

Zvorykin, A. A. (1963), 'Istoricheskii Materialism Kak Obshchesotsiologicheskikh Teoriia i Konkretnye Sotsiologicheskie Issledovaniia' ('Historical Materialism as All-Sociological Theory and Concrete Sociological Research'), *Fil Nauki*, No. 6.

Index